商务英语阅读教程

Reading Course in Business English

主审：修月祯
主编：王元歌　刘　辉
编者：李玉鹏　张　琼　孟梅艳
　　　李炳慧　冯　蕾　刘贵珍
　　　章爱民　李伟娜　张文征

图书在版编目(CIP)数据

商务英语阅读教程/王元歌,刘辉主编.—北京:北京大学出版社,2007.7
(21世纪高务英语系列教材)

ISBN 978-7-301-12259-4

I. 商⋯　II. ①王⋯②刘⋯　III. 商务－英语－阅读教学－高等学校－教材　IV. H319.4

中国版本图书馆CIP数据核字(2007)第080761号

书　　　名：	商务英语阅读教程
著作责任者：	王元歌　刘　辉　主编
组稿编辑：	刘　爽　黄瑞明
责任编辑：	黄瑞明
标准书号：	ISBN 978-7-301-12259-4/H·1778
出版发行：	北京大学出版社
地　　　址：	北京市海淀区成府路205号　100871
网　　　址：	http://www.pup.cn　新浪官方微博:@北京大学出版社
电子信箱：	zbing@pup.pku.edu.cn
电　　　话：	邮购部 62752015　发行部 62750672　编辑部 62754382　出版部 62754962
印　刷　者：	三河市博文印刷有限公司
经　销　者：	新华书店
	787毫米×1092毫米　16开本　19印张　432千字
	2007年7月第1版　2020年12月第9次印刷
定　　　价：	38.00元

未经许可,不得以任何方式复制或抄袭本书之部分或全部内容。
版权所有,侵权必究
举报电话:010-62752024　电子信箱:fd@pup.pku.edu.cn

《21世纪商务英语系列教材》编审委员会

(按姓氏笔画为序)
王立非 (对外经济贸易大学 英语学院院长)
王晓红 (中央财经大学 外国语学院院长)
王晓群 (上海财经大学 外语系主任)
邓　海 (西南财经大学 语言文化学院院长)
田海龙 (天津商业大学 外国语学院院长)
许德金 (对外经济贸易大学 英语学院通用英语系主任)
林　立 (首都经济贸易大学 外语系主任)
修月祯 (北京第二外国语学院 国际经济贸易学院副院长)
黄振华 (中央财经大学 外国语学院副院长)

前言

随着我国在国际经济活动中的地位不断提高,世界著名企业纷纷涌入我国投资设厂,中国企业也加快了"走出去"的步伐。在此过程中,如何有效地运用英语这一商务活动的重要语言工具与外商进行沟通就成为了当今企业亟需解决的主要问题。商务英语是在商务活动背景下使用的英语,要熟练掌握它,不仅需要扎实的英语基础,还需要深入了解商务知识。

《商务英语阅读教程》依据国际商务活动的各个重要环节编写而成,强调英语作为语言在商务活动中的使用;旨在通过对商务英语文章的阅读和大量练习,培养学生掌握有关商务的专门术语,了解商务英语文章的语法和文体特点,提高学生阅读商务专业书刊的能力和在国际商务实践中运用英语的能力。我们希望通过本教程的学习,学生既能提高国际商务方面的英语水平,又能获得国际商务方面的重要理论和知识。

本教程的主要特点是:第一,各单元文章均选用近年来英美原版教材和报刊时文,语言规范,难度适中,反映当今世界经贸领域的最新动态,为教学提供鲜活的商务英语素材,具有很强的时代感和国际通用性;第二,按国际商务的主要领域由浅入深编写,各单元内容互相连贯,系统地介绍国际商务方面的知识,内容丰富,涵盖面广;第三,每单元集中讨论一个专题,既包括相关的理论知识,也包括实例分析。

《商务英语阅读教程》共18个单元,内容包括国际贸易、国际金融、国际营销、国际投资、国际商法、公司治理、物流、电子商务、国际商务组织等方面。每单元都由 Text A 和 Text B 两篇文章组成:Text A 是主课文,Text B 是在主课文的基础上提供的阅读材料,对主课文的内容进行补充;Text A 包括课文,并对课文中的重点单词、短语、专有名词和商务术语进行释义,对课文中的难句进行注释,并附有大量练习;Text B 包括课文和阅读理解型问题。

本教程可供高等院校国际贸易、国际金融、国际经济法、国际旅游、国际政治、英语等专业以及其他相关专业的高年级学生使用,可供辅修经济、贸易、管理、金融等专业的学生使用,也可用做高年级学生商务英语选修课的教材,同时也可作为国际经贸工作者进一步进修国际商务英语的教材或读物。

建议本教程教学在一个学期内完成,实际授课18周,每周4课时,全学期共计72课时。

本教程由王元歌、刘辉主编,各单元的编者如下:第一、八、十三单元由王元歌编写;第二、十单元由东北财经大学章爱民编写;第三、十四单元由张琼编写;第四、十七单元由刘辉编写;第五、十六单元由孟梅艳编写;第六单元由李炳慧编写;第七、十五单元由冯蕾编写;第九、十一单元由刘贵珍编写;第十二单元由李伟娜编写;第十八单元由张文征编写。

本教程由北京第二外国语学院"人才强教"项目资助编写,在编写过程中得到了主审修月祯教授的支持和指导,并经过修月祯教授的审阅,在此深表谢意。

由于编者水平有限,书中不妥之处在所难免,恳请专业人士和各位读者提出宝贵意见,以便改进。

编者

2007年5月

Contents

Unit 1 **Entering Foreign Markets** 1
    Text A   Deciding How to Enter Foreign Markets 1
    Text B   Cooperative Joint Ventures in China 11

Unit 2 **International Trade Theories** 15
    Text A   Basic Theories of International Trade 15
    Text B   Protectionism Versus Free Trade 26

Unit 3 **International Trade in Services** 31
    Text A   The Importance of Services in International Trade:
              Defining Trade in Services 31
    Text B   Services in the World Economy 40

Unit 4 **Technology Transfer** 45
    Text A   Understanding Technology Transfer 45
    Text B   International Technology Transfer and Intellectual
              Property Rights 54

Unit 5 **Trade Barriers** 58
    Text A   Forms of Trade Barriers 58
    Text B   How to Hurdle the Barrier 67

Unit 6 **International Trade of China** 72
    Text A   China's Trade: Growth and Diversification 72
    Text B   China, US Complementary in Trade 81

Unit 7 **Marketing Strategy** 86
    Text A   The Four P's of the Marketing Strategy 86
    Text B   Uncontrollable Variables in Marketing Strategy 97

Unit 8 **Marketing Environment** 101
    Text A   The Major Macroenvironment Forces 101
    Text B   Host Country Political and Legal Environment 110

Unit 9	**Advertising**	115
	Text A The World of Advertising	115
	Text B Television Advertising and Radio Advertising	125

Unit 10	**International Payment**	130
	Text A Basic Methods of International Payments and Settlements	130
	Text B Multinational and Foreign Exchange	140

Unit 11	**Foreign Exchange Rate**	144
	Text A The Functions of the Foreign Exchange Market	144
	Text B The Asian Crisis	153

Unit 12	**Securities Market**	158
	Text A Why Do Securities Markets Exist	158
	Text B Investment Management in the 1990s	168

Unit 13	**Monetary Policy and Fiscal Policy**	171
	Text A The Basic Idea of Monetary and Fiscal Policy	171
	Text B China's Monetary Policy in the Coming Years	180

Unit 14	**International Corporate Governance**	184
	Text A International Corporate Governance	184
	Text B Corporate Governance in China	194

Unit 15	**Human Resources Management**	199
	Text A Human Resources Management	199
	Text B Job Termination and Retirement	209

Unit 16	**Global Logistics**	213
	Text A Global Integrated Logistics	213
	Text B Logistics in Creating a Recycling Economy	223

Unit 17	**E-commerce**	227
	Text A Understanding E-commerce	227
	Text B Understanding E-commerce in China	236

Unit 18	**International Business Organizations**	240
	Text A World Trade Organization	240
	Text B Asia-Pacific Economic Cooperation	248

Key 253

Glossary 277

Unit 1

Entering Foreign Markets

Learning Objectives

Text A
- to learn the different modes that firms use to enter a foreign market
- to understand the advantages and disadvantages of each entry mode

Text B
- to understand the differences between EJV and CJV
- to learn the advantages of CJV and its application in China

Text A

Deciding How to Enter Foreign Markets

Once a firm has decided to enter a foreign market, the question arises as to the best mode of entry. Firms have six modes to use when entering foreign markets:

- indirect exporting
- direct exporting
- licensing
- joint ventures
- direct investment

Each entry mode has advantages and disadvantages. Managers need to consider these carefully when deciding which to use.

Indirect Export

The normal way to get involved in a foreign market is through export. Companies typically start with indirect exporting—that is, they work through independent intermediaries to export their products. There are four types of intermediaries:

1. *Domestic-based export merchant:* Buys the manufacturer's products and then sells them abroad.
2. *Domestic-based export agent:* Seeks and negotiates foreign purchases and is paid a commission. Included in this group are trading companies.

3. *Cooperative organization:* Carries on exporting activities on behalf of several producers and is partly under their administrative control. Often used by producers of primary products—fruits, nuts, and so on.
4. *Export-management company:* agrees to manage a company's export activities for a fee.

Indirect export has two distinct advantages. First, it involves less commitment. The firm does not have to develop an export department, an overseas sales force, or a set of foreign contacts. Second, it involves less risk. Because international marketing intermediaries bring know-how and services to the relationship, the seller will normally make fewer mistakes.

Direct Export

Companies eventually may decide to handle their own exports. The investment and risk are somewhat greater, but so is the potential return as a result of not paying an intermediary.[1] The company can carry on direct exporting in several ways:

1. *Domestic-based export department or division:* An export sales manager carries on the actual selling and draws on market assistance as needed. The department might evolve into a self-contained export department performing all the activities involved in export and operating as a profit center.
2. *Overseas sales branch or subsidiary:* An overseas sales branch allows the manufacturer to achieve greater presence and program control in the foreign market. The sales branch handles sales and distribution and might handle warehousing and promotion as well. It often serves as a display center and customer-service center also.
3. *Traveling export sales representatives:* The company can send home-based sales representatives abroad to find business.
4. *Foreign-based distributors or agents:* The company can hire foreign-based distributors or agents to sell the company's goods. These distributors and agents might be given exclusive rights to represent the manufacturer in that country or only limited rights.

Whether companies decide to enter foreign markets through direct or indirect exporting, one of the best ways to initiate or extend export activities is by exhibiting at an overseas trade show. A U.S. software firm might test the waters by showing its wares at an international software expo in Hong Kong, for instance.

Licensing

A licensing agreement is an arrangement whereby a licensor grants the rights to intangible property to another entity (the licensee) for a specified period, and in return, the licensor receives a royalty fee from the licensee. Intangible property includes patents, inventions, formulas, processes, designs, copyrights, and trademarks.

For example, in order to enter the Japanese market, Xerox, the inventor of the photocopier, established a joint venture with Fuji Photo that is known as Fuji-Xerox. Xerox, then licensed its Xerographic know-how to Fuji-Xerox. In return, Fuji-Xerox paid Xerox a royalty fee equal to 5 percent of the net sales revenue that Fuji-Xerox earned from the sales of photocopiers based on Xerox's patented know-how.[2] In this case, the license was originally granted for 10 years, and it has been renegotiated and extended several times since.

A primary advantage of licensing is that the firm does not have to bear the development costs and risks associated with opening a foreign market.[3] Thus, licensing is a very attractive option for firms lacking the capital to develop operations overseas. Licensing is frequently used when a firm possesses some intangible property that might have business applications, but it does not want to develop those applications itself. For example, Coca-Cola has licensed its famous trademark to clothing manufacturers, which have incorporated the design into their clothing.[4]

The greatest risk associated with licensing is that most firms can quickly lose control over its technology by licensing it.[5] RCA Corporation, for example, once licensed its color TV technology to a number of Japanese firms including Matsushita and Sony. The Japanese firms quickly assimilated the technology, improved it, and used it to enter the US market. Now the Japanese firms have a bigger share of the US market than the RCA brand.

Joint Ventures

A joint venture entails the establishment of a firm that is jointly owned by two or more otherwise independent firms. Establishing a joint venture with a foreign firm has long been a popular mode for entering a new market. The most typical joint venture is a 50/50 venture, in which there are two parties, each of which holds a 50 percent ownership stake and contributes a team of managers to share operating control.[6] Some firms, however, have sought joint ventures in which they have a majority share and thus tighter control.[7] Many companies have announced joint ventures, for instance:

- Coca-Cola and the Swiss company Nestle are joining forces to develop the international market for "ready to drink" tea and coffee, which currently sell in significant amounts only in Japan.
- Procter & Gamble has formed a joint venture with its Italian arch-rival Fater to cover babies' bottoms in the United Kingdom and Italy. Their diaper joint venture will give the combined group almost 60% of the U.K. market and up to 90% of the Italian market.
- Domestic appliance manufacturer Whirlpool has taken a 53% stake in the Dutch electronics group Philip's white-goods business to leapfrog into the European market.

Forming a joint venture might be necessary or desirable for economic or political reasons. The foreign firm might lack the financial, physical, or managerial resources to undertake the venture alone. Or in many countries, political considerations make joint ventures the only feasible entry mode. Even corporate giants need joint ventures to crack the toughest markets. When it wanted to enter China's ice cream market, Anglo-Dutch giant Unilever joined forces with Sumstar, a state-owned Chinese investment company.

Joint ownership has certain drawbacks. The partners might disagree over investment, marketing, or other policies. One partner might want to reinvest earnings for growth, and the other partner might want to withdraw these earnings.[8] The joint venture between AT&T and the Italian computer maker Olivetti collapsed due to the companies' inability to formulate a clear, mutually agreeable strategy. Furthermore, joint ownership can hamper a multinational company from carrying out specific manufacturing and marketing policies on a worldwide basis.

Direct Investment

The ultimate form of foreign involvement is direct ownership of foreign-based assembly or manufacturing facilities. The foreign company can buy part or full interest in a local company or build its own facilities. In a wholly owned subsidiary, the firm owns 100 percent of the stock. Establishing a wholly owned subsidiary in a foreign market can be done two ways. The firm can either set up a new operation in that country or it can acquire an established firm and use that firm to promote its products in the country's market.

As a company gains experience in export, and if the foreign market appears large enough, foreign production facilities offer distinct advantages:

- ❖ The firm could secure cost economies in the form of cheaper labor or raw materials, foreign-government investment incentives, freight savings and so on.[9]
- ❖ The firm will gain a better image in the host country because it creates jobs.
- ❖ The firm develops a deeper relationship with government, customers, local suppliers, and distributors, enabling it to adapt its products better to the local environment.
- ❖ The firm retains full control over its investment and therefore can develop manufacturing and marketing policies that serve its long-term international objectives.
- ❖ The firm assures itself access to the market in case the host country starts insisting that purchased goods have domestic content.[10]

The main disadvantage of direct investment is that the firm exposes its large investment to risks such as devalued currencies, worsening markets, or expropriation. The firm will find it expensive to reduce or close down its operations, since the host country might require substantial severance pay to the employees. The firm has no choice but to accept these risks if it wants to operate on its own in the host country.

New Words

intermediary	/ˌɪntəˈmiːdiəri/	n.	中介人,中间商
commission	/kəˈmɪʃən/	n.	佣金
primary	/ˈpraɪməri/	adj.	初级的,初级品的
commitment	/kəˈmɪtmənt/	n.	投入,承担的义务
know-how	/ˈnəʊ haʊ/	n.	技术诀窍
self-contained	/selfkənˈteɪnd/	adj.	设备齐全的,有独立设施的
subsidiary	/səbˈsɪdiəri/	n.	子公司
warehousing	/ˈwɛəhaʊzɪŋ/	n.	仓储,仓储业务
promotion	/prəˈməʊʃən/	n.	促销
display	/dɪˈspleɪ/	n.	展示,陈列
distributor	/dɪˈstrɪbjʊtə/	n.	分销商,经销商
agent	/ˈeɪdʒənt/	n.	代理人
exclusive	/ɪkˈskluːsɪv/	adj.	独家的,专用的
whereby	/wɛəˈbaɪ/	adv.	以……的方式,凭借……
grant	/grɑːnt/	v.	授予,给予
intangible	/ɪnˈtændʒəbəl/	adj.	无形的
entity	/ˈentɪti/	n.	实体
specified	/ˈspesɪfaɪd/	adj.	规定的,明确的
patent	/ˈpeɪtnt/	n.	专利
formula	/ˈfɔːmjʊlə/	n.	配方,处方
copyright	/ˈkɒpɪraɪt/	n.	著作权,版权
trademark	/ˈtreɪdmɑːk/	n.	商标,商号
revenue	/ˈrevɪnjuː/	n.	收入,(国家的)税收,岁入
incorporate	/ɪnˈkɔːpəreɪt/	v.	使并入,融入
assimilate	/əˈsɪmɪleɪt/	v.	吸收
entail	/ɪnˈteɪl/	v.	使……成为必需,需要
arch-rival	/ɑːtʃˈraɪvəl/	n.	主要竞争对手
bottom	/ˈbɒtəm/	n.	臀部,屁股
diaper	/ˈdaɪəpə/	n.	尿布
stake	/steɪk/	n.	股权,股份
white-goods	/waɪt gʊdz/	n.	白色织物,白色货物
leapfrog	/ˈliːpfrɒg/	v.	超越,越级
crack	/kræk/	v.	挤入,闯入
state-owned	/steɪt əʊnd/	n.	国有的
withdraw	/wɪðˈdrɔː/	v.	提取,收回

hamper	/ˈhæmpə/	v.	阻碍, 妨碍, 牵制
interest	/ˈɪntrɪst/	n.	股份, 股权
stock	/stɒk/	n.	股权
acquire	/əˈkwaɪə/	v.	收购, 获得, 购买
secure	/sɪˈkjʊə/	v.	获得
incentive	/ɪnˈsentɪv/	n.	激励, 奖励
freight	/freɪt/	n.	运输费用, 运费
content	/ˈkɒntent/	n.	含量, 成分
devalue	/diːˈvæljuː/	v.	(货币)贬值
expropriation	/ɪksˌprəʊpriˈeɪʃən/	n.	征用

Phrases

as to	有关, 关于
carry on	进行, 经营
draw on	利用
test the waters	进行尝试
leapfrog into	跳入, 跃入
crack the market	挤入市场
on a ... basis	在……的基础上
expose... to...	使……暴露于……
close down	关闭

Special Terms

indirect export	间接出口
direct export	直接出口
licensing	许可证贸易
joint venture	合资企业
direct investment	直接投资
entry mode	进入方式
export merchant	出口商, 出口贸易商
export agent	出口代理商
primary products	初级产品, 初级品
export management company	出口管理公司(简称 EMC)
exclusive rights	独家权利
trade show	商业展览, 商展
intangible property	无形财产

royal fee 特许权使用费
wholly owned subsidiary 独资子公司
cost economies 成本节约
host country 东道国
severance pay 遣散费,解雇费,离职金

Notes

1. The investment and risk are somewhat greater, but so is the potential return as a result of not paying an intermediary.
   投资和风险会增高,但是由于无需支付中间商的费用,潜在的收益也会增大。

2. ...the net sales revenue that Fuji-Xerox earned from the sales of photocopiers based on Xerox's patented know-how.
   从销售影印机中获得的净收入,这些影印机是在专利技术的基础上生产的。

3. A primary advantage of licensing is that the firm does not have to bear the development costs and risks associated with opening a foreign market.
   许可证贸易最主要的优势在于企业无需承担开拓国外市场的开发成本和风险。
   句中 bear the costs and risks 表示"承担成本和风险";associated with 表示"与……相关的"。

4. Coca-cola has licensed its famous trademark to clothing manufacturers...
   可口可乐将自己著名的商标以许可证的形式授予服装生产商……

5. The greatest risk associated with licensing is that most firms can quickly lose control over its technology by licensing it.
   许可证贸易最大的风险在于,大多数企业都会因为将技术许可给他人而失去对技术的控制。
   句中 lose control over 表示"失去对……的控制"。

6. The most typical joint venture is a 50/50 venture, in which there are two parties, each of which holds a 50 percent ownership stake and contributes a team of managers to share operating control.
   最典型的合资企业是50/50型的企业,也就是说,合资双方各持有50%的股权,并共同组建经理人团队,共享经营控制权。
   句中 ownership stake 表示"所有权股份"或"股权"。

7. ... have a majority share and thus tighter control.
   拥有过半数的股权并因此可以施加更为严格的控制。

8. One partner might want to reinvest earnings for growth, and the other partner might want to withdraw these earnings.
   或许这个合伙人希望将收益再次投资用于合资企业的发展,而另一个合伙人则希望抽走收益。

9. The firm could secure cost economies in the form of cheaper labor or raw materials, foreign-government investment incentives, freight savings and so on.
企业能够节约成本,可以从廉价的劳动力或原材料、外国政府的投资激励措施、运费等方面获得节约。

10. ... in case the host country starts insisting that purchased goods have domestic content.
以防东道国开始坚持要求所购买的商品中要具有国产的成分。

Exercises

I. Discuss the following questions.

1. According to the article, what are the modes that firms can use to enter a foreign market?
2. What are the advantages of indirect and direct exporting?
3. What is licensing? What are the advantages and disadvantages of licensing?
4. What are the major risks of establishing a joint venture with the local partner?
5. What are the advantages and disadvantages of direct investment?

II. Analyze the case below and discuss the questions.

A small Canadian firm that has developed valuable medical products using its unique biotechnology know-how is trying to decide how best to serve the EU market. Its choices are:

a. Manufacture the products at home and let foreign sales agents handle marketing.
b. Manufacture the products at home and set up a wholly owned subsidiary in Europe to handle marketing.
c. Enter into a strategic alliance with a large European pharmaceutical firm. The product would be manufactured in Europe by the 50/50 joint venture and marketed by the European firm.

The cost of investment in manufacturing facilities will be a major one for the Canadian firm, but it is not outside its reach.

Questions:
If these are the firm's only options, which one would you advise it to choose? And why?

III. Match the terms in column A with the explanations in column B.

A	B
1. core competence	A. any business that engages in international trade or investment
2. merger and acquisition	B. exclusive legal rights of authors, composers, playwrights, artists, etc., to publish and dispose of their work
3. economies of scale	C. skills within the firm that competitors cannot easily match or imitate
4. home country	D. reduction in the unit cost achieved by producing a large volume of a product
5. patent	E. designs and names, often officially registered
6. trademark	F. combining of two or more entities through the direct acquisition by one of the net assets of the other
7. location economies	G. document giving the inventor exclusive rights to the manufacture, use, or sale of that invention
8. international business	H. the country in which a multinational corporation's headquarters is based
9. exporting	I. producing goods at home and shipping them to the receiving country for sale
10. copyright	J. economies that arise from performing a value creation activity in the optimal location for that activity

IV. Fill in the blanks of the following sentences with the words or phrases given below. Make changes when necessary.

commitment	secure	crack	assimilate	incorporate
withdraw	expose	grant	exclusive	hamper

1. The municipal government _____ them permission to develop the small island as a tourist center.
2. That would help Tsingtao beer to _____ the list of 25 best-selling foreign brands in the U.S.—now topped by Mexico's Corona beer.
3. These services may be requested by the recipient firm until the technical "know-how" or expertise has been _____.
4. Individual consumers and business executives will be able to_____ international business considerations into their thinking and planning.
5. Compared to other entry modes, exporting requires a far less _____ of capital, management, and other company resources.
6. The 5% tax on imports is bound to _____ Chinese companies from

entering European markets.

7. The aim of WTO dispute settlement mechanism is to _____ a positive solution of the dispute.

8. During the financial crisis, many foreign companies _____ their investment from the Asian countries.

9. Because it _____ low assets to political risk and economic risk, the firm retains the maximum flexibility to switch its geographical target areas.

10. Export agencies, regardless of their form, usually ask for _____ rights to sell the product in certain markets.

V. Put the following into English.

1. 专门从事出口销售的企业
2. 控制了制造业贸易和投资的相当大的份额
3. 在生产技术方面具有相对的竞争优势
4. 遵守特许人的经营策略
5. 收购东道国现有的企业
6. 丧失了对被许可人在技术上的控制
7. 充分吸收公司总部提供的最新技术知识
8. 在全球范围内从事经营
9. 将新产品推向外国市场
10. 持有合资企业半数以上的股权

VI. Translate the following sentences into English.

1. 企业可以通过制定蓝图,也可以通过收购东道国的企业开设独资公司。
2. 在不能通过出口或其他进入方式的情况下,企业可以利用许可证贸易进入和开拓国外市场。
3. 出口是企业走向国际市场最简便易行的方法,因为其经济损失的风险可以降到最低程度。
4. 一个公司进入国外市场的选择取决于多种因素,比如公司的所有权优势、市场区位优势等。
5. 许多经济学家一直在研究由国际商务活动的扩展所引起的各种理论和实际问题。

VII. Translate the following passage into Chinese.

Access to valued and scarce human resources with appropriate education and cultural background is a key factor in joint venture formation. One of the critical reasons why European and American companies enter joint ventures in Japan is the inability of companies on their own to attract local management as a result of their "outsider" status. Indeed numerous joint ventures have been formed with the express intention of recruiting nationals with managerial ability. The local partner's participation in the development of the joint ventures imposes less of a burden on its managerial capabilities than would a wholly-owned subsidiary.

Access to capital is another resource frequently sought when firms enter a joint venture. Capital markets are characterized by significant transaction costs and credit markets are likely to be imperfect for young firms with little or no track record or experience. Transaction costs are also high for investments in risky projects that have no collateral, e.g. research and development. Small-scale technology based firms frequently encounter severe difficulty in securing funds for expansion, hence the attractiveness of joint ventures.

Text B

Cooperative Joint Ventures in China

Since China's World Trade Organization entry and the PRC government's relaxation of investment regulations, foreign investors have been choosing to establish more wholly foreign-owned enterprises (WFOEs). WFOEs cannot be used in every sector, however, because the PRC government requires Chinese company participation or control in some sectors. In such cases, foreign companies must consider a joint venture structure. Even when they are not required, joint ventures can benefit foreign investors when a Chinese partner has certain strengths, such as central or local government support, brand reputation, land, licenses, distribution, and access to suppliers—that reduce start up costs and improve the foreign investor's chances of success.

In China, most joint ventures are equity joint ventures (EJVs), though some investors establish cooperative (or contractual) joint ventures (CJVs). CJVs and EJVs are similar in many respects. The PRC government approval process, approval authorities, format of agreements, tax breaks, legal standing, and the means, laws, and authorities for dispute resolution are identical. The general management structure and governance procedures are also virtually the same.

But CJVs and EJVs differ in two important ways. First, unlike an EJV, a CJV does not need to be a separate legal person under PRC law. (A CJV that is not a separate legal person may benefit from lower costs, but also may expose the parties to greater liability than if they were legal persons, because CJVs with legal person status confer limited liability on parties to the joint venture.)

Second, the CJV parties' profit, control, and risks are divided according to negotiated contract terms. In contrast, an EJV's profit, control, and risk are divided in proportion to the equity shares invested by the parties.

CJV Disadvantages

As is true for any investment structure, CJVs have their drawbacks.

First, since all CJV contract details need to be negotiated, establishing a CJV can be time consuming and expensive. Indeed, CJV negotiations can derail potential ventures as parties discover that they cannot reach agreement on every detail.

Second, CJVs are sometimes not the most appropriate business structure for the project. For example, a Western automotive technology company recently signed a memorandum of understanding for a CJV with a Chinese state-owned enterprise (SOE) for the manufacture and sale of its patented system in China. The venture did not proceed, however, because the SOE ultimately determined that it preferred an EJV so that profit sharing ratios would match shareholdings and future changes in registered capital. In the end, the foreign company decided to form a WFOE, but planned to maintain and develop options to work with its Chinese partners in the future.

Why Choose a CJV?

A CJV parties' profit, control, and risks are divided according to negotiated contract terms. CJVs nevertheless can offer investors several advantages. Compared to EJVs, cooperative joint ventures—

Allow access to restricted sectors

In a CJV, Chinese partners can hold and "lend" assets and licenses that are forbidden to foreign investors under PRC law, or that are undesired by the foreign partner, until the venture terminates or foreign ownership rules are relaxed. Undesirable assets may include those with a high transfer tax, or those that are too complicated or costly for the foreign investor to obtain, such as land. A Chinese company would not be permitted to transfer such a license to an EJV because the license, if forbidden to foreign owners, would be considered part of the whole company's assets.

A CJV could also allow negotiated levels of management and financial control, as well as methods of recourse associated with equipment leases and service contracts; in an EJV, foreign investors cannot always obtain such control since EJVs typically rely on equity levels to assign board seats and key staff and to determine other rights.

Alleviate capital contribution difficulties

The CJV's foreign partner can contribute or lease to the joint venture expensive Western technology and equipment, such as medical diagnostic equipment. The CJV can then repay the foreign partner at an "advanced rate" from revenues before profit sharing. This strategy can be used in sectors in which the law caps foreign ownership and when the Chinese partner cannot afford to fund assets up front. Under an EJV ownership structure, such an arrangement is impractical or impossible unless the Chinese side can contribute the amount of cash or assets needed to fund its equity up to the minimum Chinese ownership level required.

Allow more foreign management control

Foreign partners can often obtain the desired level of control by negotiating management, voting, and staffing rights into a CJV's articles of association. Because these rights do not have to be allocated according to equity stakes, the CJV again provides more flexibility than an EJV.

Reduce risks

The CJV structure also tends to force partners to address rights and responsibilities in advance. The PRC government must approve all CJV investments to determine that the venture may legally engage in the specified business scope. Government approval of detailed CJV contracts has the added benefit of sanctioning the detailed agreements and deterring local partner noncompliance. Thus, CJV contracts commonly provide better recourse than EJV contracts if one partner fails to comply with agreements.

Are easier to terminate or modify

Ending a CJV may be easier than ending an EJV—particularly if the partners held assets separately and clarified contingency dissolution terms in advance. In some sectors, when risk of failure in the development phase of a project is high, CJV contracts can be modified without terminating a partnership and forgoing investments and goodwill.

Offer tax advantages

Though CJVs and EJVs have the same tax advantages, CJVs offer some extra tax benefits. For instance, CJVs can sometimes appropriately avoid the asset transfer tax.

Cooperative Joint Ventures Case Study: A Chinese Toll Road CJV

Typically, toll road projects in China involve construction and operation of roads that have been classified and approved for toll collection. The PRC government sees toll roads as a way to encourage foreign investment in the development of China's transportation infrastructure.

CJVs are almost always used for such investments because other investment structures cannot effectively address the financial risk to investors that contribute a large amount of cash. A CJV enables such investors to recoup their investment more quickly than other structures, since the parties can negotiate how and when profits are ultimately divided. Because toll roads are "build-operate-transfer" projects (the assets—the road—will return to the government at the end of a project's life), foreign investors are concerned about how much time it will take to recoup the investment and focus on more than just the total investment return by the end of the project. Since the value of cash flows declines over time, most foreign investors measure investment returns by internal rate of return.

Foreign investors typically negotiate to get more than a proportionate share of the cash relative to share capital in the early years. For example, a foreign investor could negotiate to receive up to 100 percent of the available cash for an initial period (perhaps the first 5 to 15 years). In the next 5 to 10 years, available cash could be split to match the parties' shareholding. In a final period, perhaps the last 5 to 10 years, the foreign party could receive a share in the available cash less than proportionate to its shareholding. All agreements and definition of rights should be carefully spelled out in the detailed CJV contract.

In many toll road CJVs, the foreign party owns the majority of share capital. Most toll road CJVs have two categories of investors: financial and local government affiliate. Financial investors may be foreign or local; for the sake of simplicity they are called "foreign investors" here. This side contributes most of the needed cash. The second category of partners, which usually includes a subsidiary of the local traffic bureau, contributes licenses, construction, and the workforce. This side, for simplicity's sake called "local investors" here, puts in assets but may also contribute cash.

In one example of a toll road CJV, a project included an expressway and a Class 2 road (a parallel or connecting road giving access to the expressway). Most of the cash was used to build the expressway, and a lesser portion was used to repair and upgrade the Class 2 road. The foreign party maintained management control by assigning 60 percent of board seat—matching its share capital. The foreign party appointed the general manager and the financial controller so that it would be on top of daily operations and in charge of the material fund flows. The CJV set up checks and balances to communicate among foreign parties, local parties, and authorities. The CJV, a legal person with limited liability, had a four-year construction period and has a 30-year life. The parties divide profits based on the schedule described above. All of this was written into the CJV contract.

In toll road projects, the CJV structure should not inhibit exit strategies. Some investors view toll road projects as being similar to a utility with a limited life. Others have a strategy to expand their projects by adding more roads and by focusing on projects within a region or on key city-to-city projects. Thus, a successful exit strategy in this sector has been to pool toll roads and package them into a holding company for listing on a public stock exchange.

Answer the following questions:
1. What is EJV and what is CJV?
2. What are the differences between EJV and CJV?
3. What are the disadvantages of CJV?
4. Compared with EJV, what are the advantages of CJV?
5. Why do foreign investors typically negotiate to get more than a proportionate share of the cash relative to share capital in the early years?

Unit 2

International Trade Theories

Learning Objectives

Text A
- to understand the main theoretical explanations put forward by economists for how and why countries trade with each other and factors that determine the pattern of world trade

Text B
- to learn something about free trade and trade protectionism; and to understand their practical application

Text A

Basic Theories of International Trade

Classical Theories of Trade

The trade theory Mercantilism formed the foundation of economic thought from about 1500–1800. The theory held that a country's wealth was measured by its holdings of treasure, usually in the form of gold. Therefore countries should export more than they import and, if successful, would receive the value of their trade surpluses in the form of gold from the countries that ran deficits. In order to export more than they imported, governments established monopolies over their countries' trade, imposed restrictions on most imports, and subsidized many exports.

Mercantilism is wrong for two reasons. First, if one country succeeds in achieving a large export surplus, it can only do so if other countries run an equivalent trade deficit. It follows that, if all countries pursue such a policy, the result will be conflicting among them. Second, the accumulation of a large hoarding of gold through running an export surplus does not make a country materially better-off. On the contrary, a country may be able to achieve a large export surplus by denying its citizens goods which could satisfy their wants, that is, by deliberately underconsuming.

Mercantilists assumed trade was a zero-sum game—that it couldn't mutually benefit all parties.[1] On the contrary, trade should benefit all countries by enabling them to enjoy more goods at lower cost than could be obtained in the absence of trade. In *The Wealth of Nations* (1776), Adam Smith argued that trade is beneficial because of differences of production costs between countries, which reflected differences in labor efficiencies in each country. However, rather than each country striving to produce all the products which they could, each should concentrate on those products in which they enjoy a cost advantage over other countries. The result will be that all are better off. Smith's Absolute Advantage theory of trade identified differences in absolute costs as the basis for trade.[2] What if one country has an absolute cost advantage in the production of both goods? Is it still worthwhile for the two countries to specialize? The answer provided by classical political economist, David Ricardo, was that it might still be so, because the basis for trade is comparative and not absolute advantage. In his text, *Principles of Political Economy* (1816), Ricardo demonstrated that the reason why it pays countries to trade is the existence of different relative or comparative costs in the production of different goods.[3] So long as each country possesses a comparative advantage in at least one activity, it still pays to specialize in that activity and engage in trade.

The Factor-Proportions Theory—HO Theory

One of the weaknesses of the classical theory of trade is that it provided no explanation for why relative efficiencies and, hence, comparative costs should differ between countries. It was left to the neo-classical school to suggest an explanation. This was provided simultaneously, but independently, by two economists, Eli Heckscher and a Swedish economist, Bertil Ohlin, writing in the early 20th century. They explained differences in comparative costs in terms of differences in the amounts of different factors with which countries were endowed and differences in the factor proportions required for the production of different goods.[4] Different goods require for their production different proportions of the various factors of production (land, labor, capital). At the same time, countries possess different amounts of these factors. Some countries are well endowed with land, others with labor and still others with capital. This means that the relative prices of these factors will differ in different countries. Because factor prices differ, the cost of producing labor-intensive

goods will be lower in countries where labor is relatively abundant. In short, countries will enjoy a comparative advantage in the production of those goods, which use relatively large amounts of the country's most abundant factor of production. Thus, countries in which labor is abundant will possess a comparative advantage in labor-intensive goods. Other countries in which capital is the most abundant factor will enjoy a comparative advantage in capital-intensive goods.

One of the attractions of the HO theory is that it provides us with a set of fairly simply and readily testable predictions. However the labor-to-capital relationship in foreign trade does not always follow the rule set by HO theory. One of the first attempts made to test the theory was made by Leontief in 1954. Using the 1947 input-output tables for the U.S., he sought to test the proposition that the US had a comparative advantage in capital-intensive goods and therefore traded these goods for imported labor-intensive products. Interestingly, Leontief's results showed that U.S. imports were more capital-intensive than U.S. exports, the exact opposite of what the theory predicted. This surprising finding is known as Leontief Paradox. Several possible explanations for it have been proposed. One explanation challenged Leontief's research method. For example, the year 1947 he chose was not very representative or he used import replacements rather than imports. Another explanation is that his assumption of identical consumer preferences is invalid. In addition he failed to distinguish human capital from physical capital. The most plausible explanation preferred by Leontief was that U.S. labor was superior to that of other countries. Factor-proportions theory assumes production factors to be homogeneous. Labor skills are, in fact, very different within and among countries, since different people have different amounts and types of training and education. Training and education require capital expenditures that do not show up in traditional capital measurements, which include only plant and equipment values. If the factor-proportions theory is modified to account for different labor groups and the capital invested to train these groups, it seems to hold. If labor is viewed not as a homogeneous commodity but rather by categories, the industrial countries actually have a more abundant supply of highly educated labor than of other types. Industrial countries like U.S. export a high proportion of professionals and expertise; thus those countries are using their abundant production factors. Exports of less developed countries (LDCs), on the other hand, show a high intensity of less skilled labor.

It is widely agreed that, in its simple form, the HO theory is unsatisfactory as an explanation for trade. At best, it may provide some explanation for trade between developed and less developed countries. This is not surprising given the fact that these countries differ greatly in factor endowments. Actually the determinants of trade are more complex than the HO theory maintains. In particular, the theory breaks down completely when countries with similar resources endowments and at a similar stage of development trade with each other. Yet, the fastest growth in world trade in the past half century has occurred in trade in manufactured goods between developed market economies. How can trade theories explain this?

Demand-Side Theories of Trade and Country-Similarity Theory

This can be explained by demand-side theories of trade or country-similarity theory. It holds that once a producer has developed a new product in response to observed market conditions in the home market, it will turn to markets that are perceived to be the most similar to those at home.[5] Staffan Linder, a Swedish economist, argued that while factor endowments play the major role in determining patterns of trade in primary commodities, consumer preferences are the more important for trade in manufactures. Linder's theory of overlapping demand shows that, where consumer preferences determine trade flows, trade is more likely to occur between countries with similar levels of per capita income. In other words, consumers in industrial countries will have a high propensity to buy high quality and luxury products, whereas consumers in lower-income countries will buy few of these products. The basic assumption of this theory is that consumer's preferences vary among countries, although whether or not they differ sufficiently to materially affect the pattern of trade is less clear.[6] This is opposite of the major assumption of HO theory that consumer preferences are identical among countries.

Although the markets within the industrial countries might overall have similar demands, countries also specialize in order to gain acquired advantages (product technology). Countries do this through the apportionment of their research efforts. Further, those domestic industries in which there is intense competitive rivalry will probably innovate faster and develop international advantages.[7] In addition, consumers in industrial countries want and can afford to buy products with a wide variety of characteristics. Thus companies from different countries produce different product models, and each may gain some markets abroad. The relative importance of developed countries in world trade is also attributable to these countries' economic size.[8] Where the value of production is high, there is more that is available to sell both domestically and internationally. Further, when incomes are high, people tend to buy more from both domestic and foreign sources. In recent years as China's economy has grown much more rapidly than world economy as a whole, our share of global imports and exports has also increased. Our imports may be largely explained by country-similarity theory.

Technology-based Theory of Trade

The fact that so much trade takes place among industrial countries is also due to the growing importance of acquired advantage (product technology) as opposed to natural advantage (agricultural products and raw materials) in world trade. One weakness of factor-proportions trade theory is its largely static framework within which trade takes place. Countries are assumed to possess a given and constant amount of the various factors of production. The relative abundance or scarcity of a particular factor is assumed never to change. Consequently patterns of trade and specialization do not change. These assumptions are clearly not satisfactory. A country's factor endowments change over time. Plenty of evidence has shown that technological change and the process of technological creation and diffusion internationally exert a strong influence on patterns of trade.

One of the first economists to address the issue of how technological change can influence patterns of trade was Michael Posner. In Posner's model, innovating countries may enjoy a temporary advantage in the manufacture of a particular product because of time lags in the diffusion of knowledge internationally.[9] Posner considered the case of where a U.S. manufacturer discovered a new and cheaper method of producing a particular product. The innovation gives the United States a temporary cost advantage in the production of those goods. The United States' exports of the product accordingly increase. Because the knowledge about how to produce the product more cheaply is not immediately available to producers in other countries, the United States may enjoy technological superiority for a considerable period of time. Posner identified two kinds of time lags in the diffusion of knowledge. First, there is a demand or reaction lag, which is the time it takes for consumers to respond to the emergence of new, lower cost supplies of the product. The quicker they respond, the faster will U.S. exports of the products grow and the more producers in other countries will be forced to react to the competition posed by the innovation. Second, there is an imitation lag, which is the time it takes for foreign producers to imitate the innovating firm in the United States. This will depend partly on the extent to which the innovator is protected by patent law in his own and the foreign country. The occurrence of these lags gives rise to technological-gap trade.

Hufbauer (1966) developed a similar model of trade in which a temporary technological superiority enabled a country to enjoy a comparative advantage in high-technology goods for a finite period of time. However, Hufbauer introduced a further ingredient to the model that serves to lengthen the imitation lag, namely the occurrence of long-run dynamic economies of scale. In many industries, important cost savings result from learning-by-doing. The expertise of the labor force is enhanced by constant repetition of the same process. As a result, average costs fall as the cumulative volume of output increases. Consequently, the innovator is able to hold on to his comparative advantage for much longer even after the new method of production has been copied by producers in other countries. Like Posner, Hufbauer attached importance to the factors that cause innovation to occur more in some countries than in others.[10] Hufbauer advanced the theory that technological advances are more likely to occur in high-wage economies because high wages create an incentive for both producers and consumers to find ways of economizing on labor. Producers must seek out ways of introducing labor-saving techniques of production, while high wages increase the opportunity cost of leisure for households and generate a demand for goods that save time. This leads to the prediction that technology-gap exports will tend to flow from high-wage to low-wage economies.

The Product Life-Cycle Model of Trade

Another approach to the analysis of trade patterns in the context of technological change was provided by R. Vernon (1966). He attempts to explain world trade in manufactured products on the basis of stages in a product's life. Products have a limited market life. The life span depends on the time that it takes for producers to develop a new and superior substitute. The theory of the International Product Life Cycle (PLC) states that certain kinds of products go through a continuum, or cycle, that consists of roughly four stages—introduction, growth, maturity, and decline[11] —and that the location of production will shift from one country to another depending on the stage in the product's life cycle.

New Words

Mercantilism	/ˈmɜːkəntaɪlɪzəm/	n.	重商主义
surplus	/ˈsɜːpləs/	n.	剩余,过剩,[会计]盈余
deficit	/ˈdefɪsɪt/	n.	赤字,不足额
monopoly	/məˈnɒpəli/	n.	垄断,垄断者
subsidize	/ˈsʌbsɪdaɪz/	v.	资助,补贴
equivalent	/ɪˈkwɪvələnt/	adj. & n.	相当的,相等的;等价物
accumulation	/əˌkjuːmjʊˈleɪʃən/	n.	积聚,累积
deliberately	/dɪˈlɪbərɪtli/	adv.	故意地
under-consuming	/ˈʌndəkənˈsjuːmɪŋ/	n.	压低消费,抑制消费
mutually	/ˈmjuːtʃʊəli/	adv.	互相地,互助地
simultaneously	/ˌsɪməlˈteɪnɪəsly/	adv.	同时地
endow	/ɪnˈdaʊ/	vt.	捐赠;赋予
identical	/aɪˈdentɪkəl/	adj.	同一的,相同的
plausible	/ˈplɔːzəbəl/	adj.	似是而非的
homogeneous	/ˌhəʊməˈdʒiːnɪəs/	adj.	同类的,同质的
monopolize	/məˈnɒpəlaɪz/	vt.	垄断,独占
diffusion	/dɪˈfjuːʒən/	n.	扩散,传播
substitute	/ˈsʌbstɪtjuːt/	n.	替代,替代品

Phrases

in the form of	以……的形式
to impose restrictions on	对……实施限制
to succeed in doing	成功做成某事
better-off	境况更好的
to enable sb. to do sth.	使某人能做某事
to strive to do	努力做某事
to specialize in	专门从事……
in terms of	根据,按照;在……方面
to account for	解释,说明
at best	最多,充其量

per capita	人均
to have a high propensity to do sth.	有强烈的做某事的倾向
acquired advantage	后天(获得性)优势
as opposed to	与……相反,与……相对比
over time	随着时间的过去
technological creation and diffusion	技术创造和技术传播
to exert a strong influence on	对……施加/产生强烈的影响
to respond to	对……做出反应/反馈
patent law	专利法
to attach importance to	认为……重要

Special Terms

trade surplus/deficit	贸易盈余(顺差)/赤字(逆差)
zero-sum game	零和博弈
The Wealth of Nations	《国富论》(亚当·斯密)
absolute advantage	绝对优势
comparative advantage	比较优势
The Factor-Proportions Theory—HO Theory	要素禀赋理论
the neo-classical school	新古典学派
factor proportions	要素比例
labor-intensive	劳动密集型
capital-intensiv	资本密集型
Leontief Paradox	里昂惕夫之谜
consumer preferences	消费者偏好
human capital	人力资本,技能资本
physical capital	实物资本,有形资本
factor endowment	要素禀赋
manufactured goods	成品,工业制成品
demand-side theories of trade	需求方贸易理论
country-similarity theory	国家相似性理论
demand or reaction lag	需求或反应滞后
imitation lag	模仿滞后
economies of scale	规模经济
opportunity cost	机会成本
the International Product Life Cycle	国际产品生命周期(理论)

Notes

1. Mercantilists assumed trade was a zero-sum game—that it couldn't mutually benefit all parties.
   重商主义认为,贸易是一种零和博弈——贸易各方不能共同受益。

2. Smith's Absolute Advantage theory of trade identified differences in absolute costs as the basis for trade.
   斯密的绝对优势贸易理论认为贸易的基础在于成本的绝对差异。

3. Ricardo demonstrated that the reason why it pays countries to trade is the existence of different relative or comparative costs in the production of different goods.
   李嘉图证明了国家可以从贸易中获利的原因在于,不同商品的生产具有不同的相对(比较)成本。

4. They explained differences in comparative costs in terms of differences in the amounts of different factors with which countries were endowed and differences in the factor proportions required for the production of different goods.
   他们根据各国要素禀赋的数量差异以及生产不同商品所需的要素比例差异对比较成本的差异进行了解释。

5. It holds that once a producer has developed a new product in response to observed market conditions in the home market, it will turn to markets that are perceived to be the most similar to those at home.
   它(需求方贸易理论或国家相似性理论)认为,某个厂商一旦针对国内已观察到的市场环境开发出新产品,就会将其产品投入到(被认为)跟国内市场最相似的(国际)市场。

6. The basic assumption of this theory is that consumer's preferences vary among countries, although whether or not they differ sufficiently to materially affect the pattern of trade is less clear.
   该理论的基本假设是,消费者偏好存在国别差异,尽管这些差异是否很大、对贸易方式构成了实质性影响尚不甚清楚。

7. Further, those domestic industries in which there is intense competitive rivalry will probably innovate faster and develop international advantages.
   进而,这些存在激烈竞争的国内产业很可能会加速创新并开发国际优势。

8. The relative importance of developed countries in world trade is also attributable to these countries' economic size.
   发达国家在全球贸易中相对来说很重要,这也可归因于这些国家(庞大)的经济规模。

9. In Posner's model, innovating countries may enjoy a temporary advantage in the manufacture of a particular product because of time lags in the diffusion of knowledge internationally.

在波斯纳的模型里，创新型国家可能会在生产某种特定产品方面具有暂时的优势，其原因是知识在国际间扩散存在时滞。

10. Like Posner, Hufbauer attached importance to the factors that cause innovation to occur more in some countries than in others.

和波斯纳一样，哈夫鲍尔也认为那些使某些国家比其他国家创新更频繁的要素很重要。

11. introduction, growth, maturity, and decline

此为国际产品生命周期理论中关于产品的四个阶段：引入阶段、成长阶段、成熟阶段和衰退阶段。

Exercises

I. Discuss the following questions.

1. What did trade theory Mercantilism hold? Why do many economists believe that Mercantilism is wrong?
2. Why should comparative costs differ between countries? Which theory answered this question?
3. What are the attractions and inadequacies of factor-proportions theory?
4. What problem was addressed by demand-side theories of trade or country-similarity theory?
5. How can technological change—the process of technological creation and diffusion internationally—exert a strong influence on patterns of trade?
6. What are the four stages in International Product Life Cycle?

II. Analyze the case below and discuss the question.

Computers have made inroads into cartoon production, especially for blockbuster movies, but much of the industry remains highly labor-intensive. Each small movement of a cartoon character requires thousands of panels of patient drawings and paint by artist and animators. Approximately 90 percent of the animation for television cartoons happens in labor-abundant Asia, especially the Philippines, where costs run about half of those in the U.S.

As wages of Filipino artists and animators rise, cartoon studios are lured toward low-wage countries such as China and Vietnam. But the Philippines claim a non-wage advantage: the workers there speak English and live in a former U.S. colony. They argue that the result is better cartoons because the workers understand cartoon dialog and "get the joke"— an unlikely but important source of comparative advantage.

> **Questions:**
> Undoubtedly, here "getting the joke" is also a source of comparative advantage. Many terms of economics can also make sense in our daily life. Define the "comparative advantage" first and then discuss: in your daily life how do you use "comparative advantage" to your best advantage?

III. Match the terms in Column A with the explanations in Column B.

A	B
1. Mercantilism	A. a term used in economics, to mean the cost of something in terms of opportunity foregone, the highest-valued forgone activity
2. comparative advantage	B. For some goods, the average cost of production depends on the scale of output, or the number of units of the good produced. If the average cost per unit of a good falls as the scale of production rises, it's the right phenomenon.
3. factor proportions	C. the time it takes for consumers to respond to the emergence of new, lower cost supplies of products
4. labor-intensive	D. skills acquired by a worker through formal education and experience that improve the worker's productivity and increase his or her income
5. Leontief Paradox	E. consumers' attitude toward or feelings on certain goods or service, which may affect the consumer's ultimate purchasing decision
6. consumer preferences	F. In 1954, he made a test to the theory of factor-proportions. The results showed the exact opposite of what the theory has predicted. This surprising finding is called like this.
7. human capital	G. With character like this, an industry such as textile or methods of doing things needs a lot of workers.
8. demand or reaction lag	H. the ratios of factors employed in different industries; the ratios of factors with which different countries are endowed
9. economies of scale	I. It is used to justify free trade and oppose protectionism, and it is based on differing opportunity costs reflecting the different factor endowments of the countries involved.

10. opportunity cost   J. The theory held that a country's wealth was measured by its holdings of treasure, usually in the form of gold. Therefore countries should export more than they import and, if successful, would receive the value of their trade surpluses in the form of gold from the countries that ran deficits.

IV. Fill in the blanks of the following sentences with the words or phrases given below. Change the form if necessary.

| unlike | as well | such as | except for | productivity |
| nonetheless | in addition | likely | competitive | as |

Some people worry that __1__ low-wage countries acquire technology and capital, their productivity will rise, giving them a __2__ edge. But there are two reasons not be concerned about this. First, as productivity in a country rises, wages tend to rise __3__, so the competitiveness edge in low-wage lessens. Second, other factors, __4__ low levels of human capital (knowledge and skills) as well as poor public infrastructure and transportation services, tend to hold down __5__ in low-wage countries, even when they acquire new physical capital (computers and factories). __6__ products and production processes that require large amounts of unskilled labor, these factors offset the appeal of low-wages for companies considering relocating their production to poor countries. __7__, developing countries may have higher costs of other inputs, such as capital, energy, and raw materials. Prices of these inputs are more __8__ than wage rates to be similar across all countries, because, __9__ labor, non-labor inputs can be moved across borders in response to international price differences. __10__, capital, energy, and raw material costs per unit of output could be higher in developing countries if these countries use non-labor inputs less efficiently than developed countries.

V. Put the following into English.
1. 对进口进行限制,对出口给予补贴
2. 成功实现了较大的贸易顺差
3. 先天有利的自然禀赋
4. 后天有利的生产条件
5. 出口劳动密集型产品,进口资本密集型产品
6. 没能区分人力资本和有形资本
7. 工业国家的市场需求相似
8. 时滞的出现产生了技术缺口贸易

VI. Translate the following sentences into English.

1. 如果一个国家获得大量贸易顺差,它一定是以另一个国家的大量逆差为代价。
2. 相反,贸易应当使所有国家受益。它可以使这些国家比没有贸易时享受更多物美价廉的商品。
3. 劳动力丰富的国家在从事劳动密集型产业上具有成本优势;同样,资本丰富的国家在生产资本密集型产业上有优势。
4. 实践证明,技术创新和向国际的扩散、渗透的过程对国际贸易格局发挥了重要影响。
5. 有迹象表明,耐用消费品的国际贸易格局与国际产品生命周期理论是一致的。

VII. Translate the following passage into Chinese.

Free trade can provide gains from specialization both at inter-industry level and intra-industry level. The long-term gains are 1) gains from economies of scale; 2) efficiency gains from increased competition; 3) stimulus to capital investment; 4) an increase in the rate of technological innovation; 5) output expansion from reduced inflation. On the whole free trade can increase global economic welfare.

Trade protectionism can take on two forms: tariff and non-tariff barriers. Governments impose protection measures for a variety of reasons: to protect domestic industry; to correct balance of payment disequilibria; to collect more revenues. Trade protection measures are: tariff, import quotas, import licenses, embargoes, voluntary export restraints, etc.

ext

Protectionism Versus Free Trade

THE DEBATE OVER PROTECTIONISM

Arguments in favor of protectionism date back hundreds of years. During the 15th century mercantilists supported protectionism as a means of raising revenue, building surpluses of gold or precious metals, and protecting domestic industries against the predatory practices of foreigners. Since that time challenges to free trade have proliferated. Some have based their defense of protectionism on purely economic grounds; others have claimed protectionism to be appropriate for social or political reasons. Six of the most widely discussed reasons for protectionism are outlined below.

National Security

One of the most politically persuasive arguments for protectionism is that trade barriers may be necessary to protect national security. According to this line of reasoning, any country that wishes to be a major world power must maintain certain key sectors. If a nation does not have a steel industry, armament industry, and dozens of others considered to be strategic, then that country could be vulnerable in wars.

Unfair Competition

Another politically popular position is that low wages in foreign countries constitute unfair competition. Labor-intensive industries in more developed countries have tended to be the most vocal exponents of this view.

Low wages, however, are only one type of unfair competition noted by advocates of protectionism. The theory of comparative advantage and subsequent refinements assumed perfect competition, free mobility of capital and labor, and ample time for markets to adjust. If the marketplace was allowed to "rationalize" production, all countries would benefit by comparative specialization. Yet in the 1980s, rarely has the marketplace been allowed to operate fully. Countries with industrial policies have been able to mold comparative advantage through public policies such as special tax incentives, subsidies and selected protection. The use of industrial policies has led many business and labor leaders to proclaim the irrelevance of Ricardian comparative advantage. Thus, if only some countries play by the rules of free markets while others do not, firms in the free market economy will be at an unfair disadvantage.

Multinational Investment and Intrafirm Advantage

A third political argument in favor of trade barriers is that the growth of multinational corporate investment created a network of international trade never foreseen by Adam Smith or David Ricardo. Large corporations, with branches all over the world, have increasingly organized their production and marketing on a worldwide basis. The result, according to critics, has been that a large percentage of world trade has not been conducted on the basis of comparative advantage. Rather, trade has become a product of intrafirm transactions.

Labor unions, in particular, have argued that the spread of multinational investment and intrafirm trade has been a major cause of unemployment. Countries like the United States should therefore require multinationals to manufacture a large percentage of their production within the country.

Infant Industry

While the above arguments have been reactions to

problems in the international economy, the infant industry rationale has traditionally been a more positive approach to protectionism. The persuasiveness of the infant industry argument led the United States to erect high tariff barriers in the nineteenth century. In the twentieth century most developing countries have defended their protectionist policies for infant industry reasons, and even advanced countries such as Japan have used the infant industry rationale for protecting high-tech industries in the 1980s.

Most economists, however, have been careful to limit the application of infant industry protection. J. S. Mill pointed out that "the protectionism should be confined to cases in which there is good ground of assurance that the industry which it fosters will after a time be able to dispense with it; nor should the domestic producers ever be allowed to expect that it will be continued to beyond the time necessary for a fair trial of what they are capable of accomplishing."

Terms of Trade

A second positive reason for protection is that tariffs, under certain conditions, can improve a country's terms of trade. The terms of trade can be defined as the quantity of domestic goods that must be exported to receive an imported good. The terms of trade are favorable if a nation can sell few of its own goods while it receives a large quantity of imported goods; the terms of trade are unfavorable if a country must sell a large quantity of domestic production to buy a small quantity of imports.

For tariffs have desirable effects on the terms of trade, the importing country must be very large and the export must be very important to the producing country. If the exporter does not want to have its volume of shipments reduced by a tariff, the exporter will have to cut its price. Although this type of tariff does not afford protection to a domestic producer, it will improve a country's terms of trade by allowing the importing nation to purchase the foreign products at a cheaper price.

Income Distribution and Employment

A third positive approach to justifying protectionism relates to purely social goals. Through the use of tariffs and quotas, for example, a government can redistribute income within a country or maintain domestic employment and domestic living standards. Barriers to trade in a given product usually increase the domestic price of the product; domestic firms have little incentive to price their goods at world levels if they are sheltered from international competition. Higher prices will usually encourage more production for the protected product, which in turn increases the demand for labor. Higher demand for labor in the protected industry raises wage rates relative to other sectors in the economy, which thereby redistributes income.

THE LIBERAL POLITICAL ECONOMIST DEFENSE

The above discussion of protectionism is by no means exhaustive. Almost every country and interest group has its own rationale for supporting the use of trade barriers. Some developing countries, for example, justify protection as a way to attract multinational investment and/or exclude unwanted cultural influences. Some developed countries claim that protectionism is the best way to bolster balance of payments and build industrial strength. A group of noted economists in Cambridge, England, for instance, believe that free trade strengthens the strong and weakens the weak forever. Trade barriers, they argue, are just as important for "senile" industries in Great Britain as they are for infant industries in developing nations.

Liberal political economists do not deny the rationality of protectionism in all instances. They believe that some exceptions to free trade are justified. The terms-of-trade argument is widely accepted as appropriate if a nation holds some monopoly power and wants to maximize domestic welfare at the expense of other countries. Similarly, the infant industry argument is viewed by many economists as a respectable prescription as long as the protectionism meets a number of conditions.

In general, however, liberal political economists argue that protectionism is a bad policy on both political and economic grounds. On the political side, they claim that protectionism, especially in large countries, tends to provoke retaliation by others. If this occurs, any short-run benefits derived from protection would be offset by a reduction in exports. Political economists also point out that protectionism in democratic societies tends to be politically difficult to remove. Special interest groups that prosper behind trade barriers fight to maintain their privileged position.

Equally important to political economists are the efficiency problems associated with protectionism. While they argue that political and social objectives of a country should not be ignored, liberal economists claim that protectionism is usually the least efficient way to achieve these goals. The national defense arguments, for instance, made some sense in the days of protracted conventional warfare. In an era of thermonuclear power, however, a nation's ability to protect itself may no longer depend on steel mills. Although limited conflicts such as the Korean War remain possible, it seems unlikely that such wars would isolate a country from strategic materials.

In response to the "unfair" competition argument, most economists point out that wage advantages are no more unfair than the advantage of superior capital resources or sophisticated technology. Furthermore, the notion of unfair competition based on lower wages rejects the very principle of comparative advantage. Countries benefit from international trade by specializing in those products they make the best. This means that an importing country would be better off if workers in less productive sectors moved into more productive industries. If workers have difficulties finding those jobs, the government should provide retraining skills rather than protect inefficient producers.

Liberal economists also respond to arguments about the managed nature of world trade by noting that the market is usually the most efficient way to allocate resources. Multinational corporations will not remain profitable if intrafirm transactions do not reflect global comparative advantage. And even though some intrafirm trade by multinationals does export jobs, those same multinationals are often responsible for creating jobs that lead to exports.

Finally, national industrial policies are not viewed as a sound justification for protectionism, in part for efficiency reasons and in part because free trade, in the Ricardian sense, has always been a myth. Governments have always intervened in their economies, and they have always played a part in molding national comparative advantage. This makes drawing a line on many unfair trade policies extraordinarily difficult. It is clear why predatory pricing practices and subsidies devoted explicitly to exports might qualify as unfair. But if one nation has an investment tax credit for all industry, another nation has investment tax credits for selected industries, and a third directly subsidizes capital investment, which country has the unfair advantage?

While there is little agreement among liberal economists on what should be the appropriate response to a world of industrial policies, most concur that more protectionism would be a mistake. Some believe that countries without industrial policies should adopt their own national strategies; others claim that restrictions on the use of certain industrial policy tools would be a more efficient answer to these trade problems. In any case, they argue that protectionism can only aggravate the plight of the world economy. Increasing trade barriers would reduce the effectiveness of the market, hinder the adjustment of troubled industries, and lead the world back to the beggar-thy-neighbor policies of the 1930s.

Answer the following questions:

1. What are the main reasons for trade protectionism? Which one do you think is the most persuasive?
2. Should "infant industries" be protected or not? Take some China's industries as examples to show the advantages or disadvantages of protection on them.
3. For labor-intensive industries that employ workers who cannot be easily absorbed into other sectors of the economy, how can trade protectionism do good to them?
4. Combining China's current economic conditions and our commitment to WTO, how do you think should China lay down her own trade policy?

Unit 3

International Trade in Services

● *Learning Objectives*

Text A
- to learn the nature and type of international trade in services
- to understand the correlation between service trade and trade in goods

Text B
- to understand the development of international trade in services over the history
- to learn the impact of the global world on international trade in services

Text A

The Importance of Services in International Trade: Defining Trade in Services

A discussion of trade in services is best started with a large number of examples. The following people are all exporting services:

1. An advertising executive developing a TV commercial for a foreign client
2. A secretary at a law firm answering a call from a foreign client
3. A cabby who drives a foreign businessman from the airport to the hotel
4. The cast of a television show that will be broadcast abroad
5. A doctor operating on a foreign patient
6. The doorman and the bartender at a posh hotel serving foreign guests
7. An accountant unraveling the financial affairs of a foreign corporation
8. An engineer designing a bridge to be built in another country
9. A caterer preparing a meal to be served at a foreign embassy
10. A management consultant advising a foreign client

The following persons or companies are all importing services:

1. Every reader of this paper who has taken a foreign vacation
2. An auto company that asks a foreign firm to design a new model
3. Someone who buys a ticket to a performance by a foreign orchestra
4. A student attending a foreign university

    5. A businessman who extracts information from a foreign database
    6. A housewife who goes to "Jean Pierre" for the latest French hair styling
    7. A consumer who has a camera repaired abroad
    8. An investor who buys securities at a foreign stock exchange
    9. The actress who has her legs insured in London with a Lloyd's broker
    10. A traveler who uses a credit card issued by a foreign bank

Obviously, the range of activities that lead to international trade in services is wide. In many cases the persons involved are likely to be only dimly aware that they are exporting or importing services and that their economic interests are tied to policies and events that influence trade in services.

As we observed, quite a proportion of service activity enters into international trade. By their very nature, services are much less tradable than goods. Services have to be consumed at the point where they are produced. This means that either the supplier of a service must move to where the consumer is located, or the consumer of the service must move to where the producer is located. Only a small proportion of services are capable of being traded like goods with neither the producer nor the consumer being required to move.[1] To illustrate this point, we can make use of a fourfold categorization of service activities proposed by Stern and Hoekman.

"Separated" services

"Separated" services require no movement of the provider or demander of the service between countries. Transport services such as civil aviation or shipping fit this category.[2] A civil airline can provide the citizens of another country with a service without the need for the civil airline to be located in the overseas country or for the consumer to go to the country where the airline in question is located.

Demander-located services

Demander-located services require the movement of the provider of the service only. In this case the provider of the service needs to be in close geographical proximity to the demander of the service. Banking and insurance both fit this category. A British bank which wishes to gain a share of the Japanese market for retail banking will need to establish a presence in Japan.[3] This will require foreign direct investment involving a movement of both capital and labor.[4]

Provider-located services

Provider-located services require the movement of the demander of the service only. The provider of the service supplies the service in his own country but the service is purchased by a citizen or firm based in another country. Examples of these kinds of services are tourism, education, and medical services.

Footloose, non-separated services

Footloose, non-separated services require both movement of consumers and producers. The provider of the service carries out foreign direct investment in another country and utilizes the subsidiary thus established to supply a service to the citizen of or firm based in some third country.[5] Thus a British bank with a subsidiary in Japan may, through its Japanese subsidiary, make a bank loan to a firm based in the United States. This category is included for the sake of completeness.

This fourfold categorization of services illustrates the important point that a trade in services takes place whenever "domestic factors receive income from non-residents in exchange for their services."[6] Very often we are inclined to think of trade in services in the same way as we regard trade in goods. This confines trade in services to trade in "separated" services, the first category listed above. However, this would seem to be too narrow a definition of services.[7]

The above categorization serves also to demonstrate how trade in services may also be bound up with a movement of capital and labor across national borders. Both the second and fourth categories require both foreign direct investment and/or a movement of labor from one country to another. In this case the income derived by domestic factors of production (capital and labor) from their overseas activities should be included in the country's earnings from the export of services.[8] They are just as much a part of the country's service exports as the foreign currency earnings from domestically owned civil airlines or shipping companies. In practice, as will be seen later, it is often difficult to obtain accurate data concerning these service exports. It is also important to note in passing that the issue of freer trade in such demander-located services is intimately bound up with the issue of the right of establishment for firms and individuals supplying such services.

Herbert Grubel also proposed a rather different taxonomy of ways in which trade in services takes place. He has distinguished between just two types of service trade:

1. **Disembodied services,** requiring the movement of people, capital, or firms across borders, or the movement of goods across borders for transformation. Thus tourism involves a movement of people across countries to "absorb" services supplied by another country. Education and medical care similarly presuppose a movement of people from one country to another. The wages remitted by migrant workers or guest workers are similarly generally treated as service income. The income derived by banks from their foreign subsidiaries is an example of a service requiring a movement of capital across borders. Finally, the income derived by a country from packaging, warehousing, and wholesaling of goods for re-export (so-called entrepot trade) is an example of trade in services which requires a movement of goods across borders.[9]

2. **Splintered (or separated) services,** so called because the services involved have been splintered or separated from their original

production in the sense that they are now embodied in goods for separate sale. Obvious examples of such services are films, books, scientific documents, patents and electronic discs containing data or computer programmers. In all these cases citizens or firms from the exporting country derive an income from the sale of a service embodied in a good. Thus film producers receive royalties from the showing abroad of a film which they have produced, and authors also receive royalties from the sale of books which they have written. Trade in such services requires no movement of people, capital or firms across borders. Instead, goods embodying services are transported across borders. Thus trade in these kinds of services more closely resembles trade in goods. What distinguishes such trade from merchandise trade is the proportion of added value accounted for by service as opposed to manufacturing industries.[10]

    The concept of splintered, or separated services is a useful one for understanding some of the growth in services trade in recent decades. It is apparent that part of this growth is attributable to the increase in the relative importance of service inputs in manufacturing industry. This is a reflection of greater investments of human capital in the production process. As production becomes more capital and knowledge intensive, the level of service inputs increases. What was previously treated as trade in goods now becomes categorized as trade in embodied services. As Grubel observes, it is in many ways meaningless to treat such trade in services in a different way from trade in goods. To some degree all goods embody splintered services. What separates such trade from trade in services is merely the relative importance of services input.

New Words

accurate	/ˈækjʊrət/	adj.	准确的；精确的
attributable	/əˈtrɪbjʊtəbəl/	adj.	可归因的
banking	/ˈbæŋkɪŋ/	n.	银行业
bartender	/ˈbɑːtendə/	n.	酒保
base	/beɪs/	v.	设立
broker	/ˈbrəʊkə/	n.	经纪人，掮客
cabby	/ˈkæbɪ/	n.	出租车司机
capital	/ˈkæpɪtl/	n.	资金
capital-intensive	/ˈkæpɪtl ɪnˈtensɪv/	adj.	资金密集型
cast	/kɑːst/	n.	演员阵容
categorization	/ˌkætɪɡəraɪˈzeɪʃən/	n.	分类
caterer	/ˈkeɪtərə/	n.	包办伙食人
confine	/kənˈfaɪn/	v.	限制
database	/ˈdeɪtəˌbeɪs/	n.	数据库
demander	/dɪˈmɑːndə/	n.	需求方

derive	/dɪˈraɪv/	v.	取得,得到
doorman	/ˈdɔːmæn/	n.	看门人
embody	/ɪmˈbɒdi/	v.	包含,包括
executive	/ɪgˈzekjutɪv/	n.	主管
footloose	/ˈfʊtluːs/	adj.	自由自在的
fourfold	/ˈfɔːfəʊld/	adj. & adv.	四倍,四重(性的)
insure	/ɪnˈʃʊə/	v.	保险,投保
intimately	/ˈɪntɪmɪtli/	adv.	亲密地,紧密地
knowledge-intensive	/ˈnɒlɪdʒ ɪnˈtensɪv/	adj.	知识密集型
labor	/ˈleɪbə/	n.	劳动力
loan	/ləʊn/	n.	贷款
move	/muːv/	v.	流动
packaging	/ˈpækɪdʒɪŋ/	n.	包装
posh	/pɒʃ/	adj.	豪华的
presence	/ˈprezəns/	n.	存在
presuppose	/ˌpriːsəˈpəʊz/	v.	推测
producer	/prəˈdjuːsə/	n.	生产商
proximity	/prɒkˈsɪmɪti/	n.	接近,近似性
remit	/rɪˈmɪt/	v.	汇款,汇寄
retail	/ˈriːteɪl/	adj.	零售的
royalty	/ˈrɔɪəlti/	n.	专利权税,版税
securities	/sɪˈkjʊərɪtɪs/	n.	有价证券
share	/ʃeə/	n.	份额
shipping	/ˈʃɪpɪŋ/	n.	航运业,运输业
splintered	/ˈsplɪntəd/	adj.	分裂的
supplier	/səˈplaɪə/	n.	供应商
taxonomy	/tækˈsɒnəmi/	n.	分类
tradable	/ˈtreɪdəbl/	adj.	可进行贸易的,可做交易的
unravel	/ʌnˈrævəl/	v.	弄清楚
wholesaling	/ˈhəʊlseɪlɪŋ/	n.	批发

Phrases

be attributable to	可归因于……
be bound up with	与……联在一起,与……密切相关
be in close proximity to	与……靠得很近
for the sake of	为了……起见;出于对……的考虑
in exchange for	交换

in question　　　　　　　　　　　　上述的……；讨论中的，争执中的

Special Terms

civil aviation　　　　　　　　　　民用航空
disembodied service　　　　　　　脱离式服务
electronic discs　　　　　　　　　电子软盘
entrepot trade　　　　　　　　　　转口贸易，中转贸易
factors of production　　　　　　　生产要素
free trade　　　　　　　　　　　　自由贸易
foreign currency earnings　　　　　外汇收入
foreign direct investment　　　　　外商直接投资(FDI)
manufacturing industries　　　　　制造业
merchandise trade　　　　　　　　商品贸易
migrant worker　　　　　　　　　迁徙性(或流动性)工人
splintered service　　　　　　　　分离式服务
stock exchange　　　　　　　　　股票交易所

Notes

1. Only a small proportion of services are capable of being traded like goods with neither the producer nor the consumer being required to move.
   只有少部分的服务可以像货物那样交易，而不需要生产商或消费者进行流动。

2. Transport services such as civil aviation or shipping fit this category.
   运输服务业，如民航或航运，属于这一类。
   句中 fit 表示"适合"，"符合"。

3. A British bank which wishes to gain a share of the Japanese market for retail banking will need to establish a presence in Japan.
   一家英国银行要想在日本的零售银行业市场上占有一席之地，就需要在日本设立公司。
   句中 a share of ... market 指的是"市场份额"；retail 表示"零售的"。
   establish a presence 中的 presence 本意为"存在"，句中具体指"公司"。类似的例子如：
   The Japanese presence in the U.S. consumer market is strong.
   日本货在美国消费市场占有很大比例。
   与其相搭配的动词词组有 establish/maintain/withdraw one's presence 等。

4. This will require foreign direct investment involving a movement of both capital and labor.
   这就需要外商直接投资,把资金和劳动力都流动起来。
   句中 movement 指"流动"。

5. The provider of the service carries out foreign direct investment in another country and utilizes the subsidiary thus established to supply a service to the citizen of or firm based in some third country.
   服务供应商在别国进行直接投资,设立子公司向第三国的公民或公司提供服务。

6. This fourfold categorization of services illustrates the important point that a trade in services takes place whenever "domestic factors receive income from non-residents in exchange for their services."
   服务的四类分法说明了重要的一点,即只要"一国内的生产要素从非本国居民提供的服务而获得收入"的时候,服务贸易就发生了。
   这里 domestic factors 中的 factors 是"factors of production"(生产要素,包括奖金和劳动力)的简称,指的是其中的"劳动力"。

7. However, this would seem to be too narrow a definition of services.
   但是,用这一类服务来定义服务就太狭隘了。
   句中 narrow 表示"狭义的","狭隘的",又如:"狭义相对论"就是"Narrow Theory of Relativity"。

8. In this case the income derived by domestic factors of production (capital and labor) from their overseas activities should be included in the country's earnings from the export of services.
   在这种情况下,一国内生产要素(资金和劳动力)从其国外的行为中得到的收入就应该包括在该国从服务业出口所得到的收益中。
   derive... from 意为"从……得到"。
   income 为"收入",earnings 为"收入","收益",常用复数。

9. Finally, the income derived by a country from packaging, warehousing, and wholesaling of goods for re-export (so-called entrepot trade) is an example of trade in services which requires a movement of goods across borders.
   一国将货物包装、库存和批发后再出口(即:转口贸易)取得的收入就是要求货物跨国流动的服务贸易的一个例子。

10. What distinguishes such trade from merchandise trade is the proportion of added value accounted for by service as opposed to manufacturing industries.
    此类贸易与商品贸易的区别就在于,服务带来的附加值占制造业的比例。
    as opposed to 意为"与……相比"。
    added value 附加值

Exercises

I. Discuss the following questions.

1. Why does international trade in services account for only a small proportion of international trade?
2. According to Stern and Hoekman, how may categories can international trade in services fall into?
3. Under what circumstances can we say that international trade in services take place?
4. What's the relationship between international trade in services and the movement of capital and labor across national borders?
5. What are the similarities and differences between the two kinds of categorization of international trade in services?

II. Analyze the case below and discuss the questions.

A law professor from London who
(1) teaches English common law to French law students attending the University of London under a joint degree program with the Sorbonne, (2) is on her way to Hong Kong to teach a six-week course on international commercial law at one of the Hong Kong universities, and (3) is working on a book on international commercial law for international distribution
is actually involved in international trade in services in each of her activities.

Questions:
Analyze the three activities of the professor to explain why each of the three activities can be called as international trade in services.

III. Match the terms in column A with the explanations in column B.

A	B
1. supplier	A. people who are to be engaged, are engaged or have been engaged in a remunerated activity in a place other than their homeplace
2. consumer	B. a company which is a part of a larger company
3. shipping	C. the sending and delivery of something, usually by ship and usually from one country to another
4. banking	D. a sum of money, especially one used to produce more money or to start a business
5. subsidiary	E. a payment made to people like writers and inventers as part of the profit from sales

6. free trade F. a person who buys goods or uses services
7. migrant workers G. the business of a bank or a banker
8. royalties H. trade arrangements when tariffs or other duties of goods and services are eliminated
9. merchandise trade I. exports and imports of goods
10. capital J. a person or firm that provides something, especially goods and services

IV. Fill in the blanks of the following sentences with the words or phrases given below. Make changes when necessary.

| consume | merchandise | export | base | derive |
| local | service | treat | separate | presence |

1. In its bid to build an energy saving society, China calls for less _____ of energy and resources by the whole nation.
2. The fundamental characteristics of services explain why it is important that services be discussed _____ from industrial and consumer goods and why their very nature affects the manner in which they are marketed internationally.
3. Accounting and advertising firms were among the earlier companies to establish branches or acquire _____ affiliations abroad to _____ their U.S. multinational clients.
4. By establishing their subsidiaries in another country, many of the service companies expand their client _____ to include local companies.
5. Some banking services could be _____ from one country to another on a limited basis through the use of ATMs.
6. Service firms face most of the same environmental constraints and problems confronting _____ traders.
7. Under the WTO agreements, national _____, the principle of giving others the same treatment as one's own nationals, is one of its rules on non-discrimination.
8. One quarter of the value of all international trade is estimated to be _____ from the deal of services.
9. Automobiles, computers, furniture, etc, are examples of tangible products that have a physical _____; they are a thing or object that can be stored and possessed and whose intrinsic value is embedded within its physical _____.

V. Put the following into English.
1. 服务供应商
2. 占有一定市场份额
3. 在外国设立的公司
4. 向公司提供银行贷款
5. 与资金和劳动力的跨国流动相联系

6. 服务为出口创汇
7. 国有民航
8. 吸收别国提供的服务
9. 制造业中服务投入的相对重要性
10. 增加人力资本投资

VI. Translate the following sentences into English.

1. 与工业品和消费品截然不同，服务以其特性而有别于他物，因而需要予以特殊的考虑。
2. 世界市场的扩大拉动了企业对服务需求的增长，服务公司成为市场寻找者，在全世界积极为它们所提供的服务寻找顾客。
3. 国际服务贸易占国际商品贸易额的四分之一，它在服务输出、输入国的经济发展、就业扩大和国际收支状况改善中起着重要的作用。
4. 发达国家输出高技术服务获取高额服务出口收入，而从发展中国家引进廉价劳动力既可以弥补本国人力资源的不足，又可以获得高额利润，弥补国际收支逆差。
5. 有些人力资源较丰富的发展中国家可以利用自己的劳动力优势，大力发展服务输出，以获取外汇。

VII. Translate the following passage into Chinese.

Unlike merchandise trade that requires a declaration of value when exported, most services do not have to have an export declaration nor do they always pass through a tariff or customs barrier when entering a country. Consequently, an accurate tally of service trade exports is difficult to determine.

Today the most important motive for engaging in international business for most business service firms is to seek new markets. The notable exceptions are accounting and advertising firms whose motives are about equally divided between being client followers and market seekers.

ext

Services in the World Economy

After an arduous journey of four years from Venice to Shang-Tu near modern Peking, Marco Polo arrived in 1275 at the court of Kublai Khan, the Mongol emperor of China. He brought the emperor glass and jewelry produced by Venetian craftsmen and letters from the Doge of Venice and from Pope Gregory VIII in Rome. He also brought along something even more important to Kublai Khan, knowledge and professional skills, and for the next seventeen years Marco Polo worked for Kublai Khan as an adviser and emissary before returning to Venice in 1292.

The story of Marco Polo illustrates the close relationship that has existed between trade in goods and trade in services throughout history. We could find similar reports in the clay tablets that have been unearthed from the ruins of the ancient cities of Sumer and Babylon. They have left us reports on the comings and goings of the merchants, craftsmen, storytellers, and ambassadors who carried out trade in goods and services between one city-state and another.

In some ways not much has changed. Businessmen still travel from Europe to China bringing goods, messages, knowledge, and information as in the days of Marco Polo. What has changed is that modern technology has made it possible to transport goods and people from Europe to China in a matter of hours rather than years, in relative comfort rather than at great personal risk and discomfort, and at a fraction of the cost. Communication satellites and computers have made it possible to send long messages and large sums of money to remote parts of the world in seconds.

Because it is so much easier and cheaper to move goods, money, people, and information from one country to another, the minuscule international flow of goods and services of Marco Polo's time has become so large that most people are affected by it either as consumers or as producers and the companies that supply the transportation, communications, and other international services have become large business enterprises employing hundreds of thousands of people. Increased economic importance has also brought growing influence on policy, and it has become increasingly difficult to treat international services as peripheral activities not worthy of the attention of trade policy officials. They deserve attention both because they are crucial for all international economic activity and because they are an important source of income and jobs.

The same technological advances that have made it easier to move information from one country to another have also made the creation, processing, and distribution of information the source of new economic growth in the industrialized countries. The development of increasingly powerful computers has led to an economic revolution as profound as the industrial revolution of the eighteenth century. Increasingly automated factories require fewer blue-collar workers on the production line, but more white-collar workers to program the computers, to design new products, and to process performance data.

A growing demand for information-based business services and a new capability to transmit large amounts of information without a time lag has thus created a new area of international trade. Labor-intensive processing of information can take place almost anywhere across the street or at the other end of the world and an increasing number of business enterprises are taking advantage of this possibility.

A Historical Perspective

International trade in services has existed for as long as neighboring tribes, villages, or cities have traded with each other, visited each other, financed each other, or done business with each other. As people traveled, they carried skills, knowledge, information, and artistic talent from one country to another. Scientists, engineers, astronomers, and experts on many other subjects have traveled to other countries since time immemorial, offering their advice to foreign kings and merchant princes.

Some of the earliest literature is based on an oral tradition preserved by wandering bards, who mesmerized their audiences with tales of foreign lands, spreading the fame of great heroes and kings. Artists, musicians, and actors have traveled far and wide in search of inspiration and patrons. Students traveled to attend foreign universities, to apprentice themselves to master craftsmen abroad, and to learn by seeing the world.

The earliest traders had to provide their own transportation, find their own shelter, and cook their own food. As the international flow of goods, people, money, and information increased, more and more of the services that support international travel could be purchased from enterprises along the way.

Further reductions in the real cost of travel have come as a result of new technologies—steamships, railroads, and jet aircraft, which made travel not only cheaper and faster but also easier.

The growth in the market for services has created both very large companies that are able to take advantage of large economies of scale and many small companies that are better suited to meet the needs of narrow segments of the market. In both cases, specialization has added to the reduction in the cost of support services brought about by advances in technology. This in turn has stimulated a further expansion of international trade, international travel, international finance, and international information flows.

Global Economic Integration

Today, most countries export a larger percentage of their total output and import a larger portion of what they consume than ever before. Travel to other countries has become commonplace. Vast sums of money move from one country to another in a matter of hours or even minutes. Information sometimes moves faster from Washington to London and hack then from one street to another within a city. Foreign markets have thus become more closely linked to local markets, and jobs and business profits are now tied much more closely to competition in the global marketplace.

As international competition in the context of a global market has become more of a reality, corporate users have become much more sensitive to the cost of service inputs. In a world where expanded international competition has reduced margins and businesses succeed or fail on the basis of relatively small differences in costs, the cost and quality of available services can affect the profitability of a firm. Firms with large international operations have become far more vocal than in the past about the effect of foreign government policies on the availability and cost of services such as communications and transportation. This has led to a user-oriented focus to international trade discussions of such services as telecommunications, a somewhat startling concept to officials accustomed to a world of national telecommunications monopolies.

International trade in services has also become big business. In the United States, many companies that supply international services—American Express (travel services), Citibank (financial services), Pan American (air transport services), Sea Land (ocean and land transport services), AIG (insurance), AT&T (communications), and EDS (data processing)—are among the largest companies in the country. These firms have become far more conscious than in the past of the advantage of influencing government policies that affect their ability to deliver services worldwide, and their rapid growth in recent years has given them the clout to get attention from the government. Both business executives and government officials are thus more inclined than in the past to look at barriers in services as key commercial issues.

The rapid increase in international economic activity and the resulting growth of services made it inevitable that government officials responsible for trade policy would sooner or later pay more attention to policies that affect the delivery of services.

The Information Revolution

The crucial role of information-based business services to economic growth today and the tradability of these services through modern communication and data processing facilities have convinced many governments that they should pay more attention to trade in services sooner rather than later.

Services are at the heart of an economic revolution equivalent in influence to the industrial revolution that displaced artisans with factories in the eighteenth century. In the emerging economy the creation, processing, and distribution of information are displacing manufacturing as the primary economic activity of most workers. In fact, the creation, processing, and distribution of information are so central to the new economic revolution that it may well become known as the information revolution.

The information revolution has fundamentally changed the scope, character, and significance of trade in services. Old ideas about the nature of services have become a hindrance to the efficiency of government policies affecting the organization of services activities in the world economy.

Answer the following questions:

1. What does the story of Marco Polo tell us?
2. What are the implications of modern technology to the international trade in services?
3. What other fields have been boosted by the expansion of international trade in services?
4. Why do governments pay more attention to international trade in services in the consideration of their foreign government policies?
5. What fundamental changes have taken place in international trade in services in the information era?

Unit 4

Technology Transfer

Learning Objectives

Text A
- to learn what is technology transfer
- to know the parties involved in technology transfer
- to know where the financial flows come from

Text B
- to understand the relationship between international technology transfer and intellectual property rights
- to know the conflicts between developing countries and developed countries concerning property rights

ext A

Understanding Technology Transfer

Defining Technology Transfer

There is no widely accepted definition of international technology transfer, but, generally speaking, international technology transfer is the sharing of knowledge and facilities among different countries.

The concept of technology transfer as a practical matter becomes clearer when one understands what technology transfer is designed to accomplish. The purpose of a technology transfer program is to make scientific and technological developments accessible to private industry and state and local governments. These users are then encouraged to develop the technology further into new products, processes, materials, or services that will enhance our nation's industrial competitiveness or otherwise improve our quality of life.[1]

Technology and innovation can help to:
- improve living standards,
- increase productivity,
- generate new industries and employment opportunities,
- improve public services,

- create more competitive products in world markets.

Decisions and Policies

Technology transfer is embodied in the actions taken by individuals and organizations. The investment and trade decisions made by firms, acquisition of knowledge and skills by individuals through formal education and on-the-job experience, purchase of patent rights and licenses, assimilating the published results of public or private research, development and demonstration (RD&D) activity, and migration of skilled personnel with knowledge of particular technologies, all represent different forms of technology transfer.[2] Technology transfer can also be influenced by government aid and financing programs, and by multilateral bank lending. Governments can implement policies that promote R&D programs that address global climate change concerns in sectors such as energy, forestry, and transportation.[3] The role of governments is especially important for those climate-related technologies, which are not immediately viable and profitable.

The rate of technology transfer is affected both by motivations that induce more rapid adoption of new techniques and by barriers that impede such transfers. Both types of factors can be influenced by policy. Motivations of the various stakeholders can differ markedly:

- Transnational or multinational corporations are major sources of technology. They seek international sales, market share, and cheaper production costs through equipment transfers and foreign direct investment. Corporations are primarily concerned about profits, acceptable risks and ensuring protection of intellectual property.
- Recipient-country firms are also motivated to transfer technology to minimize costs, just as with transnational corporations. But other motivations may be quite different from those of supplier firms, such as: (a) technical capabilities, quality, or cost reductions that they cannot achieve on their own; (b) the higher perceived status of "international level" technologies; (c) access to managerial and marketing expertise and sources of capital; (d) access to export markets; and (e) access to new distribution networks.
- Recipient governments may seek to increase capabilities for domestic technology development and promote foreign investment in their country. At the local level, communities and community organizations need to be reached by information networks, get organized and participate in decision-making processes to improve local living standards and the quality of the environment via appropriate technologies.[4]
- Provider or donor governments may set up policies to encourage technology transfer and fund transfers of research and expertise via Official Development Assistance (ODA) to support development and political goals, but more often are interested in policies that expand foreign markets for their national firms and

increase exports.[5]

- ❖ Multilateral agencies with development goals, such as the World Bank, the United Nations Development Program (UNDP), Regional Development Banks and Regional Organizations, pursue technology transfer to support development and as an instrument for achieving desired economic and policy reforms.[6]
- ❖ Multilateral agencies with environmental goals, such as the Global Environment Facility (GEF), have the transfer of ESTs as an explicit objective, and explore new and effective means to accomplish these objectives, by catalyzing sustainable markets and enabling private sector involvement in the transfer of these technologies.
- ❖ Non-governmental organizations have been at the forefront of concerns about technology choice and the "appropriateness" of technologies transferred through development assistance and commercial channels, the social and cultural impacts of such transfers, and the needs for technology adaptation to suit local conditions and minimize unwanted impacts.[7]

International Financial Flows

Several types of international financial flows support technology transfer. In practice, the transfer of a particular technology may involve several of them operating simultaneously or in a coordinated sequence, particularly for large, costly projects. Among the types of financial flows are:

Official Development Assistance (ODA) and Official Aid (OA). These include grants and interest free or subsidized loans to developing countries (ODA) and countries with economies in transition (OA), primarily from member countries of the Organization for Economic Co-operation and Development (OECD). ODA/OA includes both bilateral aid and that provided by governments indirectly through multilateral organizations.

Loans at market rates. These include loans from international institutions, including the multilateral development banks (MDBs), and commercial banks. As noted above, some of the grant portions of ODA and OA are also channeled through MDBs to subsidize their loan interest rates, blurring somewhat the lines between these categories.

Foreign Direct Investment (FDI). It involves direct investment in physical plant and equipment in one country by business interests from a foreign country.

Commercial sales. These refer to the sale (and corresponding purchase), on commercial terms, of equipment and knowledge.

Foreign Portfolio Equity Investment (FPEI) and Venture Capital. These involve purchase of stock or shares of foreign companies through investment funds or directly. Venture capital is characterized by being longer term and higher risk, with a greater degree of management control exerted by the investor.

Other financial flows. These include Export Credit Agencies and activities supported by non-governmental organizations active in technology transfer efforts, educational and training efforts not captured in the other indicators, and related transfers.

National Systems of Innovation and Technology Infrastructure

Technology transfers, both within a country and between countries, are influenced greatly by national systems of innovation—the institutional and organizational structures which support technological development and innovation. Governments can build or strengthen scientific and technical educational institutions and modify the form or operation of technology networks: the interrelated organizations generating, diffusing, and utilizing technologies. The presence of regional and global systems of innovation interacting with national-level systems also has important implications for policy makers.

National systems of innovation depend upon the development of so-called technology infrastructure, "a set of collectively supplied, specific, industry-relevant capabilities" such as technology centers and educational and skills development institutions.[8] "Technology infrastructure consists of science, engineering and technical knowledge available to private industry. Such knowledge can be embodied in human, institutional, and facility forms. More specifically, technology infrastructure includes generic technologies, infratechnologies, technical information, and research and test facilities, as well as less technically-explicit areas including information relevant for strategic planning and market development, forums for joint industry-government planning and collaboration, and assignment of intellectual property rights. An important characteristic of technology infrastructure is that it depreciates slowly, but it requires considerable effort and long lead times to put in place and maintain."

New Words

enhance	/ɪnˈhɑːns/	v.	提高,增强
acquisition	/ˌækwɪˈzɪʃən/	n.	采购,买进
multilateral	/ˌmʌltɪˈlætərəl/	adj.	多边的,多国的
implement	/ˈɪmplɪmənt/	v.	贯彻,实现
viable	/ˈvaɪəbəl/	adj.	可行的
induce	/ɪnˈdjuːs/	v.	劝诱,促使
impede	/ɪmˈpiːd/	v.	阻止
stakeholder	/ˈsteɪkˌhəʊldə/	n	股东,享有股份或利润的人

recipient	/rɪˈsɪpiənt/	n.	接受者，容纳者
perceive	/pəˈsiːv/	v.	感知，认识到
managerial	/ˌmænəˈdʒɪəriəl/	adj.	管理的
donor	/ˈdəʊnə/	n.	捐赠人
catalyze	/ˈkætəlaɪz/	v.	催化，刺激，促进
forefront	/ˈfɔːfrʌnt/	n.	最前部，最前线
transition	/trænˈzɪʃən/	n.	转换，过渡
blur	/blɜː/	v.	把(界线、视线等)弄得模糊不清
portfolio	/pɔːtˈfəʊliəʊ/	n.	有价证券
equity	/ˈekwɪti/	n.	资产净值；股票；权益
interrelate	/ˌɪntərɪˈleɪt/	v.	(使)相互关联
exert	/ɪgˈzɜːt/	v.	施加(压力等)；努力
diffuse	/dɪˈfjuːz/	v.	散播，传播
utilize	/ˈjuːtɪlaɪz/	v.	利用
generic	/dʒɪˈnerɪk/	adj.	属的，类的
depreciate	/dɪˈpriːʃieɪt/	v.	折旧；贬值

Phrases

at the forefront of	在……最前沿
in a coordinated sequence	按协调发展的顺序
blur the lines between	模糊了……的界线

Special Terms

technology transfer	技术转让
industrial competitiveness	工业竞争力
employment opportunity	就业机会
public service	公共服务
on-the-job experience	在职经验
patent rights and licenses	专利权和授权
bank lending	银行借贷
market share	市场份额
production costs	生产成本
intellectual property	知识产权
interest-free loans	无息贷款
commercial banks	商业银行
venture capital	风险资本
policy makers	政策制定者

Notes

1. These users are then encouraged to develop the technology further into new products, processes, materials, or services that will enhance our nation's industrial competitiveness or otherwise improve our quality of life.
   这些使用者将技术进一步转化为新的产品、过程、材料或者服务，这都将提高国家的工业竞争力或改善我们的生活质量。
   industrial competitiveness 的意思为"工业竞争力"。

2. The investment and trade decisions made by firms, acquisition of knowledge and skills by individuals through formal education and on-the-job experience, purchase of patent rights and licenses, assimilating the published results of public or private research, development and demonstration (RD&D) activity, and migration of skilled personnel with knowledge of particular technologies, all represent different forms of technology transfer.
   公司的投资和贸易决策、个人通过正式教育和在职学习获得知识和技能、购买专利权和授权、吸收公众以及私人研究、发展和示范活动所发布的成果，以及拥有特殊技术知识的人才流动，都体现了不同方式的技术转让。
   此句前面为数个并列主语。

3. Governments can implement policies that promote R&D programs that address global climate change concerns in sectors such as energy, forestry, and transportation.
   政府可以执行旨在促进研发计划的政策，解决全球气候变化给诸如能源、林业以及交通等部门带来的影响。
   climate 这里可作"气候、环境"解释。

4. At the local level, communities and community organizations need to be reached by information networks, get organized and participate in decision-making processes to improve local living standards and the quality of the environment via appropriate technologies.
   在地方上，社区以及社区组织需要信息网络的覆盖，组织起来并参与决策，通过适当的技术来提高本地的生活水平和环境质量。
   via，介词，意思是"经，由"。例：I can send him a note **via** the internal mail system. 我可以通过内部通信系统给他发个通知。

5. Provider or donor governments may set up policies to encourage technology transfer and fund transfers of research and expertise via Official Development Assistance (ODA) to support development and political goals, but more often are interested in policies that expand foreign markets for their national firms and increase exports.
   作为提供者或捐助者的国家政府，可以制定各种政策来鼓励技术转让以及通过官方发展资助的方式转移研究和专业技能基金，从而支持其发展目标和政治目标，但在多数情况下，他们更关注那些能够为其国内企业扩展国外市场以及增加出口的政策。

6. Multilateral agencies with development goals, such as the World Bank, the United Nations Development Program (UNDP), Regional Development Banks and Regional Organizations, pursue technology transfer to support development and as an instrument for achieving desired economic and policy reforms.

有着各种发展目标的多边机构,比如世界银行、联合国开发计划署、区域发展银行和地方组织等,寻求技术转让以支持发展,并将其作为实现所期待的经济和政策改革的一种工具。

7. Non-governmental organizations have been at the forefront of concerns about technology choice and the "appropriateness" of technologies transferred through development assistance and commercial channels, the social and cultural impacts of such transfers, and the needs for technology adaptation to suit local conditions and minimize unwanted impacts.

非政府组织已经站在了前沿,他们关注技术的选择,并通过资助和商业途径转让"适当的"技术,还关注技术转让所带来的社会和文化影响,以及技术适应本地条件并将有害影响降到最低的需求。

8. National systems of innovation depend upon the development of so-called technology infrastructure, "a set of collectively supplied, specific, industry-relevant capabilities" such as technology centers and educational and skills development institutions.

国家的创新机制依赖于所谓技术基础设施的发展,技术基础设施是指"一组由集体所提供的、具体的、与产业相关的能力",比如技术中心以及教育和技能发展机构。

Exercises

I. Discuss the following questions.

1. What is international technology transfer?
2. What are the benefits that technology and innovation can bring to us?
3. Why motivations of the various stakeholders differ markedly?
4. What are the major types of financial flows that support technology transfer? Try to talk about one of them in detail.
5. Why are technology transfers influenced greatly by national systems of innovation?

II. Work in groups and discuss the following question.

With the economic development between China and the U.S., there are more and more disputes on the trading of technologies. For example, according to U.S. government officials, China has obtained military navigation technology from Boeing used on advanced U.S. missiles and warplanes that was improperly approved by the State Department. How could China benefit itself through technology transfer in such a complex international environment?

III. Match the terms in column A with the explanations in column B.

A	B
1. diffuse	A. to diminish in price or value
2. assimilate	B. capable of success or continuing effectiveness; practicable
3. depreciate	C. to assist or support with a subsidy
4. implement	D. to place in or come into mutual relationship
5. viable	E. to spread about or scatter; disseminate
6. transition	F. to put into practical effect; carry out
7. competitiveness	G. to make greater, as in value, beauty, or reputation; augment
8. subsidize	H. to make similar; cause to resemble
9. interrelate	I. being determined by competition
10. enhance	J. passage from one form, state, style, or place to another

IV. Fill in the blanks of the following sentences with the words or phrases given below. Make changes when necessary.

subsidize	depreciate	transition	assimilate	address
stake	property	capital	license	equity

1. The solution lies in defining this "new" economy and in developing a practical strategy for surviving the _____ period.

2. We rightfully expect immigrants to show a sincere desire to become American citizens, speak English, and _____ themselves culturally.

3. It is an association of 27 national and regional societies, each composed of men and women who have an interest in the transfer of technology, or _____ of intellectual property rights.

4. Any country in the course of economic restructuring will encounter the problem of unemployment. It is not unique in China, and the Chinese government is trying its best to _____ the issue.

5. Indian firms need no longer worry about funds for overseas acquisitions. Whether through the syndicated loans market or from private _____, they have far easier access to funds today.

6. Just when British homeowners had settled into a comfortable pattern of rising house prices and consistently low mortgage rates, along comes a quarter percentage point hike in the base rate and horror stories of _____ repossessions and record bankruptcy levels.

7. To _____ something is to actually make it worse, whereas to deprecate something is simply to speak or think of it in a manner that demonstrates your low opinion of it.

8. The dramatic development was gained at the expense of huge _____ input, tremendous consumption of resources, low economic efficiency and inferior productivity and serious environmental pollution, as the consequences of the growth mode of the extensive economy.

9. This deal would make a lot more sense than the rumored Tom-Ebay deal, but the rumors that with this 20% _____ Tom's CEO Wang Lei will take over Sina don't make any sense.

10. China's central government will _____ community-based health services in the central and western regions starting next year, a Chinese health official said here Thursday.

V. Put the following into English.
1. 使各产业能获得科学和技术上的进步
2. 寻求国际销售、市场份额以及更为低廉的产品成本
3. 具有特殊技能的人才的流动
4. 清除阻碍技术转让的各种障碍
5. 通过适当的技术来改善当地的环境质量
6. 为本土企业扩展海外市场
7. 加强私有成分的参与
8. 按合理的顺序来发展对外贸易
9. 通过投资基金来购买国外公司的股票
10. 建立健全全球的创新机制

VI. Translate the following sentences into English.
1. 发展中国家通过购买国外公司的核心技术可以提高国家的竞争力,从而改善人民的生活质量。
2. 本土企业通过银行贷款、政府资助等各种途径来加大研发的投入,为技术的自主创新奠定坚实的基础。
3. 目前在中国,一些民营企业已经走在了技术发展的前沿。
4. 技术的引进必须要因地制宜,这样才能避免不必要的浪费,将风险降到最低。
5. 风险投资的特征是时间长、风险高,并且投资者的控制力度更强。

VII. Translate the following passage into Chinese.
Once a company has declared interest in licensing a Lab technology, the Tech Transfer licensing staff evaluates whether the company is likely to successfully develop the technology and bring it to market. A desirable licensee is able to marshal the requisite financial, R & D, manufacturing, marketing, and managerial capabilities and commit-

ment. A capable and qualified licensee is critical to ensuring that technologies developed at the Lab are successfully commercialized and that the public ultimately benefits from these innovations. Once a company is found to possess the necessary capabilities, the licensing staff negotiates a licensing agreement. Different inventions require different licensing strategies. For example, a common strategy for a new scientific tool likely to be widely used is to license it on a non-exclusive basis (e.g. to more than one company). In contrast, an invention that requires a significant investment to bring it to market is typically exclusively licensed to a single company. Licenses may also be exclusive or non-exclusive for a particular field of use or geographic region.

Text

International Technology Transfer and Intellectual Property Rights

Underdeveloped countries are at a huge technological disadvantage in the global high-tech economy today. They have immeasurably fallen behind developed countries in both acquired technology and domestically developed technology. Furthermore, the lack of protection of intellectual property (IP), which governments of developing countries view as necessary to bring their economy and social welfare up to speed with the industrialized world, is at great odds with the goals and moral convictions of the developed countries. Developing countries share a belief that industrialized countries wish to maintain their monopoly over advanced technology by demanding that developing countries implement strong intellectual property rights (IPR).

Developed countries share a belief that an inventor deserves exclusive rights to their innovation. Developed countries believe it is in their interest to protect the valuable technologies and intellectual property of their transnational companies (TNC) from being used or worse yet, copied, without compensation. In their view, underdeveloped and developing countries engage in exactly those practices. Thus, developed countries continue to push for a commitment from developing countries towards stronger protection of intellectual property.

International Protection of IP

Intellectual property rights are defined as governmental protection of private innovations and creativity. The Paris Convention of 1883 and the Berne Convention of 1886 were the first international treaties on IPR. The Paris Convention was created to ensure protection of industrial property. This included patents, utility models, trademarks, and industrial designs. It required member nations to treat both domestic and foreign patent holders and applicants equally.

In 1967, the World Intellectual Property Organization (WIPO) was created as a division of the United Nations. It is charged with protecting and promoting intellectual property throughout the world, as well as resolving international disputes over IP.

In 1994, under mounting pressure from the United States, Japan, and Europe, and Trade-related Aspects of Intellect Property Rights (TRIPs) Agreement was adopted at the Uruguay Round of the General Agreement on Tariffs and Trade (GATT). TRIPs was established as an agreement under the newly formed World Trade Organization (WTO), and today, any nation wishing to join the WTO must comply with the standards set forth in TRIPs. TRIPs defines minimum standards of protection for copyright, trademarks, patents, trade secrets, and contracts. Furthermore, it requires a twenty year protection period for all inventions, products, and processes, in every area of technology.

While developed and underdeveloped nations alike may be grouped together under the umbrella of WTO membership, their needs and views of intellectual property differ widely.

Developing Countries

Technology transfer is essential to all developing countries. Developing countries do not possess a large amount of protected technology upon which they can build new technology and research. Also, they lack a sufficient pool of trained personnel to perform research and development in new technologies. Consequently, they need technology from developed nations to assist their growth.

The "Two Gap" Theory describes constraints limiting a developing country's ability to gain technology. First, developing countries are unable to save enough capital to create and maintain their own technological base to promote growth. Second, the cost of importing technology far exceeds export (usually agriculture) revenues.

If technology from developed countries is imported and protected too strongly, the developing country—the importer of technology—will not be able to lay its own technological groundwork. Less developed countries view patents as inhibitors to technology transfer. They bring about high fees for the use of beneficial technology and hinder attempts to foster the development of high technology industries domestically. Additionally, because most patents are owned by corporations in the industrialized world, patents are regarded as instruments used by industrialized countries to exert control over the economic growth of developing countries.

By far, the most common way for developing countries to receive technologies from developed nations is via foreign direct investment (FDI) from transnational corporations. In principle, transnational companies will engage in such investing when it will provide an advantage not found in the home market. However, as transnational companies move more production to developing nations where labor and infrastructure are cheap, they need stronger patent rights to ensure that their technology and knowledge do not leak into other companies in those countries.

Currently, developing countries believe—and with good cause—that the dominant international treaties, such as TRIPs, are not geared to suit their long term interests. Namely, the current policies will not help the developing countries grow out of complete dependence upon the technology of developed countries, in the long term. Changes can be made, but only when the developed nations see the long term success of the developing nations as something which is in the best interest of all nations.

Developed Countries

Developed countries have a fundamentally different view of the role of intellectual property rights. They view IPR as a way of incentivizing innovation. The way IPR are viewed is also a reflection of the western world's views of property in general. Namely, exclusive ownership, the right to limit use, and the ownership right of control over propertized goods. TRIPs reflects all of these concepts.

Developed countries argue that patents are essential to international economic development because they provide a means to guarantee a return on invested time and capital in R&D. Thus, it is argued that transnational companies will be more likely to perform costly research, because a profit incentive will exist.

Additionally, developed countries feel that stronger IPR encourages R&D *within* the developing countries. The developed countries argue that without strong protection of patent rights, scientists will leave the developing countries because their work will not be protected.

From the perspective of the transnational companies, stronger intellectual property rights are a necessity for FDI. They are very fearful of the rampant piracy occurring in developing nations today. At the same time, they know that they posses a lot of power because the developing countries desperately need modern technology. Therefore, both the transnational companies and the developed nations in which they are located, argue that stronger IPR, particularly patent rights, in developing nations will attract more FDI.

Observations, Trends, and Outlook

The long term benefits provided by technology transfer under modern international policy on intellectual property are one-sided. Transfer of technology via FDI certainly benefits the transnational corporations, who delight in access to cheap labor, and the establishment of a particular image and reputation as an employer in a new labor market. And while it is true that FDI creates jobs in developing countries, it has done very little to plant seeds for long term prosperity. In fact, 80–85% of patents held in developing countries are held by persons foreign to that country. Since developing countries are so dependent upon what little technology is brought over to them, it becomes difficult to bargain effectively for their needs in the existing forums (WTO, etc.).

Currently, developed countries express great concerns over the explosive growth of piracy in developing countries. They frequently point to this problem when arguing for the need for stronger IPR. Ironically, in the 1700s, when the United States was a developing country, there was widespread pirating of European literature, and the government took little interest in controlling it. Today, the United States exerts its economic and political power as a trade partner to persuade developing nations to adopt stronger intellectual property rights.

We are witnessing a trend towards the adoption of stronger IPR around the world. The long term prosperity of developing countries is clearly in jeopardy as they are being figuratively strip-mined for cheap labor. Developed countries must realize that policies for technology transfer which do not help developing countries become self-sufficient, will only yield a long term financial burden for developed countries. At the risk of moving outside the scope of this paper, it should be noted that such policies will result in developing countries' continuing requirement of loans and other measures of support to prevent political and social problems, due to an artified economy.

The developed countries should address this danger immediately, but it seems that their representatives cannot see beyond the profit-driven goals of their large, high-tech companies. Indeed, the prospects for developing countries to free themselves from dependencies on western technology, and to export domestically developed technologies, is bleak for the foreseeable future.

Answer the following questions:

1. What is developing countries' attitude toward protection of intellectual property?
2. Why was TRIPs Agreement adopted at the Uruguay Round of the GATT in 1994?
3. Why is technology transfer essential to all developing countries?
4. Why do developed countries have a fundamentally different view of the role of intellectual property rights?
5. What are the prospects for developing countries to free themselves from dependencies on western technology, and why do you think so?

Unit 5

Trade Barriers

Learning Objectives

Text A
- to learn several frequently used forms of trade barriers
- to understand the purpose trade barriers are aimed at

Text B
- to learn the TBT faced by ITTO producer member countries
- to understand the possible solutions to TBT

Text A

Forms of Trade Barriers

Most economists hold that free international exchange of goods and services can potentially increase welfare for all trading partners. In reality though, very few countries or regions in the world practice free trade. Hong Kong is the only free trade port city in the world. Practically all other countries, large and small, impose some form of trade barrier on their imports from other countries.

A trade barrier is usually a trade policy or action put by a national government that interferes with the free-market buying and selling of goods and services internationally. Trade barriers can be in the form of import tariffs and non-tariff barriers.

Import Tariffs

An import tariff is a tax on imported goods. When a ship arrives in port a customs officer inspects the contents and charges a tax according to the tariff formula. Since the goods cannot be landed until the tax is paid, it is the easiest tax to collect.

There are two basic ways in which tariffs may be levied:
❖ specific tariffs
❖ ad valorem tariffs

A specific tariff is levied as a fixed charge per unit of imports. [1] For example, the U.S. government levies a 5.1 cent specific tariff on every wristwatch imported into the U.S. Thus, if

1,000 watches are imported, the U.S. government collects $51 in tariff revenue. In this case, $51 is collected whether the watch is a $40 Swatch or a $5,000 Rolex.

An ad valorem tariff is levied as a fixed percentage of the value of the commodity imported.[2] "Ad valorem" is Latin for "on value" or "in proportion to the value." The U.S. currently levies a 2.5% ad valorem tariff on imported automobiles. Thus if $100,000 worth of autos are imported, the US government collects $2,500 in tariff revenue. In this case, $2,500 is collected whether two $50,000 BMWs are imported or ten $10,000 Hyundais.

Occasionally both a specific and an ad valorem tariff are levied on the same product simultaneously. This is known as a two-part tariff. For example, wristwatches imported into the US face the 5.1 cent specific tariff as well as a 6.25% ad valorem tariff on the case and the strap and a 5.3% ad valorem tariff on the battery. Perhaps this should be called a three-part tariff.

As the above examples suggest, different tariffs are generally applied to different commodities. Governments rarely apply the same tariff to all goods and services imported into the country. Thus, instead of one tariff rate, countries have a tariff schedule which specifies the tariff collected on every particular good and service.

Non-tariff Barriers

Non-tariff barriers include laws, regulations, policies and practices that either protect domestically produced goods from foreign competition, or artificially stimulate the exports of domestic products. Their use has risen sharply after the WTO rules led to a very significant reduction in tariff use.

Non-tariff barriers take many forms, and the following are some frequently used:
- import licensing
- import quotas
- voluntary export restraint
- government procurement policies
- red tape barriers
- export subsidies
- technical barrier to trade

Import Licensing

Import licensing is an administrative procedure requiring the submission of an application and other documentation as a precondition for imports. Licensing is a governmental tool to control and monitor the movement of goods through national borders. There are two kinds of import licenses.
- automatic licensing
- non-automatic licensing

Automatic licensing is granted when formal requirements are met and the application is complete.[3]

Non-automatic licensing is normally used when there are quantitative restrictions on the import of a product or when imports are permitted only after explicit authorization.[4]

Import Quotas

Import quotas are limitations on the quantity of goods that can be imported into the country during a specified period of time. There are two basic types of quotas:

- ❖ absolute quotas
- ❖ tariff-rate quotas

Absolute quotas limit the quantity of imports to a specified level during a specified period of time.[5] Sometimes these quotas are set globally and thus affect all imports while sometimes they are set only against specified countries. Absolute quotas are generally on a first-come first-served basis. For this reason, many quotas are filled shortly after the opening of the quota period.

Tariff-rate quotas allow a specified quantity of goods to be imported at a reduced tariff rate during the specified quota period.[6]

Voluntary Export Restraint (VER)

A voluntary export restraint is a restriction set by a government on the quantity of goods that can be exported out of a country during a specified period of time.[7] Often the word voluntary is placed in quotes because these restraints are typically implemented upon the insistence of the importing nations.

Typically VERs arise when the import-competing industries seek protection from plenty of imports from particular exporting countries. VERs are then offered by the exporter to appease the importing country and to avoid the effects of possible trade restraints on the part of the importer. Thus VERs are rarely completely voluntary.

Government Procurement Policies

A government procurement policy requires that a specified percentage of purchases by the federal or state governments be made from domestic firms rather than foreign firms.[8] This policy amounts to disallowing foreign firms to bid for government's infrastructure projects. In the past, the government of Japan would keep U.S. firms from bidding on government projects for building roads, schools, hospitals, etc. in Japan. The new rule of the WTO prohibits discrimination against foreign bidders except in matters of national security.

Red Tape Barriers

This is another method by which governments try to restrict imports into their countries. It refers to costly administrative procedures required for the importation of foreign goods.

A red-tape barrier may arise if multiple licenses must be obtained from a variety of government sources before importation of a product is allowed. Customs officials of a country may take samples of imported food items for "testing" that may take forever. One such claim was made by a wine official from California, charging that the Korean customs' officials have kept their wine at the border warehouses in R.O. Korea and have taken bottles of wine for testing. After a few months and an inquiry by the exporters, they claimed they were still testing the wine!

Export Subsidies

Export subsidies are payments made by the government to lower the price and encourage the export of specified products. The most common product groups where export subsidies are applied are agricultural and dairy products. Most countries have income support programs for their nation's farmers. These are often motivated by national security or self-sufficiency considerations.

Technical Barrier to Trade (TBT)

In international trade, most governments set out technical requirements to protect the health and safety of domestic consumers and establish product-quality conformity among producers. However, there exists the potential to create barriers to market access.

A standard or technical regulation becomes a technical barrier to trade if used in a way to impede international trade rather than for the purposes of achieving a legitimate objective.[9]

Requirements that have the potential to be TBTs include product standards, product quality and grading requirements and other technical regulations.

As an example, in 1994, the U.S. banned the import of gharga skirts from India with the argument that they are a fire hazard. Of course, according to Indian officials, the U.S. is using the argument as a protectionist policy to keep this type of skirts from the U.S. market.

Most trade barriers work on the same principle: the imposition of some sort of cost on trade that raises the price of the traded products. The purpose is not only to raise revenue for the government, but also

- to reduce the level of imports by making them more expensive relative to domestic substitutes;
- to counter the practice of dumping by raising the import price of the dumped good to market level;
- to retaliate against trade barriers imposed by another country;
- to protect key industries such as agriculture;
- to protect a new industry until it is sufficiently well established to compete on the international market.

However, economists generally agree that trade barriers are detrimental and decrease overall economic efficiency. Free trade encourages firms to export and import. This should encourage a greater choice for consumers and a higher standard of living. On the contrary, trade barriers increase the cost of trading. For example, a tariff would mean that domestic companies and consumers may have to pay more for imports of raw materials or consumer goods.

To make things worse, trade barriers are imposed to keep a particular interest group happy at the cost of the whole society. It is a common practice that governments, by providing subsidies and favorable policies to domestic companies with little competitiveness and imposing tariff and non-tariff barriers on imports, raise the price of the importable good to protect the income of domestic companies. This is a highly inefficient way to help the losers because it creates distortions in the price and hence the resource allocation mechanism of the economy.

New Words

practice	/'præktɪs/	v. & n.	实施,实践;惯例,做法
impose	/ɪm'pəʊz/	v.	征收;强加
inspect	/ɪn'spekt/	v.	视察,检查
charge	/tʃɑːdʒ/	v.	收费;控诉
levy	/'levi/	v.	征收,征税
commodity	/kə'mɒdɪti/	n.	商品
specify	/'spesɪfaɪ/	v.	规定
artificially	/ˌɑːtɪ'fɪʃəli/	adv.	人为地
administrative	/əd'mɪnɪstrətɪv/	adj.	管理的,行政的
procedure	/prə'siːdʒə/	n.	程序,手续
submission	/səb'mɪʃən/	n.	提交
documentation	/ˌdɒkjʊmən'teɪʃən/	n.	文件
precondition	/ˌpriːkən'dɪʃən/	n.	前提
quantitative	/'kwɒntɪtətɪv/	adj.	数量的,定量的
restriction	/rɪ'strɪkʃən/	n.	限制,约束
explicit	/ɪk'splɪsɪt/	adj.	清楚的,明确的
authorization	/ˌɔːθəraɪ'zeɪʃən/	n.	授权,认可
quota	/'kwəʊtə/	n.	定额,限额,配额
appease	/ə'piːz/	v.	平息,缓和
disallow	/ˌdɪsə'laʊ/	v.	不允许,不接受
infrastructure	/'ɪnfrəˌstrʌktʃə/	n.	基础设施
prohibit	/prə'hɪbɪt/	v.	禁止,阻止
bidder	/'bɪdə/	n.	出价人,投标人
multiple	/'mʌltɪpəl/	adj.	多样的,多重的
lower	/'ləʊə/	v.	降低
motivate	/'məʊtɪveɪt/	v.	激发
conformity	/kən'fɔːmɪti/	n.	一致
access	/'ækses/	n.	接近,进入;通路
legitimate	/lɪ'dʒɪtɪmɪt/	adj.	合法的,合理的
ban	/bæn/	v.	禁止

counter	/ˈkaʊntə/	v.	反击,反抗
dumping	/ˈdʌmpɪŋ/	n.	倾销
retaliate	/rɪˈtælieɪt/	v.	报复
detrimental	/ˌdetrɪˈmentl/	adj.	有害的
competitiveness	/kəmˈpetɪtɪvnɪs/	n.	竞争力
distortion	/dɪˈstɔːʃən/	n.	扭曲,变形
allocation	/ˌæləˈkeɪʃən/	n.	分配
mechanism	/ˈmekənɪzəm/	n.	机制

Phrases

in proportion to	按……的比例
worthy of	值得,称得上
apply... to	应用于……
first come, first served	先来先得
amount to	总计,等于
bid for	投标
in matters of	关于,在……方面
set out	规定
relative to	相对于……
at the cost of	以……为代价

Special Terms

trade barrier	贸易壁垒
non-tariff barriers	非关税壁垒
specific tariff	从量关税
ad valorem tariff	从价关税
tariff schedule	关税税率表
import licensing	进口许可证
import quotas	进口配额
voluntary export restraint	自愿出口限制
government procurement policies	政府采购政策
red tape barriers	通关环节壁垒
export subsidies	出口补贴
technical barrier to trade	技术性贸易壁垒
automatic licensing	自动许可
non-automatic licensing	非自动许可

absolute quotas	绝对配额
tariff-rate quotas	关税配额

Notes

1. A specific tariff is levied as a fixed charge per unit of imports.
   从量关税是对每单位进口商品征收固定的税额。
2. An ad valorem tariff is levied as a fixed percentage of the value of the commodity imported.
   从价关税是按进口商品的价值征收固定百分比的关税。
3. Automatic licensing is granted when formal requirements are met and the application is complete.
   当形式上达到要求，申请手续齐全时，即可授予自动许可。
4. Non-automatic licensing is normally used when there are quantitative restrictions on the import of a product or when imports are permitted only after explicit authorization.
   在对进口商品有数量限制或只有经过明确授权才能允许进口时，通常会用到非自动许可。
5. Absolute quotas limit the quantity of imports to a specified level during a specified period of time.
   绝对配额是将特定时期内进口商品的数量限制在特定的水平。
6. Tariff-rate quotas allow a specified quantity of goods to be imported at a reduced tariff rate during the specified quota period.
   关税配额是在特定的配额期限内对特定数量的进口商品给予减税的待遇。
7. A voluntary export restraint is a restriction set by a government on the quantity of goods that can be exported out of a country during a specified period of time.
   自愿出口限制是一国政府对特定时期内出口某种商品数量的限制。
8. A government procurement policy requires that a specified percentage of purchases by the federal or state governments be made from domestic firms rather than foreign firms.
   政府采购政策要求联邦或州政府的采购中特定的比例要从国内公司，而非外国公司购买。
9. A standard or technical regulation becomes a technical barrier to trade if used in a way to impede international trade rather than for the purposes of achieving a legitimate objective.
   标准或技术规定如果不是为了实现合理的目标，而是用来作为限制国际贸易的手段，就变成了技术性贸易壁垒。

Exercises

I. Discuss the following questions.

1. When is tariff levied? What is specific tariff? And what is ad valorem tariff?
2. What are non-tariff barriers? List several frequently used forms.
3. What is TBT? Can you give an example?
4. What are the purposes of building trade barriers?
5. What harm do trade barriers do to economy?

II. Calculation.

According to the U.S. tariff schedule, wristwatches imported to the U.S. are levied 5.1 cent specific tariff as well as 6.25% ad valorem tariff on the case and the strap. If 4,000 Rolex valued $5,000 (case and strap) are imported, how much tariff is expected to pay?

III. Match the terms in column A with the explanations in column B.

A	B
1. tariff formula	A. money given to export companies by the government to help or encourage export
2. free trade	B. to offer a particular amount of money for something and compete against other people
3. technical barrier	C. a tariff composed of two parts: a lump-sum fee as well as a per-unit charge
4. import licensing	D. technical standards set by a government to prevent foreign goods from entering domestic markets
5. a two-part tariff	E. the behavior of selling goods very cheaply, usually in other countries
6. dumping	F. international buying and selling of goods, without limits on the amount of goods and without special taxes on the goods
7. quota	G. official permission to buy products from another country
8. bid	H. a fixed limited amount or number that is officially allowed
9. trade deficit	I. over a period of time the value of imports of goods and services exceeding exports
10. export subsidies	J. a calculation technique to determine the amount of a tariff

IV. Fill in the blanks of the following sentences with the words or phrases given below. Make changes when necessary.

| practice | impose | stimulate | precondition | legitimate |
| specify | restraint | implement | artificially | detrimental |

1. To obtain more market share, their company decided to sell their products at _____ low prices in Asia.
2. According to the government official, the new trade policy will be _____ next year.
3. Developing economy at the cost of environment is _____ to our country in the long run.
4. The contract clearly _____ that any problem caused by misoperation of the machine is the buyer's liability.
5. He claimed at the court that the ten million dollars on his account was a _____ income.
6. A stable social environment is an essential _____ for economic development.
7. The government plans to reduce interests for a second time in order to _____ domestic consumption.
8. It is suggested that very high taxes should be _____ on cigarettes for people's health.
9. During the wartime, most governments put _____ on the dealing of essentials, such as food and cotton.
10. It is a common _____ in international trade that the seller informs the buyer of the delivery date ahead of time.

V. Put the following into English.

1. 资源分配机制
2. 价格扭曲
3. 贸易保护政策
4. 原材料和消费品的进口
5. 具有竞争力的国内企业
6. 市场准入
7. 优惠政策
8. 国内替代产品
9. 特定利益集团
10. 行政手续

VI. Translate the following sentences into English.

1. 贸易壁垒在一定程度上可以保护国内企业,但过度使用贸易壁垒会危害到国家的经济发展。
2. 很多与邻国签订了自由贸易协定的国家,对世界上其他的国家仍然实施贸易壁垒。
3. 中世纪时,关税曾经由地方政府征收。现在这种情况很少见,通常由中央政府征收。

4. 出于这样或那样的原因，几乎所有的国家都对过境的某些商品实施贸易壁垒。大多数的壁垒是用来限制进口的，两种最常用的进口壁垒是关税和配额。
5. 贸易壁垒通常是保护性的，用来保护国内的生产商，他们在自由市场上无法与外国厂商竞争。

VII. Translate the following passage into Chinese.

Most economists hold that free international exchange of goods and services can potentially increase welfare for all trading partners. In reality though, very few countries or regions in the world practice free trade. Hong Kong is the only free trade port city in the sense. Practically all other countries and regions, large and small, impose some form of trade barrier on their imports from other countries.

Most trade barriers work on the same principle: the imposition of some sort of cost on trade that raises the price of the traded products. The purpose is not only to raise revenue for the government, but also to reduce the level of imports by making them more expensive relative to domestic substitutes, to counter the practice of dumping by raising the import price of the dumped goods to market level, to retaliate against trade barriers imposed by another country, to protect key industries such as agriculture, to protect a new industry until it is sufficiently well established to compete on the international market.

*T*ext　　　　　　　　　　　B

How to Hurdle the Barrier

ITTO (International Tropical Timber Organization) producer member countries have been worried that product standards and technical regulations in consumer markets are restricting the expansion and diversification of the international tropical timber trade. To assess these concerns, ITTO started a study to identify and assess product standards, quality grading rules and other regulations in various markets that affect the trade of wood products and in particular tropical timber.

Situation in Major Consumer Countries

In North America, grade stamp certification is required for any lumber or panel product that is to be used in structural applications. Obtaining third-party accreditation for lumber or panel grade stamps tends to be a costly and long process, which may be why very little structural material is made from tropical species. Besides, Canadian and US plant health inspection agencies require all wood packaging and crating material to be heat-treated.

Possibly more pressing TBT affecting tropical wood products in the EU, North America and some other markets is government procurement. Increasingly, federal, state and municipal governments are specifying that all their purchases of building materials, furniture and millwork derived from tropical timber should be harvested legally and originate from sustainably managed forests. This could become a serious impediment to the timber trade—and to the tropical timber trade in particular. Therefore, producers and importers of tropical timber need work together to make dialogue with EU and U.S. governing bodies to explain what is being done to improve forest management and to convey the economic and social impact that their requirements will have in many developing countries.

In Japan, the most significant TBTs for tropical timber products are the Japan Agricultural Standard (JAS) and the Japan Industrial Standard (JIS) for formaldehyde emissions (甲醛释放) pertaining to "sick-house syndrome." Products affected are plywood, particleboard, medium-density fibreboard, structural panels, overlaid panel products, flooring and stair treads. Each product category requires separate certification in accordance with the relevant standard. At present, neither Korea nor China has TBTs that are significant enough to have any impact on trade.

Situation in Major Producer Countries

Latin America

In the major producer countries of Latin America the industry has been differently affected by building codes, standards and other factors related to market access, and also the countries have different capacity to overcome the constraints.

Brazil's timber industry faces several TBTs and other market requirements, including U.S. standards for structural wood panels, U.S.-government homeland security measures, formaldehyde emissions' control, and environment related issues. However, the capacity of Brazil to deal with these barriers and requirements is higher than in most other Latin American countries. The country has a more structured framework for standards, quality certification, and testing laboratories, and it also possesses a significant number of large companies that are capable of absorbing costs related to TBTs.

Though Bolivian producers have reportedly been little affected by building codes, standards and other market requirements, its timber industry has received some signs from importers that market requirements will tighten in the next few years. This is a source of concern for the industry, as it will add new costs and further reduce the competitiveness of its products in international markets. The country has a very small capacity to deal with the issue: the forestry sector is largely based on small and medium-sized enterprises (SMEs) that will not be able to absorb the costs related to certain TBTs and market requirements.

The Ecuadorian timber industry has been affected mainly by regulations related to wood-panel formaldehyde emissions in Japan. The problem is that standards are too high and the costs involved in testing/certification make exports to Japan almost impossible. The industry is also concerned about requirements related to security and procurement procedures imposed by government agencies in the U.S., and it feels that while TBTs and other market requirements are growing, the capacity to overcome them is limited—particularly among SMEs, which comprise the majority of the industry.

Africa

The timber industry in Cameroon has, so far, not been affected by TBTs and other market requirements. This is most probably due to the fact that around 90% of its exports comprise sawn wood and logs.

The main concern of the Ghanaian timber industry in relation to TBTs and other related market requirements is European technical standards. Ghanaian companies have difficulty meeting the new technical demands due to the general lack of adequate machinery and also because it does not have in place quality-assurance and certification programs. Nevertheless, Ghana is one of the most progressive countries in Africa in terms of standards' development and product-testing facilities. The main problem, though, is with the SMEs, which are unlikely to possess the means to absorb the extra costs of overcoming such TBTs.

For Gabon's tropical timber industry, TBTs and related market requirements are not a major problem. This is largely attributable to the fact that around 80% of the country's timber exports are in log form.

Southeast Asia

The TBT issues that most concern the timber sectors in Malaysia and Indonesia are the British Standards for structural plywood, and the JAS/JIS for formaldehyde emissions. Although there is an added cost in meeting such market certification requirements, Malaysia has devised an industry solution to meet these technical requirements and Indonesia is not far behind. Similar to the situation in other regions, SMEs in both countries are finding it difficult to cope with the demands imposed upon them by the TBTs.

Recommendations

Producer countries

Three recommendations are made to this group. First, producer governments should pursue greater regional cooperation to help overcome knowledge gaps related to TBTs within and between countries.

Second, governments should establish a solid framework for developing local standards for timber products, certification systems with the aim of overcoming international market barriers and meeting requirements. Governments could, if necessary, seek international support for such development. Likewise, they could evaluate the possibility of taking this action at a regional level, since this would help efforts to harmonize standards.

Third, governments should cooperate in efforts to avoid the escalation of TBTs and to promote the harmonization of standards, building codes and other requirements among consumer countries. They should continue to raise the issue of TBTs at international fora such as ITTO and WTO.

Major consumer countries

Major consumer countries should address three main issues. First, mechanisms need to be developed or improved to ensure that third party certification does not become a major TBT. For example, governments in importing countries could simplify procedures, taking into consideration existing mutual recognition mechanisms such as the International Accreditation Forum. Another action would be to cooperate with producer countries to develop local skills through technical assistance programs, technology transfer and other activities that would aim to reduce costs associated with complying with market requirements.

Second, consumer governments should work to ensure that procurement policies at all levels of government (federal, state and municipal) do not become a market barrier for tropical timber products.

Third, consumer governments should provide technical and financial assistance to standards organizations in producer countries to put in place effective and efficient national quality assurance programs for product certification in line with market requirements. They could also provide direct technical assistance to the private sectors of producer countries with the aim of enhancing the capacity of the industry to achieve the standards, quality levels and other requirements needed to access markets.

ITTO

ITTO has a critical role to play in enhancing market access. This includes helping producers to overcome their limitations in knowledge and infrastructure and serving as a forum for discussion between producers and consumers on the issue of TBTs.

ITTO should also make funds available to initiate specific programs for overcoming identified knowledge gaps among producers, such as through increased cooperation among members on technology transfer.

Final Comments

The recent wave of TBTs has had a significant negative effect on tropical timber exporters. Some TBTs require the producer/exporter to make major structural changes in operation in order to continue doing business in that market. In most cases, such producers/exporters must also absorb significant additional costs in meeting the new requirements. There exists a general and growing perception among industrialists and industry associations in producer countries that TBTs have affected many small enterprises and even some medium-sized ones, especially those with poor market information. The inability of such enterprises to cope with new requirements will likely force many out of the markets in which significant TBTs have been imposed. This in turn could have a major impact on

employment in the timber sectors of several producer countries. It would be a tough task to remove future disruptions arising from the enforcement of new TBTs in the international tropical timber trade.

Answer the following questions:

1. According to the text, what is the problem that ITTO producer member countries are faced with?
2. What forms of TBTs do consumer countries take to restrict import of tropical timber?
3. What are the respective situations in Brazil, Ghana and Malaysia?
4. What recommendations are given to producer countries?
5. What negative effects do TBTs have on tropical timber producers?

Unit 6

International Trade of China

● *Learning Objectives*

Text A
- to learn the increasing role China has been playing in world trade
- to get familiar with changes of composition and mode in China's international trade

Text B
- to understand that Sino-U.S. trade relationship is beneficial to both sides
- to know the conflicts and frictions that Sino-U.S. trade relationship is confronting

*T*ext

A

China's Trade: Growth and Diversification

Today, products bearing the words "Made in China" can be seen everywhere across the world. Statistics indicate that there are already more than a hundred kinds of manufactured products coming first in quantity in the world. Over 50 percent of cameras, 30 percent of air conditioners and television sets, 25 percent of washing machines and nearly 20 percent of refrigerators sold worldwide are made in China.

Increasing Role in World Trade

China's international trade has expanded steadily since the opening of the economy in 1979. Exports and imports have grown faster than world trade for more than 20 years and China's share in global trade has increased steadily since 1979. This process began relatively slowly in the 1980s after the relaxation of pervasive and complex import and export controls[1], but accelerated in the 1990s with broader trade reforms, including significant tariff reductions[2].

China has increased its penetration into advanced country markets, and has simultaneously become a more important export destination, especially for regional economies. The share of advanced country imports accounted for by China has risen over the last two decades, with particularly sharp increases since the early 1990s in Japan, the

United States, and the European Union. China's role in Asian regional trade has also become increasingly important. A rising share of its imports come from within the region, and China is now among the most important export destinations for other Asian countries. For example, China now accounts for over 11 percent of Japan's exports, up from only 2 percent in 1990. While most of the dramatic increases in exports to China have occurred from within the Asian region, the share of exports from the United States and the European Union that go to China have also increased, from 1 percent in 1990 to 3.5 in 2002.

China's integration with the world economy is a landmark event with implications for both the global and regional economies. However, it is not unprecedented in either its scope or speed. The earlier experiences of Japan and the newly industrializing economies (NIEs)[3] of Asia were similar in terms of their rate of growth of exports as well as with respect to their increasing share in world exports over an extended period. This historical evidence, together with the still substantial development potential of the country, suggests that China could maintain relatively strong export growth for a number of years going forward.

Changes in Composition of Trade

China's export base has diversified from an initial heavy reliance on textiles and other light manufacturing.[4] By the end of the 1980s, China completed the shift from exporting primary products to finished industrial products. After that, China started the second shift, that is, from exporting roughly processed, low value-added products to deep processed, high value-added products. In the early 1990s, light manufacturing accounted for more than 40 percent of China's exports. These products largely consisted of footwear, clothing, toys, and other miscellaneous manufactured articles. A large part of the remaining exports was accounted for by manufactured goods (mostly textiles) and machinery and transport (small electronics). In 2001, among the total export commodities, primary products accounted for only 9.1 percent while finished industrial products accounted for 90.1 percent. From 1995 up to now, high value-added mechanical and electrical products have for eight consecutive years taken the place of textiles and garments and become the largest category of export commodities.[5] In recent years, China has made substantial gains in other export categories including more sophisticated electronics (office machines and automated data processing equipment, telecommunications and sound equipment, and electrical machinery), furniture, travel goods, and industrial supplies. According to statistics from the Customs of China, China has been for years on end the largest exporting country of labor-intensive products including textiles, garments, shoes, clocks and watches, bikes, sewing machines, etc. In recent years, the export volume of mechanical and electrical products such as mobile phones,

CD players, displays, air conditioners, containers, optical components, motor-driven tools, small electrical household appliances, etc., has also risen to the first place while color TVs and motorcycles rank second in export volume in the world. For example, the proportion of China's exports represented by machinery and transport (which includes electronics) increased from 17 percent in 1993 to 41 percent in 2003, while the share of miscellaneous manufacturing declined from 42 percent to 28 percent.

China's low-cost and high labor quality superiority has brought substantial benefits to the consumers all over the world. Thanks to China's large quantity of inexpensive but elegant products, the price of some staple commodities on world market that has kept on the high side for many years has dropped.[6] The 1994 analytical report of the World Bank pointed out that if importing commodities from other countries than China, the American consumers would have to pay US$ 14 billion more per year. Now as China-U.S. trade volume has doubly increased, American consumers must have saved much more on expenditure, and such is also the case with consumers in other countries and regions.

The composition of imports reflects the high degree of vertical specialization of production within the Asia region.[7] This can be seen from several indicators. First, a high share of imports for processing is embodied in China's exports. This ratio increased from about 35 percent of all imports in the early 1990s to about 50 percent by 1997 and has remained at about that level since then. Similarly, imports for processing are estimated to be embodied in over 40 percent of China's exports. The impact of increased vertical specialization can be clearly seen in the rapid increase in imports of electronic integrated circuits and microassemblies—key components used in the assembly of electronic products. Second, strong foreign direct investment (FDI) inflows in China have come primarily from industrial economics, and especially the Asian NIEs. During 2000–2001, these NIEs plus Japan accounted for about 20 percent. Finally, the pattern of trade has changed substantially, with increasing imports from Asia and exports going to developed economies, largely the United States and Europe.

Modes of Trade

There are over 220 countries and regions that have trade contacts with China. In 2001, China's key trade partners included Japan, the U.S., China's Hong Kong, ROK, China's Taiwan, Germany, Singapore, Russia, Great Britain, Malaysia, Australia, Holland, France, Italy, Canada, Thailand, and Indonesia.

China conducts various modes of trade such as processing with customer's materials, processing with consumer's samples, assembling with customer's parts, compensation trade, processing with imported materials in additions to general trade. Other trade forms such as consignment sale, marketing on commission, exclusive sales, sole agency, leasing trade, auction, public bidding, futures trading are also adopted in specific businesses.[8] In import and export of technology, various forms such as providing technology licensing, consultation, technical service, and cooperative production are adopted. Since 1979 China has started counter trade with some developing countries. From the 1980s onwards, border trade has been widely established. In the 1990s as enterprises in China experienced a rapid growth, business people started to develop processing trade in developing countries using mature technology, equipment and raw and processed materials. Later on the development of information technology has brought along electronic commerce, that is, conducting import and export trade on the Internet. Starting from 1996, China has started to promote its own E-commerce. By establishing China international E-business center, opening up online "China Commodities Trading Market" and "China Technical Commodities Trading Market," this new trading form is gradually extended.

Among various newly developed trading forms, processing trade is more prominent than all the others. Firstly with the import of foreign capital, it has become a leading trading form in China after 20 years' development. In 2001, its total import-export amount reached US $241.43 billion, accounting for 50.9 percent of the total foreign trade turnover.

Currently the key issue confronting China's foreign trade is that the export commodities remains at a lower structural level and that the export competitiveness needs to be raised. The technical content and added value of China's export commodities are still not high. Some labor-intensive products that have been energetically developed since the 1980s have already acquired a considerable share on international market, leaving not much room for further development.

New Words

diversify	/daɪˈvɜːsɪfaɪ/	v.	使不同,使变得多样化
diversification	/daɪˌvɜːsɪfɪˈkeɪʃən/	n.	多样化
statistics	/stəˈtɪstɪks/	n.	统计数字,统计资料
relaxation	/ˌriːlækˈseɪʃən/	n.	放松,放宽;消遣,娱乐
pervasive	/pəˈveɪsɪv/	adj.	渗透的,遍布的,蔓延的
accelerate	/əkˈseləreɪt/	v.	(使)加快,加速,促进
penetration	/ˌpenɪˈtreɪʃən/	n.	穿透,透过,突入,打入
integration	/ˌɪntɪˈɡreɪʃən/	n.	融合,融入
implication	/ˌɪmplɪˈkeɪʃən/	n.	行动、决定等可能产生的影响
unprecedented	/ʌnˈpresɪdentɪd/	adj.	空前的,前所未有的
substantial	/səbˈstænʃəl/	adj.	大量的,重大的
composition	/ˌkɒmpəˈzɪʃən/	n.	构成,组成,结构;组合方式
reliance	/rɪˈlaɪəns/	n.	依靠,依赖;信任,信赖
miscellaneous	/ˌmɪsəˈleɪnɪəs/	adj.	不同种类的,多种多样的
article	/ˈɑːtɪkəl/	n.	一件物品;条款,条目

consecutive	/kən'sekjʊtɪv/	adj.	连续的,连贯的
sophisticated	/sə'fɪstɪkeɪtɪd/	adj.	复杂的;精密的;高级的
optical	/'ɒptɪkəl/	adj.	视觉的,视力的;光学的
automated	/'ɔːtəmeɪtɪd/	adj.	自动化的
volume	/'vɒljuːm/	n.	量,分量
expenditure	/ɪk'spendɪtʃə/	n.	消费,开销,开支
indicator	/'ɪndɪkeɪtə/	n.	指示器,记录器,指示物
component	/kəm'pəʊnənt/	n.	成分,组成部分;零部件
inflow	/'ɪnfləʊ/	n.	流入,流入物(量)
consignment	/kən'saɪnmənt/	n.	托付货物;托运;交付
auction	/'ɔːkʃən/	n.& v.	拍卖
consultation	/ˌkɒnsəl'teɪʃən/	n.	商量,咨询;协商会
prominent	/'prɒmɪnənt/	adj.	显著的,卓越的,突出的
turnover	/'tɜːnˌəʊvə/	n.	成交量;营业额

Phrases

in quantity	大量地
account for	是……的原因;占……部分
landmark event	具有重大意义的事件
with respect to	关于,至于
take the place of	代替,接替,取代
on end	连续地,继续地
on the...side	有点……,有几分……
later on	将来,后来,过些时候

Special Terms

manufactured products	制成品
tariff reduction	关税减让
newly industrializing economies (NIEs)	新兴工业化经济体
export base	出口基地
light manufacturing	轻工制造业
finished industrial products	工业制成品
roughly processed, low value-added products	粗加工,低附加值产品
deep processed, high value-added products	深加工,高附加值产品
labor-intensive products	劳动密集型产品
trade volume	贸易量

vertical specialization	垂直专业化
compensation trade	补偿贸易
consignment sale	寄售
exclusive sales	包销
leasing trade	租赁贸易
public bidding	公开投标
futures trading	期货交易
counter trade	对销贸易
border trade	边境贸易
processing trade	来料加工贸易
technical content	技术含量

Notes

1. the relaxation of pervasive and complex import and export controls
   提示：在计划经济体制下，我国对外贸商品进出口、外汇、经营权曾有多种限制。

2. significant tariff reductions
   为了恢复中国在"关税及贸易总协定"中的地位，中国分别于 1992 年、1993 年、1996 年和 1997 年四次降低进口关税总水平，平均关税水平由 35.9%降至 17%，并在 2000 年将关税总水平降至 15%。非关税措施涉及的进口商品已从 1247 种降至 384 种。

3. ...the newly industrializing economies (NIEs)
   第一代新兴工业化国家指中国香港、韩国、新加坡和中国台湾，即所谓的亚洲四小龙。第二代新兴工业化国家包括马来西亚、泰国和中国。

4. China's export base has diversified from an initial heavy reliance on textiles and other light manufacturing.
   中国的出口基础由原来过分依赖于纺织业和其他轻工业变得多样化。

5. From 1995 up to now, high value-added mechanical and electrical products have for eight consecutive years taken the place of textiles and garments and become the largest category of export commodities.
   从 1995 年至今，高附加值的机械和电子产品已经连续 8 年取代纺织品和服装而成为最大的出口商品种类。
   句中 take the place of 表示"取代……"。

6. Thanks to China's large quantity of inexpensive but elegant products, the price of some staple commodities on world market that has kept on the high side for many years has dropped.
   由于中国的产品物美价廉，世界市场上一些大宗商品居高不下的价格也已有所下降。

7. The composition of imports reflects the high degree of vertical specialization of production within the Asia region.

   进口构成反映了亚洲地区生产的高度垂直专业化。

   垂直专业化分工及贸易是当今国际分工和国际贸易的主要特征之一，也是经济全球化的发展趋势。它指某一国(或某一地区)利用进口的中间产品，去制造最终产品而出口。以 Nike 运动鞋的垂直专业化分工为例，其研发和产品设计在美国，鞋品元件的制造在中国台湾和韩国，鞋品的组合(组装)在中国台湾、中国大陆、泰国、马来西亚、菲律宾等地，最终产品的营销和配送主要在北美和西欧。

8. Other trade forms such as consignment sale, marketing on commission, exclusive sales, sole agency, leasing trade, auction, public bidding, futures trading are also adopted in specific businesses.

   在特定行业中也会采用其他的贸易形式，例如寄售、佣金销售、包销、独家代理、租赁贸易、拍卖、公开投标和期货交易等。

Exercises

I. Discuss the following questions.

1. From which aspects can we say China's role in world trade has been increasingly important?
2. What are the changes in composition of China's export?
3. What is the impact of increased vertical specialization on import?
4. Which modes of trade does China conduct? What is processing trade?
5. What is the current key issue confronting China's foreign trade?

II. Tell whether the following statements are true or false according to the text.

1. China is the most important export destination for other Asian countries.
2. Exports to China are mainly from the United States and the European Union.
3. China's integration with the world economy is unprecedented in either its scope or speed.
4. Textiles are the largest category of export commodities in China now.
5. Thanks to China, the price of some staple commodities on world market has dropped.
6. E-commerce is the leading trade form in China.

III. Match the terms in column A with the explanations in column B.

A	B
1. indicator	A. the amount of business done in a particular period, measured in money
2. commodity	B. the sale of goods or services that are paid for in whole or part by the transfer of goods or services from a foreign country
3. turnover	C. the act of building productive capacity directly in a foreign country
4. tariff	D. Delivery of merchandise to the buyer or distributor, whereby the latter agrees to sell it and only then pay the exporter. The seller retains ownership of the goods until they are sold, but also carries all of the financial burden and risk.
5. lease	E. a fact, quality, or situation that indicates something
6. consignment	F. an article of trade, or that which can be bought or sold
7. counter trade	G. Someone who represents another to sell products in the target market. He does not take possession of and assumes no responsibility for the goods.
8. agent	H. taxes on imported goods and services, levied by governments to raise revenues and create barriers to trade
9. Foreign Direct Investment	I. a contract in which one party conveys the use of an asset to another party for a specific period of time at predetermined rate

IV. Fill in the blanks of the following sentences with the words or phrases given below. Make changes when necessary.

| pervasive | accelerate | unprecedented | consecutive | embody |
| consultation | penetrate | integrate | | implication | miscellaneous |

1. The country's constitution _____ the ideals of freedom and equality.
2. The new economic policies have _____ the decline of manufacturing industry.
3. All the department reports should be _____ into one annual report.
4. The company has had a successful first year at home but _____ of the international market has been slow.
5. Why was I not _____ before you made the decision?
6. The streets of New York City are numbered in _____ order.

7. He worked so hard that weariness _____ his whole body.
8. There are categories for all major areas of expenditure, and then one at the end for _____ items.
9. The air crash caused an _____ number of death.
10. What are the _____ of the government's announcement for the future of our project?

V. Put the following into English.
1. 印有"中国制造"的商品
2. 劳动密集型产品的最大出口国
3. 国外直接投资
4. 提供技术许可和合作生产
5. 开展网上进出口贸易
6. 加工贸易为主要贸易形式
7. 出口量占世界第二位
8. 争取在国际市场上占有更大份额
9. 亚洲其他国家的重要出口基地
10. 中国占日本出口的11%

VI. Translate the following sentences into English.
1. 中国加快了打入发达国家市场的步伐,同时也成为一个对区域经济体更加重要的出口目的地。
2. 历史事实和这个国家一直强劲的发展潜力都表明,中国在随后的许多年里仍能保持快速的出口增长。
3. 进口的一大部分用于来料加工,然后再以成品出现在中国的出口里。
4. 除了一般贸易外,中国还从事其他各种贸易形式,例如客户材料加工、客户样品加工、客户部件组装、补偿贸易和来料加工。
5. 从20世纪80年代起,中国企业经历了一个快速发展的阶段,商人开始利用成熟的技术、设备和原材料、加工过的材料在发展中国家实施加工贸易。

VII. Translate the following passage into Chinese.
China's imports and exports have expanded continuously since the 1990s. China's trade has grown at a much faster rate than its gross domestic product, and its trade dependency ratio in 2001 was 44 percent, or 1.47 times higher than in 1990. China exports much more than it imports, and, with the exception of 1993, it enjoyed fast-growing trade surpluses in the 1990s. Foreign trade became China's main engine of economic growth in the 1990s, contributing 7.5 percent on average to GDP growth. A 10 percent increase in China's exports was, for example, found to have resulted in a 1 percent increase in GDP in the 1990s, if both direct and indirect contributions were considered.

Text B

China, US Complementary in Trade

Since the beginning of this century, bilateral trade between China and the United States has risen rapidly, benefiting both sides.

Exports

According to China customs statistics, China's exports to the United States were US$52.1 billion in 2000 and reached US$162.9 billion in 2005, an increase of 212 percent. According to U.S. customs statistics, the US exports to China were US$16.2 billion in 2000 and reached US$41.8 billion in 2005, an increase of 157 percent. Among the top 15 trade partners of the United States, U.S. exports to China had the fastest increase.

According to U.S. statistics, China was the United States' fourth-largest trade partner, the fourth-largest import trade partner and the 11th-largest export trade partner in 2000. However, by 2005, China had become its third-largest trade partner, the second-largest import trade partner and the fourth-largest export partner, next to Canada, Mexico and Japan. China is the strategic trade partner[1] of the United States, as stated by President George W. Bush on March 9 last year.

According to US statistics, China's export to the United States was US$243.5 billion last year, accounting for 32 percent of China's US$762 billion total exports and 14.6 percent of US total imports. This demonstrates the fact that China and the United States are big markets to each other. In 1994, the U.S. Department of Commerce listed China as the head of its top 10 newly emerging markets, which has been proven over the past 10 years.

Capital Investment

Like commodities, capital also needs markets and can dwindle[2] without high capital profits. According to statistics, by the end of 2005, the U.S. actual investments in China reached US$51 billion. This demonstrates that China has become a big overseas market for U.S. capital, next to Western Europe, North, Central and South America, and Japan.

China and the United States boast remarkable achievements in financial co-operation. By the end of November 2005, China held US$254.4 billion in U.S. treasury bonds and a considerable amount of U.S. enterprise stocks and private securities. By the end of 2005, China's foreign reserves[3] reached more than US$810 billion, with 60 per cent of them being U.S. capital.

Conflicts and Frictions

Since the beginning of 2005, the economic and trade relationship between the two countries, however, has encountered some trouble, as demonstrated by increasing conflicts and frictions. In future years, the economic and trade relationship between China and the United States is expected to face many challenges, for example: intellectual property rights, RMB exchange rate, trade balance, textile trade and market access in the services area.

It must be noted that most of these are the conflicts of economic interests among some industrial sectors rather than the conflicts of fundamental interests between the two countries and they can be settled through mutual understanding and negotiations. Besides, these frictions are only the minor ones in the Sino-U.S. economic and trade relationship and should not affect the mainstream economic and trade co-operation between the two countries.

The two sides should deal with any friction and dispute from a far-reaching perspective without intensifying the issue. Equality and mutual benefit are the foundations of economic and trade co-operation; complementary partners are an important condition for economic and trade co-operation; and friendly negotiation is an effective tool to settle frictions and disputes. The threat of sanctions and retaliation is not advisable[4], because it not only violates the multilateral trade system, but also intensifies the disputes rather than helping settle them.

Trade wars can only hurt both sides and economies having close economic and trade ties with China and the United States. Therefore trade wars are not acceptable or supported by most businesspeople within the two countries.

This has been demonstrated by the restrictions and counter-restrictions in the textile trade between the two countries. From June 17 to November 8 last year, the government delegations of China and the United States underwent seven rounds of hard negotiations and finally signed a memorandum of understanding (MOU)[5] on the trade of textiles and apparel.

The MOU reflects the co-operative principle of mutual understanding and mutual benefit, setting a good example for the settlement of frictions and disputes in Sino-US economic and trade relations; it is also helpful for the further development of Sino-US economic and trade co-operation.

Trade Imbalance

At present a relatively prominent issue is the U.S. trade imbalance with China. According to China's customs statistics, China's trade surplus with the United States reached US$114.2 billion; while according to the statistics of the U.S. Chamber of Commerce, the U.S. trade deficit with China reached as high as US$201.6 billion.

The United States imports a large amount of daily necessities from China that are of good quality and low price and that satisfy the needs of U.S. markets. The products benefit most consumers and help relieve U.S. inflation.

Trade deficit[6] is a trade behaviour and should be analyzed from the perspective of market needs. China exported to the United States 40 or 50 million pairs of shoes in exchange for one big Boeing 747. Therefore it should not be easily concluded that a developing country has trade advantages when it relies on the export of a large amount of labour-intensive consumer goods in exchange for a small amount of high-tech equipment and technology.

In the economic and trade co-operation between China and the United States, trade advantage stays with the United States. Since the beginning of 1993, the US trade deficit has been mainly attributed to the fact that the U.S. advantage in high technology has not been brought into full play[7]. To deregulate the management of technology export is the way to reduce China's trade surplus. The initiative of reducing trade deficit with China lies in the hand of the United States.

The U.S. trade deficit is the consequence of economic globalization and the restructure of world industries and is the natural product of the world labour division. U.S. trade deficit is a structural one and is irretrievable.

How should we look at the issue of trade imbalance between China and the United States?

First, one main feature of Sino-US trade is that most Chinese exports to the United States are processed products, accounting for about 70 per cent, which means that China only gets a small amount of processing fees.

Take the Barbie doll for example. One Barbie doll is sold at US$9.99, but only costs US$2 when imported from China. Its raw materials come from the Middle East and are made into semi-products in Taiwan, the wigs are made in Japan, and the packing materials are provided by the United States, the total of these three parts makes up US$1. Transportation and management costs US$0.65, and the Chinese mainland is left with only US$0.35 for processing. In light of the rule of origin, these US$2 are put into China's export to the United States. Obviously it cannot tell the real case of the trade between the two countries.

Second, 70 per cent of China's foreign investments are from East Asia. For many years, Japan, the Republic of Korea, Singapore, Malaysia, Thailand, and the Philippines have shifted their former trade surplus products to China, thus causing the "shift of trade imbalance." So, the products made by these co-operative or 100 per cent overseas-owned enterprises are actually Made in Asia instead of Made in China, and China's trade surplus is shared by the above countries rather than owned by China alone.

According to U.S. customs statistics, the U.S. imports from the above countries in 2000 were US$302.3 billion, while in 2005 the imports did not increase but fell to US$294.7 billion by 2.5 per cent. During the same period, its imports from China jumped to US$243.5 billion from US$100 billion, an increase of 140 per cent.

According to China's customs statistics, China's trade surplus with the United States was US$114.2 billion in 2005, but it had a trade deficit of US$140 billion with the above countries.

In this sense, China is an Asian processing centre. As Li Deshui, former director of the National Bureau of Statistics, said, China's trade surplus with the United States and Europe is in fact a passer-by, a reality of having more flowers than fruits.

Third, the economic and trade relationship between China and the United States is reflected in four areas: commodity trade, technology trade, service trade and mutual investment. The trade deficit generally refers to that of commodity trade.

The U.S. advantage in its trade lies in the last three areas. By the end of 2005, the actual investment in China by U.S. enterprises was US$51.1 billion, with 49,000 businesses set up. Most of the products made by these enterprises are sold in the Chinese market, with only a small portion of them sold to the U.S. market.

Take GM and Motorola for example. There is a strong demand for their cars and mobile phones made in China, which, as a matter of fact, replace China's import of cars and mobile phones from the United States. These US enterprises enlarge their investments with the profits made in China and remit the remainder to the United States, which in fact makes up part of the U.S. trade deficit.

According to incomplete statistics from the Chinese Ministry of Commerce, in 2004 US-owned firms' sales in China reached as high as US$75 billion, which can offset 46 per cent of the US$162 billion U.S. trade deficit with China that year.

Conclusion

During the five years from 2001 to 2005, China's total imports were US$2.173 trillion. During the next five years from 2006 to 2010, China is expected to have imports worth US$4 trillion. This really is a big newly emerging market.

As long as the Bush administration can greatly deregulate export management with China like the Reagan administration did, the U.S. large- and medium-sized enterprises will have the ability and the possibility to capture more shares in China's rapidly growing new market, and China will surely become a big market for U.S. exports.

The industrial structures of China and the United States can strongly complement each other, which guarantees a bright future and greater development for broad economic and trade co-operation between the two nations.

The combination of U.S. capital, technology and management experience with China's huge market, low-cost labour and resources will surely bring great benefits to the economic development of both countries.

China's modernization needs a large amount of U.S. capital, technology and equipment, which can push and promote U.S. economic development. Therefore, economic and trade co-operation between China and the United States is mutually beneficial and a win-win situation with bright prospects.

Notes

1. strategic trade partner
   建设性贸易伙伴
2. dwindle
   逐渐减少
3. foreign reserves
   外汇储备
4. The threat of sanctions and retaliation is not advisable.
   威胁进行制裁和报复是不可取的。
5. a memorandum of understanding (MOU)
   理解备忘录
6. trade deficit
   贸易赤字(亏损)
7. ...the US trade deficit has been mainly attributed to the fact that the U.S. advantage in high technology has not been brought into full play.
   美国贸易赤字主要是由于美国在高科技领域的优势没有充分表现出来。

Answer the following questions:

1. Why did President George W. Bush say that China is the strategic trade partner of the US? Can you find any facts and figures to support his view?
2. What kind of conflicts and frictions is Sino-U.S. trade relationship facing?
3. How should we deal with these conflicts and frictions?
4. What's the trade imbalance between China and the United States? Why?
5. How should we look at the trade imbalance between China and the United States?
6. In which aspects of trade do China and U.S. complement each other?

Unit 7

Marketing Strategy

Learning Objectives

Text A
- to define marketing and describe the functions it performs
- to identify and describe the elements of the marketing strategy

Text B
- to understand the uncontrollable variables in the marketing strategy
- to know the importance of the buying behaviour of consumers

Text A

The Four P's of the Marketing Strategy

Marketing is the process of planning and executing the conception, pricing, promotion, and distribution of ideas, goods, and services to create exchanges that satisfy individual and organizational objectives. Marketing performs eight basic functions, namely, collecting and analyzing market information, selling, financing, grading and standardization, transporting, storing, buying, and assuming risks. Marketing can be examined from two different perspectives of buyer and seller. The marketer's major tools that summarize the seller's activities are those called "Four P's," which in many strategies is called the marketing mix:

- ❖ Product strategy
- ❖ Price strategy
- ❖ Place (distribution) strategy
- ❖ Promotion strategy

Product Strategy

A product is a good, a service, an idea, or any combination of the three that may be the subject of an exchange. Product strategy calls for much more than just deciding to make a product.[1] Among the crucial factors a manufacturer must determine are:

- ❖ New-product development
- ❖ Branding

❖ Packaging
❖ Labeling

The challenge all firms face is to develop products that meet their customers' needs and wants. Markets are rarely static and business cannot be either. A well-planned new-product development process, the six-step of testing, developing, and selling a product, reduces the risk of falling behind the competition. It also holds out the promise of achieving a competitive advantage.

Phase One: Idea generation. In the present context, an idea is the starting point of the new-product development process. The more ideas a firm can generate, the better the chances are that one can be commercialized.

Phase Two: Screening. In the screening phase of new-product development process, a firm sifts the good ideas from the bad. Companies should develop decision criteria to eliminate ideas that have little promise, do not relate to customer satisfaction, or do not fit their objectives or resources.[2]

Phase Three: Business Analysis. In this phrase, the firm studies the proposed products' potential costs and revenues. The business analysis can be seen as a continuation of the screening phase, except that the criteria used are more precise.

Phase Four: Product Development. The firm begins to give an idea a form. Research and development staff will prepare and test the prototype against the customer's needs and wants.

Phase Five: Test Marketing. Once the product is ready from a business and development standpoint, the company may begin limited production, usually sold in a test market. Test-marketing results can lead to product packaging refinements.

Phase Six: Commercialization. Only a few products reach the final phase, commercialization. If the results of the test marketing are positive, the firm will then introduce the product to the entire market.

Many consumers buy brand-name products to assure themselves of consistent quality. To secure consumer loyalty, however, manufacturers must promote their brand and tightly control the quality and consistency of their products.[3] Business has a wide range of branding strategies to choose from. At one extreme is what might be called the ***no-brand strategy.*** Many companies do not use brands, preferring to sell generic or unbranded goods.[4] And ***family or blanket brand strategy*** is an approach based on the use of one brand name for all of a firm's products. ***Individual brand strategy*** refers to the approach that calls for a different brand name for each product.

The development of a container and a graphic design for a product are called ***packaging***. The functions of packaging are to preserve, protect, and provide utility. A package may serve to prevent spoilage or damage. Packaging not only protects a product but also insures its uniformity. In this sense, packaging does not just contain the product; it is an integral part of the product.

A label is that part of the package that contains information. **Labeling** is therefore the presentation of information on a package product. Typically, a label contains the brand name and symbols, the size and contents of the package, directions for use, safety precautions, and the Universal Product Code and symbol. A well-designed package can serve an invaluable promotion function.

Price Strategy

Pricing is a critical element in the marketing mix. The major pricing decision is whether to assign a price above, below, or about even with the competitors'. Of course, a firm must consider other factors too, such as product cost, consumer demand, and the need to offer discounts. Setting prices is not a simple process. The first step in the pricing decision is to determine the firm's objectives. The most common ones are:

- *Profit Maximization:* Many firms try to set their prices to maximize their profits, but it is very hard to determine just what price will precisely do that. Profit maximizers aim for a price as high as possible without causing a disproportionate reduction in unit sales.[5]
- *Target Return on Investment:* The firm has analyzed its other investment opportunities for its money and determined that in order to justify its investment in the product, it must receive a certain return.
- *Market Share:* Management may decide that the strategic advantages of an increased market share overweigh the temporary reduction in profits necessary to obtain it.
- *Status Quo:* Many firms follow what is called *status quo* pricing, a strategy that might also be called "follow the leader" pricing.
- *Survival:* Survival pricing is generally a short-term objective and is often aimed at generating enough cash to pay current or past-due bills.

A company chooses a method that will help it meets its pricing objectives. Firms have four basic methods to choose from: economic theory-based pricing, cost-based pricing, demand-based pricing, and competition-based pricing. Once a price has been set using the chosen pricing method, the firm adjusts this price in accordance with its pricing strategy.

First, let's look at the new-product pricing strategy. The pricing strategy for a new product must be consistent with the overall marketing strategy developed for it. Two choices here are the **skimming strategy** and the **penetration strategy**. A skimming price strategy involves charging a high price when the product is first produced. A penetration pricing strategy calls for introducing a new product at a low price, to attain a strong grip on a sizeable market share.[6]

Many of the more specifically targeted pricing strategies are based on consumer behavior. These psychological strategies often influence the product's image. **Odd/even pricing** is most popular. For example, when the price ends in an odd number (usually nine), it's meant to give the impression of low prices and convey the idea that the firm has cut prices to the last possible penny. **Multiple-unit pricing** is the practice of providing discounts for purchases of two or more units. **Prestige pricing** involves setting a very high price on an item to give an impression of high quality. **Price lining** is a pricing strategy used primarily by retailers in which the firm selects a limited number of key prices or price points for certain classes or products.

Place (Distribution) Strategy

To facilitate the flow of products to their ultimate purchasers, most businesses that produce goods have created extensive **channels of distribution**, paths or routes composed of marketing intermediaries or middleman that direct products to consumers. A channel of distribution, which is sometimes called a marketing channel or distribution channel, always begins with a producer and ends with a consumer or end user. Between them, a number of different types of firms may handle the goods. In designing a distribution strategy, a manufacturer focuses primarily on selecting the marketing intermediaries such as wholesalers and retailers. Wholesalers and retailers are the major marketing intermediaries, found in the channel of distribution of both consumer and industrial products.

Wholesalers are those infamous middlemen whose profits so many people talk about eliminating.[7] It is divided into two groups: full-service wholesalers and limited-service wholesalers. **Full-service wholesalers** offer the widest variety of services to their customers, including maintaining inventories, gathering and interpreting market information, extending credit, distributing goods, and promotional activities. **Limited-service wholesalers** offer a narrow range of services than do full-service wholesalers, and they often tend to specialize.

Retailers sell goods or services—or both—to consumers. Retailers vary in size from the "mom and pop" store to the giant store operated by major chains like the R.H. Macy Company, Inc. Retail stores are categorized according to their operational structure. Independent retailers are often sole proprietorship or partnerships. Chain stores are groups of retail outlets under common (usually corporate) ownership and management. In-store retailers can also be categorized by the type of store they run, such as department store, specialty store, catalogue showroom and so on.

Promotion Strategy

Promotion describes the communications that an organization uses to inform, persuade, or remind a target market about its products, its services, or itself. Business uses promotion not just to increase sales but also to manage sales. They use promotion to increase sales of specific products, increase sales at a given time, or even decrease sales or demand temporarily.[8] Promotion can also be used to shape the image of a business.

Effective promotion requires careful planning. Promotional planning begins with the need to make a choice between two distinct promotional strategies:

- ❖ Push promotion strategy
- ❖ Pull promotion strategy

A push strategy is directed at selling goods or services directly to the next intermediary in the channel of distribution. The success of a push strategy depends largely on the effectiveness of an organization's sale force. It is often appropriate for low-volume, high-value items like mainframe computers or construction equipment.[9] The other approach, the pull strategy, promotes a product or service directly to the consumer, primarily through advertising or sales promotion. A pull strategy is most effective with high-volume, low-value products like laundry soap or chewing gum.

The push and pull strategies are, of course, not mutually exclusive, and firms often use both of them together.

New Words

concept	/ˈkɒnsept/	n.	观念,概念
perspective	/pəˈspektɪv/	n.	观点,看法;前途
distribution	/ˌdɪstrɪˈbjuːʃən/	n.	销售;分配
branding	/ˈbrændɪŋ/	n.	商标,牌子
combination	/ˌkɒmbɪˈneɪʃən/	n.	结合
labeling	/ˈleɪbəlɪŋ/	n.	商标,标志
contact	/ˈkɒntækt/	v.	接触,联系
static	/ˈstætɪk/	adj.	静态的
generate	/ˈdʒenəreɪt/	v.	产生,发生
commercialize	/kəˈmɜːʃəlaɪz/	v.	使商业化,使商品化
criteria	/kraɪˈtɪərɪə/	n.	标准
eliminate	/ɪˈlɪmɪneɪt/	v.	排除,除去,消除
potential	/pəˈtenʃəl/	adj.	潜在的,可能的
continuation	/kənˌtɪnjuˈeɪʃən/	n.	继续,延长
prototype	/ˈprəutətaɪp/	n.	原型
standpoint	/ˈstændpɔɪnt/	n.	立场,观点
refinement	/rɪˈfaɪnmənt/	n.	精致,文雅,精巧
consistency	/kənˈsɪstənsi/	n.	一致性,连贯性
container	/kənˈteɪnə/	n.	容器,集装箱
graphic	/ˈgræfɪk/	adj.	绘画似的,图解的
integral	/ˈɪntɪgrəl/	adj.	完整的,整体的,基本的

preserve	/prɪˈzɜːv/	v.	保护,保持,保藏
utility	/juːˈtɪlɪti/	n.	效用,有用
spoilage	/ˈspɔɪlɪdʒ/	n.	损坏
uniformity	/ˌjuːnɪˈfɔːmɪti/	n.	同样,一式,一致
precautions	/prɪˈkɔːʃəs/	n.	预防,警惕,防范
mix	/mɪks/	n.	混合,混合物
maximization	/ˌmæksəmaɪˈzeɪʃən/	n.	最大值化,极大值化
disproportionate	/ˌdɪsprəˈpɔːʃnɪt/	adj.	不成比例的
past-due	/pɑːst djuː/	adj.	过期的
grip	/grɪp/	n.	掌握,控制
odd	/ɒd/	adj.	基数的,单数的
even	/ˈiːvən/	adj.	偶数的
facilitate	/fəˈsɪlɪteɪt/	v.	帮助,促使,使容易
convey	/kənˈveɪ/	v.	搬运;传达;转让
outlet	/ˈaʊtlet/	n.	出口,出路
inventory	/ˈɪnvəntri/	n.	详细目录;存货
sole	/səʊl/	adj.	单独的,唯一的
proprietorship	/prəˈpraɪətəʃɪp/	n.	所有权
mainframe	/ˈmeɪnfreɪm/	n.	主机
infamous	/ˈɪnfəməs/	adj.	声名狼藉的

Phrases

call for	要求,提倡
hold out	提供;维持;制止
sift...from...	从中筛选
relate to	使联系
assure of	使确信,使保证
a wide range of	大规模的
in accordance with	与……一致,依照
consistent with	与……保持一致

Special Terms

marketing mix	市场营销组合
place strategy	分销策略
market testing	市场调研
commercialization	商品化,商业化

target market	目标市场
no-brand strategy	无商标策略
blanket brand	统一商标
universal product code	通用产品码,通用货单代码
target return	目标收益
status quo	现状
skimming price strategy	撇奶油式定价策略
penetration price strategy	渗透定价策略
odd pricing	奇零定价策略 (指产品的定价为单数与零数)
multiple-unit pricing	多重定价
prestige pricing	声望定价
price lining	底价
channel of distribution	分销途径
wholesaler	批发商
retailer	零售商
high-volume product	大量生产制品
push promotion strategy	推动促销策略
pull promotion strategy	拉引促销策略

Notes

1. Product strategy calls for much more than just deciding to make a product.
   产品策略所需要的远远大于下决定制造一个产品。
   句中 much more than 指"大于,远多于"。

2. Companies should develop decision criteria to eliminate ideas that have little promise, do not relate to customer satisfaction, or do not fit their objectives or resources.
   公司应该制定决策标准,从而将那些前途渺茫、无法满足顾客需要,或是不符合公司的目标或资源的产品清除。
   have little promise 在这里表示"没有希望,没有前途",而 do not relate to customer satisfaction 是指"与顾客的满意毫无联系"。

3. To secure consumer loyalty, however, manufacturers must promote their brand and tightly control the quality and consistency of their products.
   但是,为了保证顾客的忠诚度,制造商必须提升品牌,并且牢固地控制产品的质量和一致性。
   句中的 secure consumer loyalty 是指保证顾客对产品的忠诚。

4. At one extreme is what might be called the no-brand strategy. Many companies do not use brands, preferring to sell generic or unbranded goods.

其中一个极端的做法就是"无商标策略"。许多公司在销售普通产品或是无标记的产品时,倾向于不用商标。

at one extreme 指"在一个极端"。

5. Profit maximizers aim for a price as high as possible without causing a disproportionate reduction in unit sales.

奉行利润最大化的销售商的目的在于:在不会造成单位销售不成比例地减少的前提下,尽可能的高定价。

6. A penetration pricing strategy calls for introducing a new product at a low price, to attain a strong grip on a sizeable market share.

渗透定价策略要求以低价格引介一个新产品,从而牢固地获得一份相当大的市场份额。

at a low price 表示"以低价";attain a strong grip on 表示"紧紧抓住",相似的还有 hold/take a grip on something/somebody,意思是"控制住某事或某人"。

7. Wholesalers are those infamous middlemen whose profits so many people talk about eliminating.

批发商指的是那些声名狼藉的中间人,而且人们正在议论要消除他们所获得的利润。

句中 talk about eliminating 即 talk about eliminating their profits。

8. They use promotion to increase sales of specific products, increase sales at a given time, or even decrease sales or demand temporarily.

他们(经销商)利用促销来增加特定产品的销售,增加特定时间的销售,甚至是暂时地减少销售或是需求。

at a given time 意思是"在一个特定的时间段里"。

9. It is often appropriate for low-volume, high-value items like mainframe computers or construction equipment.

它(促销策略)适用于小量生产的、高价值的制品,例如计算机主机或是建筑设备。

句中的 appropriate for 意为"适合于……,适用于……"。

Exercises

I. Discuss the following questions.

1. What is marketing? What major functions does marketing perform?
2. What are the elements of the marketing mix? Define each element.
3. What are the basic steps in the new-product development process? Describe each of them.
4. Identify the major pricing methods. How is each different from the others?

5. Provide an overview of the channels of distribution.
6. What is the primary difference between a push-oriented promotion strategy and a pull-oriented strategy?

II. Analyze the case below and discuss the questions.

A Rich Dessert

Since 1921, Reuben Mattus's family had produced hand-turned ice cream for local consumption. Theirs was one of dozens of small firms vying for distribution in New York City's neighborhoods. By the time Reuben took over the business, the competition was fierce; it got worse in the 1950s, when the large ice cream manufacturers began to use their economic power to drive small local firms out of supermarkets. Mattus decided he'd had enough of that kind of competition, and he searched for something that would get him out of it. What he came up with, in 1960, was the first of so-called "super-premium" ice creams—twice as rich as mass-produced ice cream, and made with only natural ingredients. Because he believed that Danish made superior ice cream, Mattus made up a Danish sounding name for his product: Haagen-Dazes. He also gave it a high price, betting that plenty of people would pay more for a quality product with a foreign-sounding name. He was right. At first he had trouble getting local supermarkets to carry Haagen-Dazes, because they didn't believe people would pay the price. Mattus refused to advertise his produce, because he didn't trust advertising. But his persistence and a higher-than-usual markup convinced some supermarkets to carry it, and word-of-mouth advertising convinced the rest. Competitors soon followed Mattus's lead; the market for super-premium ice cream now is estimated at $2 billion annually, and growing by about 25 percent each year.

Questions:
1. What risks were involved in Reuben Mattus's marketing effort?
2. Describe and evaluate the Haagen-Dazes marketing mix.

III. Match the terms in column A with the explanations in column B.

A	B
1. channel of distribution	A. sample market areas, the sales from which are used to predict the behaviour of the entire market
2. product	B. a pricing strategy derived from the cost of producing or purchasing a product
3. test market	C. strategy that takes advantage of all available retail outlets
4. generic name	D. wholesaler who offers the widest variety of services to its customers

5. packaging   E. strategy that promotes a product or service directly to the customer
6. cost-based pricing   F. a group of intermediaries or middlemen that direct products to customers
7. intensive distribution strategy   G. the communications that an organization uses to inform, persuade, or remind a target market about its products, its services, or itself
8. full-service wholesaler   H. a trademark that has passed into common, every-day language
9. promotion   I. a good, service, an idea, or any combination of the three that may be the subject of an exchange
10. pull strategy   J. the development of a container and a graphic design for a product

IV. Fill in the blanks of the following sentences with the words or phrases given below. Make changes when necessary.

| concept | distribution | contact | generate | eliminate |
| standpoint | integral | grip | convey | exclusive |

1. From my _____, the reform of the committee will bring great changes to the performance of the employees.
2. The first government-to-government _____ will improve the mutual understanding to a large extent.
3. We have no _____ that most of the workers didn't accept the company's decision by not cooperating with the new boss.
4. After having made great efforts, the producer eventually got the _____ right to film the popular novel.
5. More and more graduates realized that English and computer skill are the _____ parts of finding a job in the big city.
6. A company's successful management greatly depends on the rational _____ of its factories throughout the country so much as the world.
7. It is indeed a hard task to get rid of the hatred _____ by racial prejudice in a short time.
8. Words cannot _____ how delighted I am when hearing that my book will be published soon.
9. The little boy tried hard to take a _____ on himself and said to the thief, "What did you want to get from me?"
10. To keep healthy, one needs to _____ the waste material from the body through dieting and exercise.

V. Put the following into English.
1. 分销渠道
2. 市场概念
3. 新产品的开发流程
4. 以竞争为基础的定价
5. 市场中间商
6. 市场覆盖
7. 独立零售商
8. 商标策略
9. 资源分配
10. 利益最大化

VI. Translate the following sentences into English.
1. 良好的包装在促进产品销售上起着举足轻重的作用。
2. 公司在制定产品的价格时,既需要体现公司近期的市场目标,也要考虑到公司的长期发展策略。
3. 广告是推销产品的市场策略之一。产品广告必须要推出产品的质量、令人满意的特征以及产品的价格。
4. 大部分的零售商都囤有大量的、种类繁多的货物,而且他们的经营范围主要在商铺之中。
5. 竞争的加剧迫使许多生产厂家不得不为专业市场生产产品,从而增加了成本的费用。

VII. Translate the following passage into Chinese.

Newspapers, which are the most popular advertising media, have low costs and CPM. The CPM for a quarter-page ad in major metropolitan newspaper averages $4.64.

Newspapers are quite selective from a geographic standpoint. They permit advertisers to pinpoint their advertising to the metropolitan areas that they wish to reach. From the standpoint of interest selectivity, most newspapers reach all economic and social levels of people and have a general rather than a special appeal. A favourable characteristic of newspaper advertising is its flexibility or timelines. In most cases changes in an advertising copy can be made within a few hours ahead of the time the paper goes to press. This permits advertisers to follow with great speed any national or local event, the weather or changes in their own internal situations. For instance, the *St. Louis Post-Dispatch* requires receipt of an advertising copy only 48 hours prior to publication.

Since nearly 80 percent of all adults read a daily newspaper, the reach for newspaper is high. A newspaper provides an advertiser with the ability to reach immediately nearly all of a particular market. The frequency of a newspaper ad is directly related to the number of times the ad is inserted in the paper. The more times the ad is inserted, the more frequently a reader can see it.

Text B
Uncontrollable Variables in Marketing Strategy

Marketing managers make their decisions within a social, economic, and political environment. Although they cannot control this environment, they seek as much information as possible about it. This information helps them make more suitable decisions. In the long run the decision of marketing managers modify their environment. In the short run, however, they do not significantly change the environmental influences surrounding them. There are five uncontrollable variables, which are particularly significant to a marketing manager: competition, marketing legislation, nonmarketing costs, structure of distribution and demand.

Competition

A marketing manager should be knowledgeable about the pricing, promotion, product and place policies of all competitors. Some firm develop marketing intelligence systems in an effort to gather knowledge for better decision making. A major portion of the intelligence activity is devoted to accumulating information about competition. Important sources of intelligence for the marketing manager of a firm include:

- the firm's salespersons,
- the company's suppliers,
- government sources,
- trade associations,
- industry and competing company publications,
- marketing research,
- expert opinions,
- rumors.

Marketing Legislation

Since marketing managers must make decisions within a scope of the law, they must have a knowledge of legislation. Managers should also understand the laws so that the effect of their decisions upon public policy and social welfare can be evaluated. The body of marketing laws is designed to protect the buyer from the seller, protect the seller form the buyer, and protect one competition from another. The dominant American conviction is that uncontrolled competition among firms is an economic liability. Consequently, the bulk of marketing legislation is concerned with competition. To maintain some influence on marketing legislation at all levels of government, companies join trade associations and employ public relations personnel and lobbyists.

Nonmarketing Costs

In most cases the decisions made by a marketing manager have an impact on both marketing and nonmarketing costs. For example, a managerial decision is made to employ an additional 50 salespersons in an effort to intensify coverage in all major markets. This involves not only additional marketing costs, but also extra manufacturing costs. The expenses of manufacturing the additional products which are needed because of the intensified selling effort are nonmarketing costs. Although both costs are affected by the managerial decision, only the employment of additional salespersons is controllable by the marketing executive. Cost accountants and financial planning committees help marketing managers recognize how their decisions affect costs in other areas such as production and finance.

Structure of Distribution

The structure of distribution refers to the alternative channels of distribution that are available to move goods from producers to consumers. A channel of distribution is the path taken in the transfer of title to a good from producer or manufacturer to the final user. The structure of distribution is considered to be an uncontrollable marketing variable since the manufacturer must typically choose the firm's channel from among those in existence.

For example, a new manufacturer of electric garbage disposal, units may desire to grant an exclusive franchise, to appliance wholesalers in large metropolitan areas. An investigation shows, however, that the desired wholesalers are already handling competitive lines and that they do not care to add any additional lines. The manufacturer considers selling directly to appliance retailers, but a cost analysis reveals that this type of selling is not economically feasible. The attention of the manufacturer turns to searching for other types of middlemen to handle the firm's line. The manufacturer finally decides to use hardware wholesalers to provide the needed distribution.

Studies of market potential, distribution cost analysis, and the application of mathematical models guide the marketing manager in selecting the most efficient distribution channel.

Demand

Demand refers to the potential sales volume for a product or service in a given period of time. In order to forecast demand, a marketing manager should be conscious of population trends, income patterns and buying behaviour of consumers

Population trends

Population is the underlying market factor for consumer demand. From 1900 to 1985, the population of the United States grew from 76 million to 237 million—an increase of 212 percent. Rather than looking at total population, however, it is more significant for a marketing manager to segment the population by age group, geographical locations and income.

Income patterns

The aggregate amount for spending and saving in this country during a particular period of time is called disposable personal income. This amount is prime factors in determining consumer demand. Personal income is the most important source of consumer purchasing power. Other sources include credit and wealth. Most families spend the greatest part of their income on necessities such as food, housing, clothing, and basic transportation. The income available after necessities have been purchased and a certain living standard has been met is called discretionary income. A family's discretionary income is dependent upon family size, composition of the family, total income, social environment, and life-cycle stages. As the income of the family increases, the discretionary portion usually has more than a proportionate rise. During a business recession, discretionary income rapidly decreases, resulting in a decline in the sales of automobiles, luxury boats, expensive furniture, and other high-ticket items.

Buying behaviour of consumers

A knowledge of consumer behaviour has helped many companies in successfully marketing their products. Therefore, a firm cannot neglect the role that the consumer behaviour plays when it is making a marketing strategy. Listerine mouthwash was introduced with the advertising heading, "Always a bridesmaid but never a bride." Many individuals drive a Cadillac because it is an easily recognized symbol of prestige.

Both psychological (or intrapersonal) forces and social (or inter personal) forces influence consumer behaviour. The psychological forces arise from within an individual and affect his or her mental process. These forces include motivation, perception, learning attitudes, and personality. The social forces are the elements in the external environment that interact on an individual and direct her or his buying behaviour. Theses elements are culture, social class, reference groups, and family.

Because of the importance of motivation in the buying process, we will examine several types of buying motives. Buying motives are difficult to classify since they are closely allied to one another, are capable of being classified into numerous groupings, and overlap in meaning. A buying motive is aroused when bodily energy is activated and selectively directly toward satisfying a need. Maslow's hierarchy of needs represents one set of buying motives. Maslow theorizes that individuals buy to satisfy the following order of needs: psychological safety, social esteem, and self-fulfillment. The following discussion identifies several other categories of buying motives.

Rational motives. Socially approved reasons for buying are called rational buying motives. In general, they tend to economize the money and time spent for a good or service. These motives include dependability, low price, economy in use, money gain, and convenience. The promotions for most industrial goods use rational buying motives.

Emotional buying motives. Emotional buying motives relate to a person's psychological drives. Some critics disapprove of these do not reduce the long-run costs for a product and may appear wasteful. Such motives include prestige, individuality, conformity, comfort, pleasure, creativity and emulation.

Dormant and conscious motives. Dormant buying motives are unknown and unrecognized by consumers until these are brought to their attention. For example, homemakers may not be aware of a need for a microwave oven until they see one demonstrated and talk with friends who have them. Conscious buying motives are known and clearly recognized by the consumer without exposure to any marketing effort. For example, the seven-year-old is absolutely conscious of the need for a dirty bike because a friend down the street already has one.

Patronage motives. Patronage motives attract buyers to a particular vendor. Those motives are different from those that attract buyers to a certain market. For example, K mart uses low prices, wide assortments, and self-service for customers. Sake Fifth Avenue uses fashion merchandise, numerous customer services, and attractive stores to attract wealthy patrons.

Answer the following questions:

1. What are the uncontrollable variables in the marketing strategy?
2. How does marketing legislation affect the marketing strategy?
3. What is the structure of distribution?
4. How do income patterns affect the marketing strategy?
5. How many buying motives are there? Explain them.
6. Explain how both psychological and social forces may influence a corporate executive to purchase a Lincoln.

Marketing Environment

Learning Objectives

Text A
- to learn the forces that will shape opportunities and pose threats to the marketers
- to understand the effects of each major macroenvironment force

Text B
- to understand the political and legal environment of the host country and the risks firms face
- to learn how to deal with the intricacies of national politics and laws

Text A

The Major Macroenvironment Forces

Companies and their suppliers, marketing intermediaries, customers, competitors and the public all operate in a macroenvironment of forces and trends that shape opportunities and pose threats. These forces represent "noncontrollables," which the company must monitor and respond to. Within the rapidly changing global picture, the firm must monitor six major forces: demographic, economic, natural, technological, political/legal, and social/cultural forces. Marketers must pay attention to their causal interactions, since these set the stage for new opportunities as well as threats. For example, the explosive population growth (demographic) leads to more resource depletion and pollution (natural environment), which leads consumers to call for more laws (political/legal). The imposed restrictions stimulate new technological solutions and products (technological), which if they are affordable (economic) may actually change people's attitudes and behavior (social/cultural).

Demographic Environment

The world population is showing "explosive" growth. This explosive world population growth has major implications for business growing human needs, but it does not mean growing markets unless these markets have sufficient purchasing power[1]. Companies that carefully analyze their markets can find major opportunities. For example, to curb its skyrocketing population, the Chinese government has passed regulations limiting Chinese families to one child per family. Toy companies are paying attention to one consequence of these regulations: Known in China as "little emperors," Chinese children are being showered with everything from candy to computers as a result of six adults' indulging. This trend has encouraged such companies as Japan's Bandai Co., Denmark's Lego Group to enter the Chinese market.

National populations vary in their age mix. At one extreme is Mexico, a country with a very young population and rapid population growth. At the other extreme is Japan, a country with one of the world's oldest populations. Products of high importance in Mexico would be milk, diapers, school suppliers, and toys. Japan's population will consume many more adult products.

The population in any society falls into five educational groups: illiterates, high school dropouts, high school degrees, college degrees, and professional degrees. In Japan, 99% of the population is literate, while in the United States 10% to 15% of the population may be functionally illiterate. However, the United States has one of the world's highest percentages of college-educated citizenry, around 36 percent. The high number of educated people in the United States spells a high demand for quality books, magazines, and travel.[2]

The "traditional household" consists of a husband, wife and children (and sometimes grandparents). In the United States today, the traditional household is no longer the dominant household pattern. Today's households also include single live-alones, adult live-togethers of one or both sexes, single-parent families, childless married couples and empty nesters. Each group has a distinctive set of needs and buying habits. For example, people in the SSWD group (single, separated, widowed, divorced) need smaller apartments; inexpensive and smaller appliances, furniture and furnishings; and food packaged in smaller sizes. Marketers must increasingly consider the special needs of nontraditional households, since they are now growing more rapidly than traditional households.

Economic Environment

Markets require purchasing power as well as people. The available purchasing power in an economy depends on current income, prices, savings, debt, and credit availability. Marketers must pay close attention to major trends in income and consumer-spending patterns.

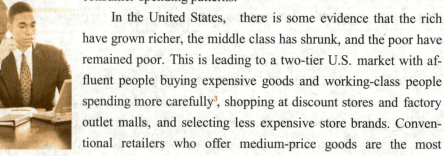

In the United States, there is some evidence that the rich have grown richer, the middle class has shrunk, and the poor have remained poor. This is leading to a two-tier U.S. market with affluent people buying expensive goods and working-class people spending more carefully[3], shopping at discount stores and factory outlet malls, and selecting less expensive store brands. Conventional retailers who offer medium-price goods are the most vulnerable to these changes.[4] The Japanese, for example, save about 18% of their income, while U.S. consumers save about 6 percent. The result is that Japanese banks have been able to loan out money to Japanese companies at a much lower interest rate than U.S. banks could offer to U.S. companies. Access to lower interest rates has helped Japanese companies expand faster.

Natural Environment

The deterioration of the natural environment is one of the major issues of the 1990s. In many world cities, air and water pollution have reached dangerous levels. There is great concern about certain chemicals causing air, soil and water pollution. Research has shown that about 42% of U.S. consumers are willing to pay higher prices for "green" products. This willingness creates a marketing opportunities for alert companies. It leads to a search for alternative ways to produce and package goods that do not cause environmental damage. New legislation passed because environmentalism has hit certain industries very hard.[5] Steel companies and public utilities have had to invest billions of dollars in pollution-control equipment and more environmentally friendly fuels. And the auto industry has had to introduce expensive emission controls in cars.

Smart companies are initiating environment-friendly moves to show their concern for the environment. AT&T uses a special software package to choose the least harmful materials, cut hazardous waste, reduce energy use, and improve product recycling in its operations. McDonald's and Burger King eliminated their polystyrene cartons and now use smaller, recyclable paper wrappings and paper napkins. The major hopes are that companies around the world will accept more social responsibility and that less expensive devices will be invented to control and reduce pollution.

Technological Environment

One of the most dramatic forces shaping people's lives is technology. Technology has released such wonder as penicillin, open-heart surgery, and the birth-control pill. It has released such horrors as the hydrogen bomb, nerve gas, and the submachine gun. It has also released such mixed blessings as the automobile and video games.

Every new technology is a force for "creative destruction." Transistors hurt the vacuum-tube industry, xerography hurt the carbon-paper business, autos hurt the railroads, and television hurt the newspapers. Instead of moving into the new business, many old industries fought or ignored them and their business declined.

As products become more technology-related, the public needs to be assured of their safety. Consequently, government agencies' powers to investigate and ban potentially unsafe products have been expanded. Marketers must be aware of these regulations when proposing, developing and launching new products.

Political/Legal Environment

Marketing decisions are strongly affected by developments in the political and legal environment. This environment is composed of laws, government agencies and pressure groups that influence and limit various organizations and individuals. Sometimes these laws also create new opportunities for business. For example, mandatory recycling laws have given the recycling industry a major boost.[6]

Legislation affecting business has steadily increased over the years. The European Commission has been active in establishing a new framework of laws covering competitive behavior, product standards, product liability, and commercial transactions for the 15 member nations of the European Union. The United States has many laws on its books covering such issues as competition, product safety and liability, fair trade, packaging and labeling and so on. Several countries have gone further than the United States in passing strong consumer-protection legislation. Norway bans several forms of sales promotion—trading stamps, contests, and premiums—as inappropriate or "unfair" instruments for promoting products. Thailand requires food processors selling national brands to market low-price brands also so that low-income consumers can find economy brands. In India, food companies need special approval to launch brands that duplicate what already exists on the market, such as another cola drink or brand of ice.

It is the marketer's responsibility to have a good working knowledge of the major laws protecting competition, consumers, and society. Companies generally establish legal review procedures and promulgate ethical standards to guide their marketing managers.

Social/Cultural Environment

The society in which people grow up shapes their beliefs, values and norms. People absorb, almost unconsciously, a worldview that defines their relationship to themselves, to others, to nature and to the universe.

The people living in a particular society hold many core beliefs and values that tend to persist. Thus most Americans still believe in work, in getting married, in giving to charity, and in being honest. Core beliefs and values are passed on from parents to children and are reinforced by major social institutions—schools, churches, business, and government.[7]

People's secondary beliefs and values are more open to change. Believing in the institution of marriage is a core belief; believing that people ought to get married early is a secondary belief.[8] Thus family-planning marketers could make some headway arguing that people should get married later than that they should not get married at all. Marketers have some chance of changing secondary values but little chance of changing core values.

Marketers have a keen interest in spotting cultural shifts that might augur new marketing opportunities or threats. Several firms offer social/cultural forecasts in this connection. One of the best known is the Yankelovich Monitor. The Monitor interviews 2,500 people each year and tracks 35 social trends, such as "living for today," "away from possessions." It describes the percentage of population who share the attitude as well as the percentage who are antitrend. For example, the percentage of people who value physical fitness and well-being has risen steadily over the years, especially in the under-thirty group, the young women and upscale group, and people living in the west. Marketers of health foods and exercise equipment cater to this trend with appropriate products and communications. This trend plays itself out even in the fast-food industry, where companies are now racing to see who can come up with the healthiest new products.

New Words

macroenvironment	/ˌmækrəʊɪnˈvaɪrənmənt/	n.	宏观环境
noncontrollable	/ˌnɒnkənˈtrəʊləbəl/	n.	不可控制的变量
demographic	/deməˈɡræfɪk/	adj.	人口的
marketer	/ˈmɑːkɪtə/	n.	营销者
depletion	/dɪˈpliːʃən/	n.	耗尽,枯竭
curb	/kɜːb/	v.	控制,抑制
skyrocket	/ˈskaɪˌrɒkɪt/	v.	(物价、数量等)猛涨,剧增
illiterate	/ɪˈlɪtərɪt/	n. & adj.	不识字的人,文盲;文盲的
dropout	/ˈdrɒpaʊt/	n.	退学者,中途辍学者
citizenry	/ˈsɪtɪzənri/	n.	(旧用法)全体公民
spell	/spel/	v.	带来,意味着
quality	/ˈkwɒlɪti/	n.	优质
appliance	/əˈplaɪəns/	n.	工具,器具
tier	/tɪə/	n.	层次,等级
affluent	/ˈæfluənt/	adj.	富裕的
mall	/mɔːl/	n.	购物中心,商场
retailer	/ˈriːteɪlə/	n.	零售商
vulnerable	/ˈvʌlnərəbəl/	adj.	易受攻击的
deterioration	/dɪˌtɪərɪəˈreɪʃən/	n.	恶化
environmentalism	/ɪnˌvaɪərənˈmentlɪzm/	n.	环境保护主义
emission	/ɪˈmɪʃən/	n.	排放
initiate	/ɪˈnɪʃɪeɪt/	v.	发起,启动,开始实施
environment-friendly	/ɪnˈvaɪərmənt ˈfrendli/	adj.	有利于环境保护的
polystyrene	/ˌpɒlɪˈstaɪriːn/	n.	聚苯乙烯
carton	/ˈkɑːtn/	n.	塑料盒
wrapping	/ˈræpɪŋ/	n.	包装
napkin	/ˈnæpkɪn/	n.	餐巾

transistor	/træn'zɪstə/	n.	晶体管
xerography	/zɪə'rɒgrəfi/	n.	静电印刷
carbon-paper	/'kɑːbən'peɪpə/	n.	复写纸
mandatory	/'mændətəri/	adj.	强制性的
liability	/ˌlaɪə'bɪlɪti/	n.	责任,义务
premium	/'priːmiəm/	n.	优惠
duplicate	/'djuːplɪkeɪt/	v.	复制,复印
promulgate	/'prɒməlgeɪt/	v.	公布,颁布(法令、教规等)
reinforce	/ˌriːɪm'fɔːs/	v.	加强,强化
institution	/ˌɪnstɪ'tjuːʃən/	n.	机构;制度
spot	/spɒt/	v.	找出,认出,看出
augur	/'ɔːgə/	v.	预卜,预示,预言
upscale	/'ʌpskeɪl/	adj.	上层的,有声望的,有地位的

Phrases

set the stage for	为……做准备,促成
fall into	可分为,分成
be vulnerable to	易受攻击的,暴露于危险面前的
make headway	取得进展
cater to	迎合,满足某种需要或要求
play out	演出或现出某事物

Special Terms

supplier	供应商
marketing intermediary	市场营销中间商
age mix	年龄组合
empty nesters	空巢者
purchasing power	购买力
discount store	折扣店
factory outlet mall	工厂分销商店区
public utilities	公用事业
mixed blessing	祸福皆有的事物,有好处也有坏处的事物
product safety and liability	产品安全与责任
fair trade	公平贸易
trading stamp	交易券(商店给顾客的赠券,可换物品或现金)

Notes

1. ...but it does not mean growing markets unless these markets have sufficient purchasing power.
   但是除非这些市场有足够的购买力，否则就并不意味着市场在不断扩大。

2. The high number of educated people in the United States spells a high demand for quality books, magazines, and travel.
   美国有大量受过教育的人口，这就表明了对高品质的书籍、杂志和旅游有强烈的需求。

   句中的 spell 表示"意味着"、"表明"或"带来"。

3. This is leading to a two-tier U.S. market with affluent people buying expensive goods and working-class people spending more carefully, ...
   这就使美国市场分为了两个层次，富人购买昂贵的产品，而工薪阶层则对支出非常谨慎……

4. Conventional retailers who offer medium-price goods are the most vulnerable to these changes.
   传统零售商提供的是中等价位的产品，因此他们最容易在这些变化中遭受损失。

5. New legislation passed because environmentalism has hit certain industries very hard.
   由于环境保护主义曾经沉重地打击了某些产业，因此颁布了新的法律。

6. For example, mandatory recycling laws have given the recycling industry a major boost.
   强制性的再循环法极大地促进了再循环产业的发展。

   句中 give...a major boost 表示"极大地促进或推动"。

7. Core beliefs and values are passed on from parents to children and are reinforced by major social institutions—schools, churches, business, and government.
   核心信念和价值观由父辈传给了下一代，同时主要的社会机构，如学校、教堂、商业和政府也强化了核心信念和价值观。

8. Believing in the institution of marriage is a core belief; believing that people ought to get married early is a secondary belief.
   对婚姻制度的信仰是核心信念，而认为人们应该早结婚则属于从属信念。

   句中 institution 的意思是"制度"，而注释 7 中 institution 则表示"机构,组织"。

Exercises

I. Discuss the following questions.

1. What are the six major forces that must be monitored by international marketers?

2. What are the effects of national populations on international marketing?
3. Why should marketers pay close attention to the changes in income and consumer-spending patterns?
4. What are the effects of natural environment on international marketing?
5. Why should international marketers be aware of regulations related to the safety of the products?
6. What is political/legal environment? What are its effects on international marketing?
7. What is social/cultural environment? What are its effects on international marketing?

II. Analyze the case below and discuss the question.

On April 23, 1985, Roberto C. Goizueta, chairman of Coca-Cola, announced that "the best has been made even better." Coke's 99-year-old formula had been abandoned, and a new, sweeter tasting Coke would replace the old Coke. By July 11, 1985, Coca-Cola admitted that it had made a mistake and that it was bringing back the old Coke under the name "Coca-Cola Classic." Business schools will dissect this case for years to come and wonder how the Coca-Cola Company (known for years as an astute marketer) could have made such a blunder.

But that was then. This is now and you are part of a marketing team at Coca-Cola charged with launching a new marketing campaign. Before you make any further decisions, discuss in some depth how the six macroenvironmental forces discussed in text A may affect the marketing of Coca-Cola by the year 2008.

III. Match the terms in column A with the explanations in column B.

A	B
1. intermediary	A. merchandise offered at a relatively low cost or free as an incentive to purchase a particular product
2. trading stamp	B. a legal requirement that an organization must pay damages to anyone who is harmed because their products are faulty
3. premium	C. a shop, etc. that sells goods for a particular company
4. discount store	D. the amount of money that a person, an organization or a country has to buy goods and services
5. purchasing power	E. a type of department store, which sell products at prices lower than those asked by traditional retail outlets
6. outlet	F. stamp that is given by certain shops, etc. to their customers and may be exchanged for goods or cash
7. product liability	G. putting a piece of paper, cloth, metal on or beside an object that describes its nature, name, owner, destination, etc.

8. labeling   H. a person or service that is involved as a third party between two or more end points in a communication or transaction

IV. *Fill in the blanks of the following sentences with the words or phrases given below. Make changes when necessary.*

curb	vulnerable	mandatory	liability	promulgate
spot	augur	play out	quality	skyrocket

1. The accession countries worry that until they join the euro-zone their borrowing costs will be higher and their currencies more _____ to attack.
2. Since high inflation is very destructive, we must do our utmost to fight it, _____ it, or bring it under control.
3. The company has accepted _____ for the damage to the cargo.
4. Because of the _____ of house prices, people in large cities are shouldering a heavy burden in their life.
5. The inferior quality of its products does not _____ well for its exports this year.
6. What has happened to the food industry over the past decade will now _____ in entertainment industry over the next couple of years.
7. For strategic materials and all shipments to unfriendly countries, a validated export license is _____.
8. In nearly all countries, the government _____ Patent Law and Trademark Law to protect the industrial property right from infringement.
9. The _____ furniture earned a good name for this factory.
10. International marketers should know how to _____ the differences between opportunities and risks.

V. *Put the following into English.*

1. 影响营销决策的宏观环境
2. 意识到人们购买行为的变化
3. 把经济变量综合起来考虑以适应营销目的
4. 衡量市场潜力的总体指标
5. 城市人口和农村人口存在的巨大收入差距
6. 占有笔记本电脑市场90%的份额
7. 将通货膨胀率保持在单位数的水平
8. 对新的营销环境做出战略性的回应
9. 在不断改变的市场中保持长期的竞争优势
10. 限制国际营销的各种具体规则和条例

VI. Translate the following sentences into English.

1. 为了培养文化敏感度和接受组织内部新的行事方式,管理层必须制定内部培训规划。
2. 对一国市场环境的评估应该从评估与市场的规模和性质相关的经济变量开始。
3. 中国市场的复杂性和巨大变化通常都是对西方营销者最严峻的挑战;由于中国各地区文化和经济背景的差异如此明显,西方营销者都认为中国市场实际上是许多小市场的组合。
4. 一些政府对外国投资者实行经济开放,仅对外国投资者施加最低限度的约束条件,希望这样的政策能够促使本国经济快速发展。
5. WTO为其成员国定义了国际上普遍认可的经济惯例。虽然它不能直接影响个体企业,但是它的确可以通过提供一个更为稳定的国际市场环境来间接影响它们。

VII. Translate the following passage into Chinese.

The complexity and vast changes of the Chinese market have always proved the biggest challenges for Western marketers. Geographically, regional difference is so distinct that China is regarded as a combination of many small markets. The consumption pattern varies significantly between coastal and central regions, and between the south and the north, mainly due to differences in cultural and economic backgrounds. The Gallup Organization conducted a broad range of surveys to better understand Chinese consumers from different regions. For example, there is much heavier consumption of beer in northern China than in other regions. In eastern China, people most read newspapers but do not listen to the radio. This has major implications for how marketers advertise their products.

Text

Host Country Political and Legal Environment

Host country environment, both political and legal, affects the international marketing operations of firms in a variety of ways. A good manager will understand the country in which the firm operates so that he or she is able to work within the existing parameters and can anticipate and plan for changes that may occur.

Political Action and Risk

Firms usually prefer to conduct business in a country with a stable and friendly government, but such governments are not always easy to find. Managers must therefore continually monitor the government, its policies, and its stability to determine the potential for political change that could adversely affect corporate operations.

There is political risk in every nation, but the range of risks varies widely from country to country. Political risk is defined as the risk of loss when investing in a given country caused by changes in the country's political structure or policies, such as tax laws, tariffs, expropriation of assets, or restriction in repatriation of profits. For example, a company may suffer from such loss in the case of expropriation or tightened foreign exchange repatriation rules, or from increased credit risk if the government changes policies to make it difficult for the company to pay creditors. In general, political risk is lowest in countries that have a history of stability and consistency. Political risk tends to be highest in nations that do not have this sort of history.

Most businesses operating abroad face a number of other risks that are less dangerous, but probably more common, than the drastic ones already described. Host governments that face a shortage of foreign currency sometimes will impose controls on the movement of capital in and out of the country. Such controls may make it difficult for a firm to remove its profits or investments from the host country. Sometimes, exchange controls are also levied selectively against certain products or companies in an effort to reduce the importation of goods that are considered to be a luxury or unnecessary. Such regulations are often difficult to deal with because they may affect the importation of parts, components, or supplies that are vital for production operations. Restrictions on such imports may force a firm either to alter its production program or, worse yet, to shut down its entire plant. Prolonged negotiations with government officials may be necessary in order to reach a compromise agreement on what constitutes a "valid" expenditure of foreign currency resources. Because the goals of government officials and corporate managers may often be quite different, such compromises, even when they can be reached, may result in substantial damage to the international marketing operations of a firm.

Countries may also raise the tax rates applied to foreign investors in an effort to control the firms and their capital. On occasion, different or stricter applications of the host country's tax codes are implemented for foreign investors. The rationale for such measures is often the seeming underpayment of taxes by such investors, when comparing their payments to those of long-established domestic competitors. Overlooked is the fact that new investors in foreign lands tend to "overinvest" by initially buying more land, space, and equipment than is needed immediately and by spending heavily so that facilities are state-of-the-art. This desire to accommodate future growth and to be highly competitive in the early investment stages will, in turn, produce lower profits and lower tax payments. Yet over time, these investment activities should be very successful, competitive, and job-creating. Selective tax increases for foreign investors may result in much-needed revenue for the coffers of the host country, but they can severely damage the operations of the foreign investors. This damage, in turn, may result in decreased income for the host country in the long run.

The international marketing manager must also worry about price controls. In many countries, domestic political pressures can force governments to control the prices of imported products or services, particularly in sectors that are considered to be highly sensitive from a political perspective, such as food or health care. If a foreign firm is involved in these areas, it is a vulnerable target of price controls because the government can play on its people's nationalistic tendencies to enforce the controls. Particularly in countries that suffer from high inflation and frequent devaluations, the international marketer may be forced to choose between shutting down the operation or continuing production at a loss in the hope of recouping that loss once the government chooses to loosen or remove its price restrictions.

In this discussion of the political environment, laws have been mentioned only to the extent that they appear to be the direct result of political changes. However, each nation has laws regarding marketing, and the international manager must understand their effects on the firm's efforts.

Legal Difference and Restraints

Countries differ in their laws as well as in their use of these laws. For example, the United States has developed into an increasingly litigious society, in which institutions and individuals are quick to take a case to court. As a result, court battles are often protracted and costly, and simply the threat of a court case can reduce marketing opportunities. In contrast, Japan's legal tradition tends to minimize the role of law and of lawyers. Some possible reasons include the relatively small number of courts and attorneys, the delays, the costs and the uncertainties associated with litigation, the tendency of judges to encourage out-of-court settlements, and the easy availability of arbitration and mediation for dispute resolution.

Host countries may adopt a number of laws that affect a company's ability to market. To begin with, there can be laws affecting the entry of goods, such as tariffs and quotas. Also in this category are antidumping laws, which prohibit below-cost sales of products, and laws that require export and import licensing. In addition, many countries have health safety standards that may, by design or by accident, restrict the entry of foreign goods. Japan, for example, has particularly strict health standards that affect the import of pharmaceuticals. Rather than accepting test results from other nations, the Japanese government insists on conducting its own tests, which are time consuming and costly. It claims that these tests are necessary to take into account Japanese peculiarities. Yet some importers and their governments see these practices as thinly veiled protectionist barriers.

A growing global controversy surrounds the use of genetic technology. Governments are increasingly devising new rules that affect trade in genetically modified products. For example, Australia introduced a mandatory standard for foods produced using biotechnology, which prohibits the sale of such products unless the food has been assessed by the Australia New Zealand Food Authority.

Other laws may be designed to protect domestic industries and reduce imports. For example, Russia charges a 20 percent value-added tax on most imported goods; assesses high excise taxes on goods such as cigarettes, automobiles, and alcoholic beverages; and provides a burdensome import licensing and quotas regime for alcohol and products containing alcohol to depress Russian demand for imports.

Very specific legislation may also exist to regulate where a firm can advertise or what constitutes deceptive advertising. Many countries prohibit specific claims by marketers comparing their product to that of the competition and restrict the use of promotional devices. Some countries regulate the names of companies or the foreign language content of a product's label. Even when no laws exist, the marketer may be hampered by regulations. For example, in many countries, governments require a firm to join the local chamber of commerce or become a member of the national trade association. These institutions in turn may have internal regulations that set standards for the conduct of business and may be seen as quite confining to the international marketer.

Finally, the enforcement of laws may have a different effect on national and on foreign marketers. For example, the simple requirements that an executive has to stay in a country until a business conflict is resolved may be a major burden for the international marketer.

Influencing Politics and Laws

To succeed in a market, the international marketer needs much more than business know-how. He or she must also deal with the intricacies of national politics and laws. Although a full understanding of another country's legal and political system will rarely be possible, the good manager will be aware of the importance of this system and will work with people who do understand how to operate within the system.

Many areas of politics and laws are not immutable. Viewpoints can be modified or even reversed, and new laws can supersede old ones. Therefore, existing political and legal restraints do no always need to be accepted. To achieve change, however, there must be some impetus for it, such as the clamors of a constituency. Otherwise, systemic inertia is likely to allow the status quo to prevail.

The international marketer has various options. One approach may be to simply ignore prevailing rules and expect to get away with it. Pursuing this option is a high-risk strategy because of the possibility of objection and even prosecution. A second, traditional option is to provide input to trade negotiations and expect any problem areas to be resolved in multilateral negotiations. The drawback to this option is, of course, the quite time-consuming process involved.

A third option involves the development of coalitions or constituencies that can motivate legislators and politicians to consider and ultimately implement change. This option can be pursued in various ways. One direction can be the recasting or redefinition of issues. Often, specific terminology leads to conditioned though inappropriate responses. For example, before China's accession to the World Trade Organization in 2001, the country's trade status with the United States was highly controversial for many years. The U.S. Congress had to decide annually whether to grant "Most Favored Nation" status to China. The debate on this decision was always very contentious and acerbic and was often framed around the question why China deserved to be treated the "most favored way." Lost in the debate was the fact that the term "Most Favored" was simply taken from WTO terminology and indicated only that trade with China would be treated like that with any other country. Only in late 1999 was the terminology changed from MFN to NTR, or "Normal Trade Relations." Even though there was still considerable debate regarding China, the controversy about special treatment had been eliminated.

Beyond terminology, marketers can also highlight the direct linkages and their costs and benefits to legislators and politicians. For example, the manager can explain the employment and economic effects of certain laws and regulations and demonstrate the benefits of change. The picture can be enlarged by including indirect linkages. For example, suppliers, customers, and distributors can be asked to participate in delineating to decision makers the benefits of change. Such groups can be quite influential. For example, it has been suggested that it was the community of Indian businesses working as information technology suppliers to U.S. firms that exerted substantial pressure on their government to find a resolution to the Kashmiri conflict. If so, this is an encouraging example of the benefits of globalization.

> **Answer the following questions:**
> 1. What is political risk?
> 2. What are the political risks that international firms face in the host country?
> 3. What is price control and why do host country governments want to exert price control?
> 4. What are the laws host countries can adopt to affect a company's ability to market?
> 5. What should the international marketers do to influence politics and laws in host countries?

Advertising

Learning Objectives

Text A
- to understand the meaning of advertising
- to be familiar with the different types of advertising
- to understand the roles and functions of advertising

Text B
- to understand the advantages and disadvantages of television advertising and radio advertising

Text A

The World of Advertising

In this section we define advertising by analyzing its six elements. Then we examine the types and roles of advertising.

Defining Advertising

What is advertising? What are its elements? The standard definition of advertising has six elements. First, advertising is a paid form of communication, although some forms of advertising, such as public service announcements (PSAs), use donated space and time. Second, not only is the message paid for, but the sponsor is identified. Third, most advertising tries to persuade or influence the consumer to do something, although in some cases the point of the message is simply to make consumers aware of the product or company. Fourth, the message is conveyed through many different kinds of mass media, and fifth, advertising reaches a large audience of potential consumers. Finally, because advertising is a form of mass communication, it is also nonpersonal. A definition of advertising, then, includes all six elements.

Advertising is paid nonpersonal communication from an identified sponsor using mass media to persuade or influence an audience.[1]

In an ideal world every manufacturer would be able to talk one-on-one with every consumer about its product. But personal selling, a one-on-one approach, is very expensive. Today, advertisers can provide customization through interactive media such as the World Wide Web, but it is not the same as meeting with every customer individually to discuss a product or service. Still, what does this have to do with defining advertising? The key point is that interactive advertising reaches a large audience, just like traditional advertising.

The costs for time in broadcast media, for space in print media, and for time and space in interactive and support media are spread over the tremendous number of people that these media reach. For example, $ 2 million may sound like a lot of money for one Super Bowl ad, but when you consider that the advertisers are reaching over 500 million people, the cost is not so extreme.

Types of Advertising

Advertising is complex because so many different advertisers try to reach so many different types of audiences. Let's examine nine major types of advertising.

Brand Advertising The most visible type of advertising is national consumer, or brand advertising. Brand advertising focuses on the development of a long-term brand identity and image.

Retail or Local Advertising A great deal of advertising focuses on retailers or manufacturers that sell their merchandise in a restricted area. In the case of retail advertising, the message announces facts about products that are available in nearby stores. The objectives tend to focus on stimulating store traffic, and creating a distinctive image for the retailer. Local advertising can refer to a retailer or a manufacturer or distributor who offers products in a fairly restricted geographic area.

Political Advertising Politicians use advertising to persuade people to vote for them or their ideas, so it is an important part of the political process in the United States and other countries that permit candidate advertising. Critics worry that political advertising tends to focus more on image than on issues, meaning that voters concentrate on the emotional part of the message or candidate, often overlooking important difference.[2]

Directory Advertising Another type of advertising is called directory advertising because people refer to it to find out how to buy a product or service. The best-known form of directory advertising is the Yellow Pages, although there are many other kinds of directories such as trade directories, organization directories, and so forth.

Direct-Response Advertising Direct-response advertising can use any advertising medium, including direct mail, but the message is different from that of national and retail advertising in that it tries to stimulate a sale directly.[3] The consumer can respond by telephone or mail, and the product is delivered directly to the consumer by mail or some other carrier. Of particular importance has been the evolution of the Internet as an advertising medium.

Business-to-Business Advertising Business-to-business advertising includes only messages directed at retailers, wholesalers, and distributors, and from industrial purchasers and professionals to other businesses, but not to general consumers.[4] Advertisers place most business advertising in publications or professional journals.

Institutional Advertising Institutional advertising is also called corporate advertising. These messages focus on establishing a corporate identity or winning the public over to the organization's point of view. Many of the tobacco companies are running ads that focus on the positive things they are now doing.

Public Service Advertising Public service announcements (PSAs) communicate a message on behalf of some good cause, such as stopping drunk driving or preventing child abuse. These advertisements are usually created by advertising professionals free of charge and the media often donate the space and time.

Interactive Advertising Interactive advertising is delivered to individual consumers who have access to a computer and the Internet. Advertisers use Web pages, banner ads, and e-mail to deliver their messages. In this instance, the consumer can respond to the ad or ignore it.

Roles of Advertising

Advertising can also be explained in terms of the four roles it plays in business and in society:

1. Marketing
2. Communication
3. Economic
4. Societal

Let's briefly explore each of these roles.

The Marketing Role

Marketing is the process a business uses to satisfy consumer needs and wants through goods and services. The particular consumers at whom the company directs its marketing effort constitute the target market. The tools available to marketing include the *product*, its *price*, and the means used to deliver the product, or the *place*. Marketing also includes a method for communicating this information to the consumer called *marketing communication*, or *promotion*. These four tools are collectively referred to as the marketing mix or the four Ps.

Marketing communication consists of several related communication techniques, including advertising, sales promotion, public relations, and personal selling. The role of advertising, within marketing, is to carry persuasive messages to actual and potential customers. One advertising campaign that has been very effective is the "It's What's for Dinner" campaign, started over 20 years ago when the America's Beef Producers trade association decided that the decline in beef consumption, due to consumers' concern for personal health, had to be reversed. Starting with a TV commercial, featuring the voice of actor Robert Mitchum, America learned that beef went along with mom and apple pie. Since that initial ad, beef consumption has stabilized and increased 12 percent.

The Communication Role

Advertising is a form of mass communication. It transmits different types of market information to match buyers and sellers in the marketplace. Advertising both informs and transforms the product by creating an image that goes beyond straightforward facts.

The Economic Role

There are two points of view about how advertising affects an economy. In the first, advertising is so persuasive that it decreases the likelihood that a consumer will switch to an alternative product, regardless of the price charged. By featuring other positive attributes, and avoiding price, the consumer makes a decision on these various nonprice benefits.

The second approach views advertising as a vehicle for helping consumers assess value, through price as well as other elements such as quality, location, and reputation.[5] Rather than diminishing the importance of price as a basis for comparison, advocates of this school view the role of advertising as a means to objectively provide price/value information, thereby creating a more rational economy. It should be noted that neither perspective has been verified, and it is presumed that advertising likely represents both economic models.

The Societal Role

Advertising also has a number of social roles. It informs us about new and improved products and helps us compare products and features and make informed consumer decisions. It mirrors fashion and design trends and adds to our aesthetic sense. Advertising tends to flourish in societies that enjoy some level of economic abundance, in which supply exceeds demand. In these societies, advertising moves from being informational only to creating a demand for a particular brand.

The question is: Does advertising follow trends or does it lead them? At what point does advertising cross the line between *reflecting* social values and *creating* social values? Critics argue that advertising repeatedly has crossed this line, influencing vulnerable groups, such as young teenagers, too strongly. The increasing power of advertising, both in terms of money (we spend more annually educating consumers than we spend educating our children) and in terms of communication dominance (the mass media can no longer survive without advertising support), has made these concerns more prominent than ever.

Can advertising manipulate people? Some critics argue that advertising has the power to dictate how people behave. They believe that even if an individual ad cannot control our behavior, the cumulative effects of nonstop television, radio, print, and outdoor ads can be overwhelming.[6]

The evidence demonstrating the manipulative power of advertising is shaky because so many other factors contribute to the choices we make. Still, advertisers are not objective and often slant or omit information to their benefit.

Functions of Advertising

Even though each ad or campaign tries to accomplish goals unique to its sponsor, advertising performs three basic functions.

Provides product and brand information. Although many ads are devoid of information, providing the consumer with relevant information that will aid decision making is still the main function of advertising.[7] The information given depends on the needs of the target audience. In the case of purchasing a new suit, needed information might be price and outlet location. For technical products, the information is likely to be very detailed.

Provides incentives to take action. In most instances, consumers are reluctant to change their buying behavior. Even if they are somewhat dissatisfied with their current product, a habit has been established and learning about a new product is difficult. Advertising sometimes gives the consumer reasons to switch brand, if that's the goal. Convenience, high quality, lower price, warranties—these all might be stressed in advertising.

Provides reminders and reinforcement. Much advertising is directed at keeping current customers. Consumers forget why they bought a particular brand of microwave or automobile. Advertising must constantly remind the consumer about the name of the brand, its benefits, its value, and so forth. These same messages help reinforce the consumer's decision. Most TV advertising provides this function.

New Words

nonpersonal	/ˌnɒnˈpɜːsənəl/	adj.	非个人化的
manufacturer	/ˌmænjʊˈfæktʃərə/	n.	制造商
merchandise	/ˈmɜːtʃəndaɪz/	n.	商品
stimulate	/ˈstɪmjʊleɪt/	v.	刺激
candidate	/ˈkændɪdɪt/	n.	候选人
identity	/aɪˈdentɪti/	n.	个性
image	/ˈɪmɪdʒ/	n.	形象
wholesaler	/ˈhəʊlˌseɪlə/	n.	批发商
purchaser	/ˈpɜːtʃɪsə/	n.	购买者
professional	/prəˈfeʃənəl/	n.	专业人士
publication	/ˌpʌblɪˈkeɪʃən/	n.	出版物
individual	/ˌɪndɪˈvɪdʒuəl/	n.	个人
deliver	/dɪˈlɪvə/	v.	传递
societal	/səˈsaɪətl/	adj.	社会的
marketing	/ˈmɑːkɪtɪŋ/	n.	营销
commercial	/kəˈmɜːʃəl/	n.	(电视或无线电中的)广告

initial	/ɪˈnɪʃəl/	adj.	开始的，最初的
straightforward	/ˌstreɪtˈfɔːwəd/	adj.	简单的，易理解的
assess	/əˈses/	v.	评估
rational	/ˈræʃənəl/	adj.	合理的；理性的
feature	/ˈfiːtʃə/	n.	特性
aesthetic	/iːsˈθetɪk/	adj.	审美的
cumulative	/ˈkjuːmjʊlətɪv/	adj.	累积的
manipulative	/məˈnɪpjʊlətɪv/	adj.	操纵的
slant	/slɑːnt/	v.	歪曲
devoid	/dɪˈvɔɪd/	adj.	缺乏的，没有的
warranty	/ˈwɒrənti/	n.	担保

Phrases

vulnerable group	弱势群体
communication technique	沟通技巧
public relation	公共关系
mass communication	大众沟通

Special Terms

public service announcement	公益广告宣传
mass media	大众传媒
brand advertising	品牌广告
retail advertising	零售广告
political advertising	政治广告
audience	受众
directory advertising	目录广告
advertising medium	广告媒体
direct-response advertising	直接反馈广告
business-to-business advertising	企业对企业广告
institutional advertising	机构广告
public service advertising	公益广告
interactive advertising	互动广告
banner ad	旗帜广告
marketing communication	营销沟通

consumer about its product. But personal selling, a one-on-one approach, is very expensive. Today, advertisers can provide customization through interactive media such as the World Wide Web, but it is not the same as meeting with every customer individually to discuss a product or service. Still, what does this have to do with defining advertising? The key point is that interactive advertising reaches a large audience, just like traditional advertising.

The costs for time in broadcast media, for space in print media, and for time and space in interactive and support media are spread over the tremendous number of people that these media reach. For example, $ 2 million may sound like a lot of money for one Super Bowl ad, but when you consider that the advertisers are reaching over 500 million people, the cost is not so extreme.

Types of Advertising

Advertising is complex because so many different advertisers try to reach so many different types of audiences. Let's examine nine major types of advertising.

Brand Advertising The most visible type of advertising is national consumer, or brand advertising. Brand advertising focuses on the development of a long-term brand identity and image.

Retail or Local Advertising A great deal of advertising focuses on retailers or manufacturers that sell their merchandise in a restricted area. In the case of retail advertising, the message announces facts about products that are available in nearby stores. The objectives tend to focus on stimulating store traffic, and creating a distinctive image for the retailer. Local advertising can refer to a retailer or a manufacturer or distributor who offers products in a fairly restricted geographic area.

Political Advertising Politicians use advertising to persuade people to vote for them or their ideas, so it is an important part of the political process in the United States and other countries that permit candidate advertising. Critics worry that political advertising tends to focus more on image than on issues, meaning that voters concentrate on the emotional part of the message or candidate, often overlooking important difference.[2]

Directory Advertising Another type of advertising is called directory advertising because people refer to it to find out how to buy a product or service. The best-known form of directory advertising is the Yellow Pages, although there are many other kinds of directories such as trade directories, organization directories, and so forth.

Direct-Response Advertising Direct-response advertising can use any advertising medium, including direct mail, but the message is different from that of national and retail advertising in that it tries to stimulate a sale directly.[3] The consumer can respond by telephone or

Notes

1. Advertising is paid nonpersonal communication from an identified sponsor using mass media to persuade or influence an audience.

   广告是一种由特定出资人发起,通过大众传媒开展的非个人化的有偿沟通方式,其目的是说服或影响某类受众。

2. Critics worry that political advertising tends to focus more on image than on issues, meaning that voters concentrate on the emotional part of the message or candidate, often overlooking important difference.

   评论家们担心政治广告具有更关注于形象而不是具体问题的倾向,这意味着选举者全神贯注于选举中的情感信息或候选人,却通常会忽略重要的差别。

3. Direct-response advertising can use any advertising medium, including direct mail, but the message is different from that of national and retail advertising in that it tries to stimulate a sale directly.

   直接反馈广告可以使用任何广告媒体,包括直邮的形式。但它与国内广告以及零售广告的不同之处在于,直接反馈广告所传递的信息试图直接刺激销售。

4. Business-to-business advertising includes only messages directed at retailers, wholesalers, and distributors, and from industrial purchasers and professionals to other businesses, but not to general consumers.

   企业对企业广告的目标受众不是普通消费者,而是零售商、批发商和分销商,从行业购买者和专业人士到其他企业都包括在内。

5. The second approach views advertising as a vehicle for helping consumers assess value, through price as well as other elements such as quality, location, and reputation.

   第二种观点认为,广告通过提供价格以及质量、场所和声誉等其他要素来帮助消费者进行价值评估。

6. They believe that even if an individual ad cannot control our behavior, the cumulative effects of nonstop television, radio, print, and outdoor ads can be overwhelming.

   他们认为,即使单个的广告不会控制我们的行为,但没完没了的电视、广播、印刷品和各种形式的户外广告轰炸的累积效果却会改变我们的行为。

7. Although many ads are devoid of information, providing the consumer with relevant information that will aid decision making is still the main function of advertising.

   尽管许多广告的信息都不充足,但是向消费者提供有助于决策制定的相关信息仍然是广告的主要职能。

Exercises

I. Discuss the following questions.

1. According to the article, what's advertising?
2. What are the nine major types of advertising?
3. What is retail advertising?
4. What's the best-known form of directory advertising?
5. What's interactive advertising?
6. What are the four roles that advertising plays in business and in society?
7. What are the social roles of advertising?
8. What are the three basic functions of advertising?

II. Analyze the case below and discuss the question.

Tenica Ski Company makes some of the finest ski boots in the world. Its top-of-the-line boot is the Icon RX, manufactured in Italy, and then sold through Tenica USA. The boot features a variety of adjustments to fit it to the customer's foot, resulting in a superior fit that leads to higher levels of comfort on the ski slope. Another feature is a carbon cuff that stiffens up the boot for racers who need to put a lot of pressure in it, and the cuff can be injected with foam in order to form the liner to the wearer's foot. Colored bright orange, which has been the color of Tenica's past top-end boots, this one can effectively compete with any top-of-the-line boot.

The target market for the Icon RX is the expert skier or racer. These individuals usually look for a high performance boot to supplement their other high-end equipment and their superior skills. People who ski and buy their own equipment usually have a significant amount of disposable income; they often live in an area of the country that provides them with opportunities to ski, such as a mountainous region. The skier who buys this type of boot is a moderate to heavy user, usually someone who skis 20-plus times each season. While the boot is not made to perform better with one type of ski, it would benefit the company as a whole if it is bought in tandem with Volkl skis, another high-end Tenica product. Tenica would like the boot to be viewed as a complement to the whole elite ski package.

The product is positioned as the high-end boot that feels good. The advertising campaign being considered focuses on all the benefits of a tight-fitting race boot, with the added bonus of comfort.

Question:
What category of advertising would Tenica most likely employ?

III. Match the terms in column A with the explanations in column B.

A	B
1. national advertising	A. a process a business uses to satisfy consumer needs and wants through goods and services
2. target audience	B. the four tools available to marketing, including the product, its price and the means used to deliver the product (or the place), and marketing communication
3. marketing	C. advertising by a marketer of a trademarked product or service sold through different outlets, in contrast to local advertising
4. consumer	D. advertising focusing on retailers or manufacturers that sell their merchandise in a restricted area
5. marketing mix	E. small space ads with limited words and graphics whose purpose is to tease viewers to click on the banner, which links them to the sponsor's Web site
6. public relations	F. the person or organization that needs to get out a message
7. retail advertising	G. the work of forming in the minds of the general public a favorable opinion of an organization
8. advertising media	H. the group that composes the present and potential prospects for a product or service
9. banner ads	I. channels of communication that carries the message from the advertiser to the audience, and in the case of the Internet, it carries the response
10. advertiser	J. a person who (is likely to) buys and uses goods and services

IV. Fill in the blanks of the following sentences with the words or phrases given below. Make changes when necessary.

advertiser	merchandise	sponsorship	sales promotion	candidate
commercial	awareness	response	interactive	brand image

1. The _____ makes the final decisions about the target audience, the media that will carry the advertising, the size of the advertising budget, and the length of the campaign.
2. After we delivered our message on the Internet, there have been several _____ to our advertisement.
3. If a Web site is well designed, people may want to respond and _____ with the organization sponsoring the site.

4. _____ is when companies support an event, say a sporting event, concert, or charity either financially or by donating supplies and services.
5. The employers are interviewing _____ for the job of sales manager.
6. _____ is the set of ideas, feelings and attitudes that consumers have about a brand—how they value it.
7. Producing a major TV _____ may take the work of hundreds of people and cost as much as half a million dollars.
8. Whenever a marketer increases the value of its product by offering an extra incentive to purchase a brand or product, it's creating a _____.
9. Sales promotion usually includes specified limits, such as an expiration date or a limited quantity of the _____.
10. Although an action response is the goal of most sales promotions, some programs are designed to build _____ first, but always with action as the ultimate goal.

V. Put the following into English.

1. 树立与发展长期品牌个性和形象
2. 在有限的区域内销售其产品
3. 反映时尚和设计的发展趋势
4. 彻底地改变广告的面貌
5. 向目标受众传递一致的、有说服力的信息
6. 通过选择特定的媒体来接触特定的消费者
7. 对广告主和竞争对手的信息进行必要的研究核实
8. 影响公众的购买行为
9. 希望消费者信任他们的产品和广告
10. 确定各目标市场的需求、欲望和利益

VI. Translate the following sentences into English.

1. 广告是一种有偿的沟通形式,但是有些广告形式,例如公益广告宣传,使用的是免费的时段和版面。
2. 广告告诉我们新产品和改良产品的信息,并且帮助我们比较不同的产品及其特性。
3. 广告主并不客观,他们常常会为了自己的利益而歪曲或删减信息。
4. 广告应该与其他营销沟通方式相配合以吸引消费者。
5. 只有广告主(和相应的广告代理商)才知道广告宣传活动是否达到了目的,以及广告是否真正有价值。

VII. Translate the following passage into Chinese.

One reason why Internet advertising is growing in popularity is that it offers distinct advantages over other media alternatives. Most notably, advertisers can customize their message over the Internet. Thanks to database marketing, an advertiser can input key demographic and behavioral variables, making the consumer feel like the ad is just for him. Check out classmates.com for an example. Ads appearing on a particular page are for products that would appeal to that age group. Someone who graduated from high school in 1960 would see banner ads for investments that facilitate early retirement.

These same databases can be merged so that the Internet advertiser knows a great deal about the habits of the consumer. Advertisers may combine databases to develop fairly comprehensive profiles. Consider how an advertiser might tailor a message to people if it knew their travel behavior, media preferences, and credit card usage.

Text B

Television Advertising and Radio Advertising

Advantages of Television Advertising

Television has three key advantages. First, its influence on consumers' taste and perceptions is pervasive. Second, it can reach a large audience in a cost-efficient manner. Third, its sound and moving images create a strong impact.

Cost-Efficiency

Many advertisers view television as the most cost-effective way to deliver a commercial message because it has such a wide reach. Millions of people watch some TV regularly. Not only does television reach a large percentage of the population, but it also reaches people that print media misses. NMC's *Today* show averages approximately $45,000 for a 30-second spot, and the household cost per thousand (CPM) is $3.62. This mass coverage is extremely cost-efficient. Reaching the same number of people with a $60,000 ad in *Time* magazine would have a CPM of $11.85. For an advertiser attempting to reach an undifferentiated market, a 30-second spot on a top-rated show may cost a penny or less for each person reached.

Impact

Television makes a strong impact. The interaction of sight, sound, color, motion, and drama creates a level of consumer involvement that often approximates the shopping experience itself. It can make mundane products appear important, exciting, and interesting. It can also create a positive association with the sponsor if the advertising is likable.

Disadvantages of Television Advertising

Despite the effectiveness of television advertising, it has four problems: expense, clutter, nonselective targeting, and inflexibility.

Expense

The most serious limitation of television advertising is the extremely high cost of producing and running commercials. Although the cost per person reached is low, the absolute cost can be restrictive, especially for small and even midsized companies. Production costs include filming the commercial (several thousand to several hundred thousand dollars) and paying the talent—writers, directors, and actors. For celebrities such as Jerry Seinfeld, Candice Bergen, and Michael Jordan, the price tag can be millions of dollars.

The prices charged for network time simply result from supply and demand. Programs that draw the largest audiences—that supply the greatest number of viewers—can charge—demand—more for their advertising space. A 30-second prime-time spot averages about $185,000. Special shows, such as the Super Bowl, World Series, or Academy Awards, charge much more. Some experts comment that television advertising is very cheap if you can afford it.

Clutter

Television suffers form commercial clutter. In the past, the National Association of Broadcasters (NAB) restricted the allowable commercial time per hour to approximately six minutes. In 1982 the Justice Department overturned this restriction. Although there are nonrestrictions, the networks continue to honor the NAB guidelines. This could change as revenue needs increase. If the number of 30-second commercials, station break announcements, credits, and public service announcements increase, the visibility and persuasiveness of television advertising would diminish.

Nonselective Audience

Although the network attempt to profile viewers, their demographic and psychographic descriptions are quite general, offering the advertiser little assurance that appropriate people are viewing the message. Television advertising includes a great deal of waste coverage; communication directed at an unresponsive (and often uninterested) audience that may not fit the advertiser's target market characteristics.

Inflexibility

Television also suffers from inflexibility in scheduling. Most network television is bought in the spring and early summer for the next season. If an advertiser is unable to make this up-front buy, only limited time-slot alternatives remain available. Also, it is difficult to make last-minute adjustments in copy and visuals. Production of a TV commercial may take days or weeks, and is changed reluctantly.

Cable television is much more targeted than network and spot television and so it has far less waste. However, cable cannot cover a mass audience and probably is more cluttered than network TV.

Television may offer the benefits of sight and sound, many advertisers (especially local ones) want to target audience more specifically than the TV medium can. In addition, consumers may find television commercials too intrusive. In the case of these instances, radio offers a reliable medium.

Advantages of Radio Advertising

Radio has five key advantages for advertisers. Let's look at each briefly.

Target Audiences

The most important advantage radio offers is its ability to reach specific audience through specialized programming. In addition, radio can be adapted for different parts of the country and can reach people at different times of the day. For example, radio is the ideal means of reaching people driving to and from work. Known as drive time, these radio time slots provide the best audience for many advertisers. Pizza Hut, for instance, reached out to its target audience of women making dinner choices by using radio during the 4:00—7:00 P.M. time slot.

Flexibility

Radio offers advertisers flexibility. Of all the media, radio has the shortest closing period: Copy can be submitted up to airtime. This flexibility allows advertisers to adjust to local market conditions, current news events, and even the weather. For example, a local hardware store can quickly implement a snow-shovel promotion the morning after a snowstorm. Radio's flexibility is also evident in its willingness to participate in promotional tie-ins such as store openings, races, and so on.

Affordability

Radio may be the least expensive of all media. And because airtime costs are low, extensive repetition is possible. In addition, the costs of producing a radio commercial can be low, particularly if a local station announcer reads the message. Radio's low cost and high reach of selected target groups make it an excellent supporting medium. In fact, the most appropriate role for most radio advertising is a supportive one. Columbia Bank used local radio to support its print ad campaign and give the bank a strong presence.

Mental imagery

Radio allows the listener to imagine. Radio uses words, sound effects, music, and tonality to enable listeners to create their own pictures. For this reason, radio is sometimes called the theatre of the mind.

High level of acceptance

The final advantage is radio's high acceptance at the local level. Partly because of its passive nature (background sound),

radio normally is not perceived as an irritant. People have their favorite radio stations and radio personalities, which they listen to regularly. Messages delivered by these stations and personalities are likely to be accepted and retained.

Disadvantages of Radio Advertising

Radio is not without its drawbacks. Here are five key disadvantages:

Listener inattentiveness

Because radio is strictly a listening medium, radio messages are fleeting, and listeners may miss or forget commercials. Many people think of radio as pleasant background and do not listen to it carefully.

Lack of visuals

Being restricted to using sound can hamper a person's creativity. Developing radio ads that encourage the listener to see the product is a difficult challenge, and clearly, products that must be demonstrated or seen to be appreciated are inappropriate for radio advertising. Experts believe that humor, music, and sound effects may be the most effective way to create visualization.

Clutter

The number of radio stations has increased, and so has the heavy repetition of some ads. The result is tremendous clutter in radio advertising.

Scheduling and buying difficulties

Scheduling and buying radio time can be cumbersome. Advertisers seeking to reach a wide audience often need to buy time on several stations, complicating scheduling and ad evaluation. The bookkeeping involved in checking nonstandardized rates, approving bills for payment, and billing clients can be a staggering task. Fortunately, computers and large-station representatives have helped to ease much of this burden.

Lack of control

A large percentage of radio is talk shows, and most of radio's recent growth has come through talk shows. There is always the risk that a radio personality will say something that offends the audience, which would in turn hurt the audience's perception of an advertiser's product.

Answer the following questions:

1. What are the advantages of television advertising?
2. What does the phrase "cost-efficiency" mean?
3. How does television advertising make a strong impact on the audience?
4. What are the four disadvantages of television advertising?
5. What are the five advantages of radio advertising?
6. How does radio offer advertisers flexibility?

7. Why may radio be the least expensive of all media?
8. Why is radio sometimes called the theatre of the mind?
9. Why does radio have high level of acceptance at the local level?
10. What are the disadvantages of radio advertising?

Unit 10

International Payment

Learning Objectives

Text A
- to learn some methods of international payments and settlements

Text B
- to understand the importance of payment currency in international payments and settlements

Text A

Basic Methods of International Payments and Settlements

Key Factors Determining the Payment Method

International payments and settlements are financial activities conducted among different countries in which payments are effected or funds are transferred from one country to another in order to settle accounts, debts, claims, etc, emerged in the course of political, economic or cultural contracts among them. The specific payment method is generally influenced by the following factors:

- the business relationship between the seller and the buyer
- the nature of the merchandise
- industry norms
- the distance between the buyer and the seller
- the potential for currency fluctuation
- political and economic stability in both the buyer and the seller's country

Relative Security of Payment Methods

In international business, the seller and the buyer are far from each other. It is, of course, the desire of all parties for a transaction to have absolute security. The seller wants to be absolutely sure that he gets paid, while the buyer wants to make absolutely certain he gets what he has ordered. In fact, there can't be absolutes of certainty for both parties to a transaction. If one has absolute security, the other party correspondingly loses a degree of security. Also, a buyer or seller who insists on having the transaction work only for himself will find that he is losing a great deal of business. International business, therefore, often requires a compromise on the part of the seller and the buyer that leads to relative security for both parties.

Settlement on Commercial Credit

The following categories are the usual methods of payment to settle international transactions on commercial credit. All have variations and permutations, and yet here is a brief description.

Payment in Advance

It is also called advance payment. The buyer places the funds at the disposal of the seller prior to shipment of the goods or provision of services.[1] While this method of payment is expensive and contains a degree of risk, it is quite common when the manufacturing process or services delivered are specialized and capital-intensive. In such circumstances the parties may agree to fund the operation by partial payment in advance or by progressive payment. It provides greatest security for the seller and involves greatest risk for the buyer.

Characteristics:

1. Provides greatest security for the seller and greatest risk for the buyer;
2. Requires that the buyer have a high level of confidence in the ability and willingness of the seller to deliver the goods as ordered.

Basic points to be considered in using advance payment:

1. The credit standing of the exporter must be exceedingly good;
2. The economic and political conditions in the exporter's country should be very stable;
3. The importer should have sufficient balance sheet liquidity or be confident of obtaining working capital by way of import financing;
4. The importer should have the knowledge that the exchange control authorities in his country will permit advance payment to be made.[2]

Open Account

An arrangement between the buyer and the seller whereby the goods are manufactured and delivered before payment is required. Open account provides for payment at some stated specific future date and without the buyer issuing any negotiable instrument evidencing his legal commitment.[3] The seller must have absolute trust that he will be paid at the agreed date. It provides the least risk for the buyer and the greatest risk for the seller.

Essential features of open account business are:

1. The credit standing of the importer must be very good;
2. The exporter is confident that the government of the importer's country will not impose regulations deferring or blocking the transfer

of funds;

3. The exporter has sufficient liquidity to extend any necessary credit to the importer or has access to export financing.[4]

Remittance

Remittance refers to the transfer of funds from one party to another among different countries. That is, a bank (the remitting bank), at the request of its customer (the remitter), transfers a certain sum of money to its overseas branch or correspondent bank (the paying bank) instructing them to pay to a named person or corporation (the payee or beneficiary) domiciled in the country.

Collection

An arrangement whereby the goods are shipped and the relevant bill of exchange is drawn by the seller on the buyer, and documents are sent to the seller's bank with clear instructions for collection through one of its correspondent banks located in the domicile of the buyer.

1. Documentary collection: Documentary collection may be described as collection on financial instruments being accompanied by commercial documents or collection on commercial documents without being accompanied by financial instruments, that is, commercial documents without a bill of exchange.

    ❖ The seller ships the goods and obtains the shipping documents, and usually draws a draft, either at sight or with a tenor of xx days on the buyer for the value of the goods;
    ❖ The seller submits the draft(s) and / or document(s) to his bank, which acts as his agent;
    ❖ The bank acknowledges that all documents as noted by the seller are presented;
    ❖ The seller's bank sends the draft and other documents along with a collection letter to a correspondent bank usually located in the same city as the buyer;
    ❖ Acting as an agent for the Remitting Bank, the Collecting Bank notifies the buyer upon receipt of the draft and documents;
    ❖ All the documents, and usually title to the goods, are released to the buyer upon his payment of the amount specified or his acceptance of the draft for payment at a specified later date.

2. Clean collection: Clean collection is collection on financial instruments without being accompanied by commercial documents, such as invoice, bill of lading, insurance policy, etc.[5]

    ❖ An arrangement whereby the seller draws only a draft on the buyer for the value of the goods / services and presents the draft to his bank.
    ❖ The seller's bank sends the draft along with a collection instruction letter to a correspondent bank usually in the same city as the buyer.

An essential feature of collection is that although it is safer than on open account for the seller, there is the possibility of the buyer or his banker refusing to honor the draft and take up the shipping documents, especially at a time when the market is falling.[6] In such a case, the seller may not receive his payment although he is still the owner of the goods.

Settlement on Bank Credit

Letter of Credit

A letter of credit is an undertaking issued by a bank for the account of the buyer (the Applicant) or for its own account, to pay the Beneficiary the value of the draft and / or documents, provided that the terms and conditions of the documentary credit are complied with.[7]

A letter of credit provides the most satisfactory method of settling international transactions. Its primary function is relying on the bank's undertaking to pay, thereby enabling the seller or the exporter to receive payment as soon as possible after the shipment of his goods and also enabling the buyer or the importer to arrange with his bank for the financing of the payment. In other words, the documentary credit achieves a commercially acceptable compromise between the conflicting interest of buyer and seller by matching time of payment for the goods with the time of their delivery. It is, therefore, of great importance in the sense that it contributes to the smooth conducting of international trade.

Usually, the buyer requests his bank to issue a letter of credit in favor of the seller. Assuming that the credit risk is acceptable to the bank, it issues its letter of credit. The letter says, in essence, to the seller: "We, the bank, promise that we will pay you when you submit certain documents proving that you have made the agreed-upon shipment."[8] The letter of credit also protects the buyer, for he knows that he will not be called upon for payment by his bank until the evidence shows that the shipment has actually been effected.

Bank Guarantee

In international trade, the buyer wants to be certain that the seller is in a position to honor his commitment as offered or contracted.[9] The former therefore makes it a condition that appropriate security is provided. On the other hand, the seller must find a way to be assured of receiving payment if no special security is provided for the payment such as in open account business and documentary collections. Such security may be obtained through banks in the form of a guarantee. A bank guarantee is used as an instrument for securing performance or payment especially in international business.

A bank guarantee is a written promise issued by a bank at the request of its customer, undertaking to make payment to the beneficiary within the limits of a stated sum of money in the event of default by the principal. It may also be defined as the irrevocable obligation of a bank to pay a sum of money in the event of non-performance of a contract by the principal.[10]

New Words

norm	/nɔːm/	n.	标准,规范
fluctuation	/ˌflʌktjuˈeɪʃən/	n.	波动,起伏
stability	/stəˈbɪlɪti/	n.	稳定性
security	/sɪˈkjʊərɪti/	n.	安全
compromise	/ˈkɒmprəmaɪz/	n. & v.	妥协,折衷
settle	/ˈsetl/	v.	解决;支付
variation	/ˌveəriˈeɪʃən/	n.	变化,变异,变种
permutation	/ˌpɜːmjuˈteɪʃən/	n.	置换;蜕变;彻底改变
liquidity	/lɪˈkwɪdɪti/	n.	流动性,灵活性
exceedingly	/ɪkˈsiːdɪŋli/	adv.	非常地,极度地
defer	/dɪˈfɜː/	v.	使推迟,使延期
block	/blɒk/	v.	妨碍,阻塞
domicile	/ˈdɒmɪsaɪl/	n.	住所,居住地
accompany	/əˈkʌmpəni/	v.	陪伴,伴奏
undertaking	/ˌʌndəˈteɪkɪŋ/	n.	承诺,保证
irrevocable	/ɪˈrevəkəbəl/	adj.	不可撤销的
default	/dɪˈfɔːlt/	n.	拖欠;食言,不履行责任
principal	/ˈprɪnsəpəl/	n.	当事人,委托人

Phrases

relative/absolute security	相对/绝对安全
to insist on doing sth.	坚持做某事
on the part of	就……而言;关于……而言
at the disposal of	交由……处置
prior to	在……之前
to defer or block the transfer of funds	延迟或冻结资金的流动
a sum of money	一笔款项
to be accompanied by	由……伴随
to honor the draft	承兑/兑现汇票
for the account of	以……的名义
to be complied with	与……相一致
primary function	主要功能
in favor of	有利于……;以……为受益人
in essence	从本质上讲

to be in a position to do sth. 有能力做……
at the request of 应……的要求
within the limits of 在……的限度内
in the event of 如果发生……
non-performance of a contract 不履行合同

Special Terms

payment method	支付方式
currency fluctuation	汇率波动
commercial credit	商业信用
partial payment in advance	分期预付
payment in advance	预付
progressive payment	按(施工)进度(分批)付款
credit/financial standing	信用/财务状况
balance sheet	资产负债表
working capital	流动资本,周转资金
open account	赊销/记账交易
negotiable instrument	流通票据
remittance	汇付
the remitting bank	汇款行
the paying bank	付款行
payee/beneficiary	收款人;受益人
documentary/clean collection	跟单/光票托收
the correspondent bank	议付行/代理行
a bill of exchange (draft)	汇票
shipping documents	装运单据
at sight	即期,见票
with a tenor of... days	在……天的期限之内
invoice	发票,发货单
bill of lading	提单
insurance policy	保险单
bank credit	银行信用
letter of credit	信用证
bank guarantee	银行担保函
terms and conditions	条款

Notes

1. The buyer places the funds at the disposal of the seller prior to shipment of the goods or provision of services.
   买方在卖方装运货物或提供服务之前,将款项交由卖方支配。

2. The importer should have the knowledge that the exchange control authorities in his country will permit advance payment to be made.
   进口人应知道本国外汇管制当局准许使用提前支付的形式支付货款。

3. Open account provides for payment at some stated specific future date and without the buyer issuing any negotiable instrument evidencing his legal commitment.
   赊销规定买方在将来某一具体日期支付货款,而无需出具议付单据证明其法律义务。

4. The exporter has sufficient liquidity to extend any necessary credit to the importer or has access to export financing.
   出口人有充分的灵活性扩大对进口人的信用担保或是获得出口资金融通。

5. Clean collection is collection on financial instruments without being accompanied by commercial documents, such as invoice, bill of lading, insurance policy, etc.
   光票托收是指仅用金融工具(汇票)收取货款,不随附任何商业单证,例如发票、提单、保险单等。

6. ..., there is the possibility of the buyer or his banker refusing to honor the draft and take up the shipping documents, especially at a time when the market is falling.
   可能会出现买方或买方银行拒绝承兑汇票、扣留装运单据的情况,尤其是在市场不景气的时候。

7. A letter of credit is an undertaking issued by a bank for the account of the buyer (the Applicant) or for its own account, to pay the Beneficiary the value of the draft and / or documents, provided that the terms and conditions of the documentary credit are complied with.
   信用证是一种由银行为买方(开证申请人)或以其自己的名义开立的一种保证,保证在符合信用证的一切条件下,将汇票或单据的金额支付给受益人。

8. "We, the bank, promise that we will pay you when you submit certain documents proving that you have made the agreed-upon shipment."
   "我行承诺:只要贵公司提交证明已经按协议装运的相关单证,我行将支付货款。"

9. In international trade, the buyer wants to be certain that the seller is in a position to honor his commitment as offered or contracted.
   在国际贸易中,买方想要确保卖方有能力履行他提出的或是合同规定的义务。

10. It may also be defined as the irrevocable obligation of a bank to pay a sum of money in the event of non-performance of a contract by the principal.
    银行保函也可以这样定义,如果委托人不履行合同义务,银行有不可撤销的义务支付一笔款项。

Exercises

I. Discuss the following questions.

1. What are the key factors determining the payment methods?
2. How do you comprehend the relative security of each payment method?
3. What are the basic methods of international payments based on commercial credit?
4. What are the basic methods of international payments based on bank credit?
5. Which method of international payment is most widely used in current international business transactions?

II. Analyze the case below and discuss the question.

Bills of exchange, promissory notes, and checks are three important and common negotiable instruments, which function as a means of payment, credit instrument and transferable instrument. The following is a model of a bill of exchange. Can you list all the essentials of a bill of exchange?

Exchange for US$ 25, 000   Shanghai, Nov. 11th, 2006

At sight pay to the order of the Bank of China

The sum of twenty-five thousand US dollars only.

Value received.

To: The City Bank   For China National Chemicals Import & Export
New York, N. Y., U.S.A.   Corporation, S. B.
                                                                   (Signed)

III. Match the terms in column A with the explanations in column B.

A	B
1. balance sheet	A. a contract that defines the obligations of the two parties involved, the insured (your organization) and the insurer (insurance company)
2. working capital	B. a document which serves as an evidence of the contract of carriage of goods by sea, and based on which the carrier undertakes to deliver the goods against surrendering the same
3. negotiable instrument	C. a document as part of a financial transaction between two or more parties and a response to an order
4. remittance	D. the documents used to evidence shipment
5. the paying bank	E. an instrument signed by the issuer, authorizing the payer

to unconditionally pay a certain sum of money to the payee or the bearer when the bill is presented or at a specified time

6. a bill of exchange (draft)   F. the bank undertaking to carry out payment

7. shipping documents   G. a settlement method for the remitter to entrust the bank to pay a sum of money to the payee

8. invoice   H. a class of documents evidencing promises or orders to pay a certain sum of money

9. a bill of lading   I. also "operating capital"; the money you will need to keep your business going until you can cover your operating costs out of revenue

10. insurance policy   J. a financial "snapshot" of your business at a given date in time, which includes your assets and liabilities and tells you your business's net worth

IV. Fill in the blanks of the following sentences with the words or phrases given below. Make changes when necessary.

fluctuation	in favor of	accompany	to be in a position
exceedingly	for the account of	compromise	undertaking
security	commitment		

1. Please instruct your bank to issue a transferable and irrevocable letter of credit _____ our corporation.
2. Your completed passport application should be _____ by two recent photographs.
3. I've become _____ worried about the future of our nation.
4. This price _____ requires that one measure the current yield on a seasoned bond.
5. We need to increase profits without _____ employees' safety.
6. Covering an Olympics is an extraordinary _____ for any television company.
7. Many parents do not get involved in schools because they have too many other _____.
8. This insurance plan offers your family financial _____ in the event of your death.
9. For occupational accident, the full premium is _____ the employer.
10. The strategy aims to ensure that Customs are _____ to meet with their obligations in a changing world.

V. Put the following into English.

1. 用商业信用来处理(结算)国际业务
2. 出口商的资信状况
3. 在货物装运或服务提供之前
4. 具有一定程度的风险

5. 通过进口融资获得流动资本
6. 作为汇付行的代理行
7. 一俟收到汇票和单证
8. 向银行提交汇票
9. 有利于国际贸易的顺利进行
10. 确保履约或支付的工具

VI. Translate the following sentences into English.

1. 选择支付方式有一些重要的决定因素，比如买卖双方的商务关系、商品的性质、产业规范等。
2. 光票托收是指仅用金融工具（汇票）收取货款，不必随附任何商业单证，例如发票、提单、保险单等。
3. 在具备银行保函的情况下，如果当事人不履行合同，银行将有无条件支付的责任。
4. 跟单信用证通过将付款和交货的时间结合起来，取得了一种解决买卖双方之间利益矛盾的商业上的折中方式。
5. 在法律上，信用证完全独立于它所基于的交易。银行处理的是单据而不是货物。

VII. Translate the following passage into Chinese.

A Letter of Credit is a payment term generally used for international sales transactions. It is basically a mechanism, which allows importers/buyers to offer secure terms of payment to exporter/sellers in which a bank (or more than one bank) gets involved. The technical term for Letter of Credit is Documentary Credit. At the very outset one must understand is that Letters of Credit deal in documents, not goods. The idea in an international trade transaction is to shift the risk from the actual buyer to a bank. Thus an L/C (as it is commonly referred to) is a payment undertaking given by a bank to the seller and is issued on behalf of the applicant, i.e., the buyer. The buyer is the applicant and the seller is the beneficiary. The bank that issues the L/C is referred to as the issuing bank which is generally in the country of the buyer. The bank that advises the L/C to the seller is called the advising bank which is often in the country of the seller.

The specified bank makes the payment upon the successful presentation of the required documents by the seller within the specified time frame. Note that the bank scrutinizes the "document" and not the "goods" for making payment. Thus the process works in favor of both the buyer and the seller. The seller gets assured that if documents are presented on time and in the way that they have been requested in the L/C the payment will be made and the buyer on the other hand is assured that the bank will thoroughly examine these presented documents and ensure that they meet the terms and conditions stipulated in the L/C.

Text

Multinational and Foreign Exchange

It is clear that any non-instantaneous transaction involving more than one currency involves a foreign exchange risk. If the exchange rate between the relevant currencies changes significantly during the transaction, the terms of the transaction will deviate *ex post* from those originally negotiated. As reductions in transportation and communication costs have encouraged firms to become more international in their production, finance, and marketing operations, firms' exposure to foreign exchange risks has grown. Businesses and the financial institutions that serve them have developed several techniques to manage these risks.[1]

Simply speaking, multinational enterprises are firms that manage and control facilities in at least two countries. For large multinational firms, internal hedging (that is, offsetting one division's long position in a currency against another division's short position) provides the most common way of handling exchange risk. The costs involved in internal hedging often prove less than that of using a bank's forward foreign exchange services. If a firm's chemical division expects to be paid 1 million euros in 30 days for goods exported to Germany while the plastics division owes 1 million euros for imported raw materials, a simple internal transfer of the euros from chemicals to plastics can hedge against foreign exchange risk while avoiding the cost of forward contracts.

A forward contract is an agreement between two parties to buy or sell an asset (which can be of any kind) at a pre-agreed future point in time. Therefore, the trade date and delivery date are separated. It is used to control and hedge risk, for example currency exposure risk (e.g. forward contracts on USD or EUR) or commodity prices (e.g. forward contracts on oil). Allaz and Vila (1993) suggest that there is also a strategic reason (in an imperfect competitive environment) for the existence of forward trading, that is, forward trading can be used even in a world without uncertainty. One party agrees to buy, the other to sell, for a forward price agreed in advance. In a forward transaction, no actual cash changes hands. Otherwise no asset of any kind actually changes hands, until the maturity of the contract. The forward price of such a contract is commonly contrasted with the spot price, which is the price at which the asset changes hands (on the spot date, usually two business days). The difference between the spot and the forward price is the forward premium or forward discount. A standardized forward contract that is traded on an exchange is called a futures contract.

Unlike futures contracts (which occur through a clearing firm), forward contracts are privately negotiated and are not standardized. Further, the two parties must bear each other's credit risk, which is not the case with a futures contract. Also, since the contracts are not exchange traded, there is no marking to market requirement, which allows a buyer to avoid almost all capital outflows initially (though some counterparties might set collateral requirements). Given the lack of standardization in these contracts, there is very little scope for a secondary market in forwards. The price specified in a forward contract for a specific commodity. The forward price makes the forward contract have no value when the contract is written. However, if the value of the underlying commodity changes, the value of the forward contract becomes positive or negative, depending on the position held. Forwards are priced in a manner similar to futures. Like in the case of a futures contract, the first step in pricing a forward is to add the spot price to the cost of carry (interest forgone, convenience yield, storage costs and interest/dividend received on the underlying). Unlike a futures contract though, the price may also include a premium for counterparty credit risk, and the fact that there is not daily marking to market process to minimize default risk. If there is no allowance for these credit risks, then the forward price will equal the futures price.

For smaller, less internationalized firms, forward markets provide the most widely used method of managing foreign exchange risk. By allowing a firm to contract to buy or sell a currency in the future at a pre-specified price, forward markets facilitate planning by eliminating uncertainty about the domestic-currency value of future revenues earned in foreign currencies and future costs owed in foreign currencies. Forward contracts can be expensive, however, especially during times when foreign exchange market participants perceived exchange risk to be high—exactly when firms would most want to hedge. Also, banks typically offer forward contracts in only a few major currencies and only for relatively short durations (typically less than two years). For other currencies, and longer-term risks, firms must pursue other strategies to cover their foreign exchange risk.

One possibility for avoiding losses due to currency fluctuations is the design of contracts that allow flexibility in the timing of receipts and payments. A U.S. firm importing 1 billion yen of goods from Japan may request contractual terms that allow payment at any time within a 180-day period following the delivery date. If the U.S. firm expects the dollar to appreciate against the yen, the firm may postpone payment as long as possible to obtain the best expected price on the yen. If, on the other hand, the firm expects the dollar to depreciate, the firm may pay the bill right away to avoid the possibility that the dollar price of yen will rise. The same idea can be used to alter the timing of foreign-currency-denominated export receipts.

Another strategy involves holding domestic bank deposits denominated in foreign exchange. As of 1990, U.S. firms can hold such accounts, insured by the Federal Deposit Insurance Corporation. The accounts, with minimum deposits of $ 20, 000—$ 25, 000, are invested in foreign time deposits (CDs) with maturities of three months to one year. But, again, a relatively small number of currencies are available.

Still another possibility is a financial instrument called an option contract. An option contract is defined as "a promise which meets the requirements for the formation of a contract and limits the promisor's power to revoke an offer." Or, quite simply, an option contract is a type of contract that protects the individual making the offer (the offeree) from a seller's (the offeror) ability to revoke the contract. Buying an option contract guarantees the buyer the right to purchase (or sell) a specified quantity of a currency at a future date for a predetermined price called the strike price. The contracts are called options because the buyer has the option whether to exercise the contract; forward or futures contracts, on the other hand, obligate the buyer to accept delivery at the specified date and price. Option contracts for future purchases of a currency are *calls*, and option contracts for future sales are *puts*.

A call option guarantees that the holder of the contract won't have to pay a price higher than the contract's strike price, because the owner will exercise the call if the spot price exceeds the strike price. (**Why?**) A put option guarantees that the holder won't have to sell currency for a price below the strike price; the owner will exercise the put ii the spot price is below the strike price. (**Why?**) For puts, note that prices rise for contracts with higher strike prices. Option contracts therefore provide the possibility of combining hedging and speculation. The holder of an option contract can still enjoy the benefits of favorable movements in the exchange rate (the speculative element) while limiting the effects of unfavorable movements (the hedging element). The Philadelphia Stock Exchange and Chicago Mercantile Exchange dominate currency options markets in the United States.

Some firms follow the ultimate strategy to avoid foreign exchange risk. They insist on being paid in their own currencies even on foreign sales, forcing customers to bear the risk. Such arrangements occur primarily in markets where the selling firm has substantial market power; otherwise, customers can threaten to go to a competitor with more willingness to take on the risk. In 2000—2001, as the British pound appreciated dramatically against the new euro, manufacturers in Britain, including Unilever and Toyota, demanded billing from their suppliers in euros—in order to avoid the painful combination of euro revenues and pound payments.

The Asian financial crisis caused many firms that historically had left exchange risk unhedged to reconsider, especially after they were surprised by the dramatic July 1997 devaluation of the Thai baht. But many of the Asian currencies most affected by the crisis—the baht, the Korean won, the Indonesian rupiah, and the Malaysian ringgit, for example—are only thinly traded, so forward contracts are unavailable or very costly. Nonetheless, firms such as computer manufacturer Digital Equipment started to hedge.[2] Dell Computer routinely buys currency options in all currencies in which the company operates. Other firms deliberately took out loans in the Asian currencies in which they expected to earn revenues, so if a devaluation lowered the revenues' dollar

value, the firm enjoyed the offsetting benefit of repaying the loan with devalued currency. Avon Cosmetics chose to buy most of its raw materials and do most of the manufacturing for its Asian cosmetics sales in its biggest Asian markets (China, Indonesia, the Philippines, and Japan); that strategy assured that any devaluation that lowered revenues would also lower costs.[3] The company also denominated its operational loans in local currency. In addition, Avon ordered its Asian operations to convert their earnings to dollars weekly rather than monthly.

Traditionally, Asian firms hedged currency risks less than U.S. or European firms, in part because so many Asian countries pegged their currencies to dollar. Even in November 1997, well into the financial crisis, a survey of 110 chief financial officers (CFOs) at a CEO forum in the Philippines found that only 42 percent hedged their companies' foreign exchange risk. Of those that did, most relied on forward contracts. But as the Asian crisis shook those pegs, more firms began to hedge, again using a variety of techniques. Japanese auto manufacturer Mitsubishi responded to the weakness of the Thai baht by boosting production facilities in Thailand and replacing inputs previously imported from Japan with local ones. Since the Asian financial crisis, firms around the world report placing a higher priority on financial market expertise, especially foreign exchange trading, in recruiting for CFO and chief executive officer positions.

Notes

1. These techniques can't eliminate foreign exchange risks, but they transfer the risks from one party to another.
2. Darren McDermott, "Asian Turmoil in Currencies Creates Risks", *The Wall Street Journal*, August 15, 1997.
3. Fred R. Bleakley, "How U.S. Firm Copes with Asia Crisis", *The Wall Street Journal*, December 26, 1997.

Answer the following questions:

1. Why is currency problem very important in international transactions?
2. How do foreign exchange rate fluctuations affect international business?
3. How does an average firm try to avoid foreign exchange risks?
4. How do international corporations avoid foreign exchange risks especially?
5. Do you know how the option contract works as a financial instrument in terms of avoiding losses due to foreign exchange rate fluctuations?
6. Try to answer the two questions in the 9th paragraph.

Unit 11

Foreign Exchange Rate

Learning Objectives

Text A
- to be familiar with the functions of the foreign exchange market
- to understand the difference between spot and forward exchange rate
- to appreciate the role of the foreign exchange market in insuring against foreign exchange risks
- to appreciate why some currencies cannot always be converted into other currencies

Text B
- to understand the reasons why the Asian Crisis took place
- to understand the roles the IMF played in the Asian Crisis

Text A

The Functions of the Foreign Exchange Market

The foreign exchange market is a market for converting the currency of one country into that of another country. It serves two main functions. The first is to convert the currency of one country into that of another. The second is to provide some insurance against foreign exchange risk.

Currency Conversion

Each country has a currency in which the prices of goods and services are quoted. In general, within the borders of a particular country one must use the national currency. A US tourist cannot walk into a store in Edinburgh, Scotland, and use US dollars to buy a bottle of Scotch whisky. Dollars are not recognized as legal tender in Scotland; the tourist must use British pounds. Fortunately, the tourist can go to a bank and exchange her dollars for pounds. Then she can buy the whisky.

When a tourist exchanges one currency into another, she is participating in the foreign exchange market. The exchange rate is the rate at which the market converts one currency into another. It allows us to compare the relative prices of goods and services in different countries. Our US tourist may find that she must pay £25 for the bottle of Scotch whisky in Edinburgh, knowing that the same bottle costs $40 in the United States. Is this a good deal? Imagine the current dollar/pound exchange rate is $1= £0.50. Our tourist discovers that the bottle of Scotch costs the equivalent of $50, and she is surprised that a bottle of Scotch whisky could cost less in the United States than in Scotland. (This is true: alcohol is taxed heavily in Great Britain.)

Tourists are minor participants in the foreign exchange market; companies engaged in international trade and investment are major ones. International businesses have four main uses for foreign exchange markets. First, the payments a company receives for its exports, the income it receives from foreign firms or the income it receives from licensing agreements with foreign firms may be in foreign currencies.[1] To use those funds in its home country, the company must convert them to its home country's currency. Second, international businesses use foreign exchange markets when they must pay a foreign company for its products or services in its country's currency. Third, international businesses use foreign exchange markets when they have spare cash that they wish to invest for short terms in money markets. Finally, currency speculation is another use of foreign exchange markets. Currency speculation typically involves the short-term movement of funds from one currency to another in the hope of profiting from shifts in exchange rates.[2] In general, however, companies should beware of speculation for it is a very risky business; the company cannot know for sure what will happen to exchange rates. While a speculator may profit handsomely if his speculation about future currency movements is correct, he can also lose vast amounts of money if it is wrong.

Currency Convertibility

Until this point we have assumed that the currencies of various countries are freely convertible into other currencies. This assumption is invalid. Many countries restrict the ability of residents and nonresidents to convert the local currency into a foreign currency. The result is that international trade and investment are more difficult in those countries. Many international businesses have used countertrade to circumvent problems that arise when a currency is not freely convertible.

Convertibility and Government Policy

Because of government restrictions, a significant number of currencies are not freely convertible into other currencies. A country's currency is said to be freely convertible when the government allows both residents and nonresidents to purchase unlimited amounts of a foreign currency with it. A currency is said to be externally convertible when only nonresidents

145

may convert it into a foreign currency without any limitations. A currency is nonconvertible when neither residents nor nonresidents are allowed to convert it into a foreign currency.

Free convertibility is the exception rather than the rule. Many countries place some restrictions on their resident's ability to convert the domestic currency into a foreign currency (a policy of external convertibility). Restrictions on convertibility for residents range from the relatively minor (such as limiting the amount of foreign currency they may take with them out of the country on trips) to the major (such as restricting domestic businesses' ability to take foreign currency out of the country). External convertibility restrictions can limit domestic companies' ability to invest abroad, but they present few problems for foreign companies' wishing to do business in that country. Even if the Japanese government placed tight controls on the ability of its residents to convert the yen into US dollars, all US businesses with deposits in Japanese banks could convert all their yen into dollars and take them out of the country. Thus, a US company with a subsidiary in Japan is assured that it will be able to convert the profits from its Japanese operation into dollars and take them out of the country.

Serious problems arise, however, under a policy of nonconvertibility. This was the practice of the former Soviet Union, and it continued to be the practice in Russia until recently. When strictly applied, nonconvertibility means that although a US company doing business in a country such as Russia may generate ruble profits, it may not convert those rubles into dollars and take them out of the country. This is not desirable for international business.

Governments limit convertibility to preserve their foreign exchange reserves. A country needs an adequate supply of these reserves to service its international debt commitments and to purchase imports. Governments typically impose convertibility restrictions on their currency when they fear that free convertibility will lead to a run on their foreign exchange reserves. This occurs when residents and nonresidents rush to convert their holdings of domestic currency into a foreign currency—generally referred to as capital flight. Capital flight is most likely to occur when the value of the domestic currency is depreciating rapidly because of hyperinflation, or when a country' economic prospects are shaky in other respects.[3] Under such circumstance, both residents and nonresidents tend to feel that their money is more likely to hold its value if it is converted into a foreign currency and invested abroad. Not only will a run on foreign exchange reserves limit the country's ability to service its international debt and pay for imports, but it will also lead to depreciation in the exchange rate as residents and nonresidents unload their holdings of domestic currency on the foreign exchange markets (thereby increasing the market supply of the country's currency).[4] Governments fear that the rise in import prices resulting from currency depreciation will lead to further increases in inflation. This fear provides another rationale for limiting convertibility.

Insuring against Foreign Exchange Risk

A second function of the foreign exchange market is to provide insurance to protect against the possible adverse consequences of unpredictable changes in exchange rates (foreign exchange risk). To explain how the market performs this function, we must first distinguish between spot exchange rates and forward exchange rates.

Spot Exchange Rates

When two parties agree to exchange currency and execute the deal immediately, the transaction is referred to as a spot exchange. Exchange rates governing such "on the spot" trades are referred to as spot exchange rates. The spot exchange rate is the rate at which a foreign exchange dealer converts one currency into another currency on a particular day. Thus, when our US tourist in Edinburgh goes to a bank to convert her dollars into pounds, the exchange rate is the spot rate for that day.

Although it is necessary to use a spot rate to execute a transaction immediately, it may not be the most attractive rate. The value of a currency is determined by the interaction between the demand and supply of that currency relative to the demand and supply of other currencies. For example, if lots of people want US dollars and dollars are in short supply, and few people want Swiss francs and Swiss francs are in plentiful supply, the spot exchange rate for converting dollars into Swiss francs will change. The dollar is likely to appreciate against the Swiss franc (or the franc will depreciate against the dollar).

Forward Exchange Rates

The fact that spot exchange rates change daily as determined by the relative demand and supply for different currencies can be problematic for an international business. A US company that imports laptop computers from Japan knows that in 30 days it must pay yen to a Japanese supplier when a shipment arrives. The company will pay the Japanese supplier ¥200,000 for each laptop computer, and the current dollar/yen spot exchange rate is $1=¥120. At that rate, each computer costs the importer $1,667 (i.e., 1,667=200,000/120). The importer knows she can sell the computers the day they arrive for $2,000 each, which yields a gross profit of $333 on each computer ($2,000−$1667). However, the importer will not have the funds to pay the Japanese supplier until the computers have been sold. If over the next 30 days the dollar unexpectedly depreciated against the yen, say to $1=¥95, the importer will still have to pay the Japanese company ¥200,000 per computer, but in dollar terms that would equal $2,105 per computer, which is more than she can sell the computers for. A depreciation in the value of the dollar against the yen from $1=¥120 to $1=¥95 would transform a profitable deal into an unprofitable one.[5]

To avoid the risk of this occurring, the US importer might want to engage in a forward exchange. A forward exchange occurs when two parties agree to exchange currency and execute the deal at some specific date in the future. Exchange rates governing such future transactions are referred to as forward exchange rates. For most major currencies, forward exchange rates are quoted for 30 days, 90 days, and 180 days into the future. In some cases, it is possible to get forward exchange rates for several years into the future. Let us assume the 30-day forward exchange rate for converting dollars into yen is $1 = ¥110. The laptop computer importer enters into a 30-day forward exchange transaction with a foreign exchange dealer at this rate and is guaranteed that she will have to pay no more than $1,818 for each computer (1,818=200,000/110). This guarantees her a profit of $182 per computer ($2,000–$1,818), and she insures herself against the possibility that an unanticipated change in the dollar/yen exchange rate will turn a profitable deal into an unprofitable one.

In this example, the spot exchange rate ($1=¥120) and the 30-day forward rate ($1=¥110) differ. Such differences are normal; they reflect the expectations of the foreign exchange market about future currency movements. When this occurs we say the dollar is selling at a discount on the 30-day forward market (i.e., it is worth less than on the spot market). The opposite can also occur. If the 30-day forward exchange rate were $1=¥130, for example, $1 would buy more yen with a forward exchange than with a spot exchange, In such a case, we say the dollar is selling at a premium on the 30-day forward market. This reflects the foreign exchange dealers' expectations that the dollar will appreciate against the yen over the next 30 days.

New Words

convert	/kən'vɜːt/	v.	改变(某物)的形式或用途
insurance	/ɪn'ʃʊərəns/	n.	安全保障
spare	/speə/	adj.	剩余的;多余的;备用的
invalid	/ɪn'vælɪd/	adj.	无道理的;站不住脚的
circumvent	/ˌsɜːkəm'vent/	v.	设法避免
resident	/'rezɪdənt/	n.	居民
prospect	/'prɒspekt/	n.	前程;前景
unload	/'ʌn'ləʊd/	v.	转手
rationale	/ˌræʃə'nɑːl/	n.	基本原理;理论基础
adverse	/'ædvɜːs/	adj.	不利的
consequence	/'kɒnsɪkwəns/	n.	结果;影响
execute	/'eksɪkjuːt/	v.	完成;执行;履行
transaction	/træn'zækʃən/	n.	交易
dealer	/'diːlə/	n.	商人;交易商
interaction	/ˌɪntər'ækʃən/	n.	相互作用;相互影响
problematic	/ˌprɒblə'mætɪk/	adj.	难处理的
shipment	/'ʃɪpmənt/	n.	装载的货物;运输的货物
unanticipated	/ˌʌnæn'tɪsɪpeɪtɪd/	adj.	意料之外的

Phrases

participate in	参加；参与（某活动）
engage in	从事
home country	本国
beware of	谨防
place tight control on	严格控制
laptop computer	便携式电脑

Special Terms

foreign exchange market	外汇市场
quote	报价；开价
currency conversion	货币兑换
legal tender	合法货币；法定货币
exchange rate	汇率；兑换价
currency speculation	货币投机
currency convertibility	货币可兑换性
convertible	可兑换的
freely convertible currency	可自由兑换货币
domestic currency	本国货币
ruble	卢布
nonconvertibility	不可兑换性
foreign exchange reserve	外汇储备
service	支付(贷款的)利息
capital flight	资本流失
depreciation	贬值
inflation	通货膨胀
hyperinflation	恶性/极度通货膨胀
foreign exchange risk	外汇风险
spot exchange rate	即期汇率
forward exchange rate	远期汇率
appreciation	增值
gross profit	毛利
at a discount	贴水
at a premium	溢价
spot market	现货市场

Unit 11

149

Notes

1. First, the payments a company receives for its exports, the income it receives from foreign firms or the income it receives from licensing agreements with foreign firms may be in foreign currencies.
   首先,公司收到的出口商品的款项,从外国公司那里获得的收入,或因和外国公司签订许可证协议而获得的收入,这些都有可能以外币的方式付款。

2. Currency speculation typically involves the short-term movement of funds from one currency to another in the hope of profiting from shifts in exchange rates.
   典型的货币投机牵涉到资金短期内从一种货币兑换成另一种货币,希望从汇率的浮动中获利。

3. Capital flight is most likely to occur when the value of the domestic currency is depreciating rapidly because of hyperinflation, or when a country' economic prospects are shaky in other respects.
   当恶性通货膨胀造成本国货币迅速贬值,或本国经济前景在其他方面不太乐观时,更有可能出现资本流失。

4. Not only will a run on foreign exchange reserves limit the country's ability to service its international debt and pay for imports, but it will also lead to depreciation in the exchange rate as residents and nonresidents unload their holdings of domestic currency on the foreign exchange markets(thereby increasing the market supply of the country's currency).
   外汇储备的流失不仅限制了国家支付国际贷款的利息和进口商品的能力,也会造成汇率贬值,因为本国居民和非本国居民将他们手中持有的本国货币转移到了外汇市场上(从而增加了对本国货币的市场供应)。

5. If over the next 30 days the dollar unexpectedly depreciated against the yen, say to $1=¥95, the importer will still have to pay the Japanese company ¥200,000 per computer, but in dollar terms that would equal $2,105 per computer, which is more than she can sell the computers for. A depreciation in the value of the dollar against the yen from $1=¥120 to $1=¥95 would transform a profitable deal into an unprofitable one.
   如果未来30天后,美元对日元突然贬值,比如说,1美元兑换95日元,而进口商仍要付给日本公司每台电脑200000日元,折合成美元即每台2105美元,这一价位甚至超出了电脑的销售价。美元对日元从1美元兑换120日元贬值到1美元兑换95日元,一桩有利可图的交易也就无利可图了。

Exercises

I. Discuss the following questions.

1. According to the article, what are the two main functions of the foreign exchange market?
2. What four main uses do international businesses have for the foreign exchange market?
3. What's the difference between spot exchange rate and forward exchange rate?
4. How does the foreign exchange market insure against foreign exchange risks?
5. Why cannot some currencies always be converted into other currencies?

II. Analyze the case below and discuss the question.

An interesting exchange rate side effect was occurring the summer of 1997 during the currency crisis in Southeast Asia. The currency crisis led to a dramatic political crisis in Indonesia, which caused the overthrow of President Suharto and much unrest in the streets of many major cities. The peaceful beaches of Bali were affected, too, as tourism collapsed. The spot exchange rate moved from 2,500 to 16,000 rupiah to the US dollar, which meant that costs in Bali dropped so much that a suite in the best resort could be had for $40 a night.

Question:
Please imagine the impact of the currency crisis on the local economy.

III. Match the terms in column A with the explanations in column B.

A	B
1. deposit	A. to pay interest on a loan
2. service	B. to lose value over a period of time
3. exchange rate	C. the rise in prices resulting from an increase in demand for goods and services
4. depreciate	D. a company of which at least half the share capital is owned by another company, called a parent or holding company
5. subsidiary company	E. the buying and selling of goods, currency or securities that are available for immediate delivery
6. inflation	F. an amount of money received from the sale of goods minus the cost of manufacturing or buying them
7. gross profit	G. a form of money that must be accepted if offered as payment

8. spot market   H. a sum of money paid into a bank or savings account
9. legal tender   I. the rate at which the market converts one currency into another

IV. Fill in the blanks of the following sentences with the words or phrases given below. Make changes when necessary.

| participant | quote | insurance | transaction | circumvent |
| interaction | anticipate | service | unload | consequence |

1. The company hasn't enough cash to _____ its debts.
2. He hoped to make a 5% profit on each _____.
3. Please _____ a price for updating this computer system.
4. All the _____ in the debate had an opportunity to speak.
5. I hadn't enough money to pay our bus fare, and in _____ we had to walk back home.
6. We _____ meeting a lot of opposition to the new plan for the traffic control.
7. I bought some new locks as an additional _____ against burglary.
8. The company opened an office abroad in order to _____ the tax laws.
9. There should be a lot more _____ between the social services and local doctors.
10. They've brought up thousands of cheap videos which they want to _____ on the British market.

V. Put the following into English.

1. 为预防外汇风险提供安全保障
2. 比较不同国家的货物和服务的相对价格
3. 将剩余现金短期内投入外汇市场
4. 无限制地将本国货币兑换成外币
5. 限制货币的可兑换性以保存外汇储备
6. 货币贬值造成的进口价格上涨
7. 每笔交易获得10%的净利润
8. 从日本进口便携式电脑
9. 参与外汇市场

VI. Translate the following sentences into English.

1. 然而，对于货币投机，通常情况下，公司应该十分谨慎，因为货币投机风险很大，公司很难预知下一步汇率会怎样变化。
2. 外汇交易商在某一特定时期将一种货币兑换成另一种货币时的汇率叫做即期汇率。

3. 货币的价值是由相对于其他货币的供需而言这一货币的供需间的相互作用决定的。
4. 许多跨国公司采取对销贸易的形式来避免货币不能自由兑换而产生的问题。
5. 一个国家需要足够的外汇储备来支付其跨国债务的利息和进口产品。

VII. Translate the following passage into Chinese.

A company can deal with the nonconvertibility problem by engaging in countertrade. Countertrade refers to a range of barterlike agreements by which goods and services can be traded for other goods and services. Countertrade can make sense when a country's currency is nonconvertible. Consider the deal that General Electric struck with the Romanian government in 1984, when that country's currency was nonconvertible. When General Electric won a contract for a $150 million generator project in Romania, it agreed to take payment in the form of Romanian goods that could be sold for $150 million on international markets. The Venezuelan government negotiated a contract with Caterpillar in 1986 under which Venezuela would trade 350,000 tons of iron ore for Caterpillar heavy construction equipment. Caterpillar subsequently traded the iron ore to Romania in exchange for Romanian farm products, which it then sold on international markets for dollars.

Text B

The Asian Crisis

The financial crisis that erupted across Southeast Asia during the fall of 1997 has emerged as the biggest challenge the IMF has had to deal with. Holding the crisis in check required IMF loans to help the shattered economies of Indonesia, Thailand, and South Korea stabilize their currencies. In addition, although they did not request IMF loans, the economies of Japan, Malaysia, Singapore, and the Philippines were also badly hurt by the crisis.

The seeds of this crisis were sown during the previous decade when these countries were experiencing unprecedented economic growth. Although there were and remain important differences between the individual countries, they shared a number of elements. Exports had long been the engine of economic growth in these countries. The nature of these exports had also shifted in recent years from basic materials and products such as textiles to complex and increasingly high-technology products, such as automobiles, semiconductors, and consumer electronics.

The Investment Boom

The wealth created by export-led growth fueled an investment boom in commercial and residential property, industrial assets, and infrastructure. The value of commercial and residential real estate in cities such as Hong Kong and Bangkok soared. This fed a building boom. Heavy borrowing from banks financed much of this construction, but as long as the value of property continued to rise, the banks were happy to lend. The success of Asian exporters encouraged them to make bolder investments in industrial capacity.

As added factor behind the investment boom in most Southeast Asian economies was the government. In many cases the governments had embarked on huge infrastructure projects. Throughout the region, governments also encouraged private businesses to invest in certain sectors of the economy in accordance with "national goals" and "industrialization strategy." By the mid-1990s Southeast Asia was in the grips of an unprecedented investment boom, much of it financed with borrowed money.

Excess Capacity

As the volume of investments ballooned during the 1990s, often at the request of national governments, the *quality* of many of these investments declined significantly. Often the investments were based on unrealistic projections about future demand. The result was significant excess capacity.

The Debt Bomb

Massive investments in industrial assets and property had created excess capacity and plunged prices and left the companies that had made the investments groaning under huge debt burdens they found difficult to service.

To make matters worse, much of the borrowing had been in US dollars. Originally this had seemed like a smart move. Throughout the region local currencies were pegged to the dollar, and interest rates on dollar borrowings were generally lower than rates on borrowings in domestic currency. Thus, it often made economic sense to borrow in dollars if possible. However, if the governments in the region could not maintain the dollar peg and their currencies started to depreciate against the dollar, this would increase the size of the debt burden that local companies would have to service, when measured in the local currency. Currency depreciation would raise borrowing costs and could result in companies defaulting on their debt obligations.

Expanding Imports

A final complicating factor was that by the mid-1990s although exports were still expanding across the region, so were imports. The investments in infrastructure, industrial capacity, and commercial real estate were sucking in foreign goods at unprecedented rates. To build infrastructure, factories, and office buildings, Southeast Asian countries were purchasing capital equipment and materials from America, Europe, and Japan. It was becoming increasingly difficult for these governments to maintain the peg of their currencies against the US dollar. If that peg could not be held, the local currency value of dollar-denominated debt would increase, raising the specter of large-scale default on debt service payments. The scene was now set for a potentially rapid economic meltdown.

The Crisis

The Asian meltdown began in mid-1997 in Thailand when it became clear that several key Thai financial institutions were on the verge of default. These institutions had been borrowing dollars from international banks at low interest rates and lending Thai baht at higher interest rates to local property developers. However, due to speculative overbuilding, these developers could not sell their commercial and residential property, forcing them to default on their debt obligations to Thai financial institutions. In turn, the Thai financial institutions seemed increasingly likely to default on their dollar-denominated debt obligations to international banks. Sensing the beginning of the crisis, foreign investors fled the Thai stock market, selling their positions and converting them into US dollars. The increased demand for dollars and increased supply of Thai baht pushed down the dollar/Thai baht exchange rate while the stock market plunged.

Foreign exchange dealers and hedge funds started to speculate against the baht, selling it short. For the previous 13 years the Thai baht had been pegged to the US dollar at an exchange rate of around $1=Bt25. The Thai government tried to defend the peg, but only succeeded in depleting its foreign exchange reserves. On July 2, 1997, the Thai government abandoned its defense and announced it would allow the baht to float freely against the dollar. The baht started a slide that would bring the exchange rate down to $1=Bt55 by January 1988. As the baht declined, the Thai debt bomb exploded. The 55 percent decline in the value of the baht against the dollar doubled the amount of baht required to serve the dollar-denominated debt commitments taken on by Thai financial institutions and businesses. This increased the probability of corporate bankruptcies and further pushed down the battered Thai stock market. The Thailand Set stock market index ultimately declined from 787 in January 1997 to a low of 337 in December of that year; this was on top of a 45 percent decline in 1996.

On July 28 the Thai government took the next logical step and called in the International Monetary Fund. With its foreign exchange reserves depleted, Thailand lacked the foreign currency needed to finance its international trade and service debt commitments and desperately needed the capital the IMF could provide. It also needed to restore international confidence in its currency, and it needed the credibility associated with gaining access to IMF funds. Without IMF loans, the baht was likely to increase its free fall against the US dollar, and the whole country might go into default. The IMF agreed to provide the Thai government with $17.2 billion in loans, but the conditions were restrictive. The IMF required the Thai government to increase taxes, cut public spending, privatize several state-owned businesses, and raise interest rates—all designed to cool Thailand's overheated economy. The IMF also required Thailand to close illiquid financial institutions. In December 1997 the government shut 56 financial institutions, laying off 16,000 people in the process and further deepening the recession that now gripped the country.

Following the devaluation of the Thai baht, wave after wave of speculation hit other Asian currencies. In a period of weeks the Malaysian ringgit, Indonesian rupiah and the Singapore dollar were all marked sharply lower. With the exception of Singapore, these devaluations were driven by factors similar to those behind the earlier devaluation of the Thai baht. Although both Malaysia and Singapore were able to halt the slide in their currencies and stock markets without the help of the IMF, Indonesia was not. Indonesia was struggling with a private-sector dollar-denominated debt of close to $80 billion. With the rupiah sliding precipitously almost every day, the cost of servicing this debt was exploding, pushing more Indonesian companies into technical default. On October 31, 1997, the IMF announced that in conjunction with the World Bank and the Asian Development Bank it had put together a $37 billion rescue deal for Indonesia.

The final domino to fall was South Korea. During the 1990s South Korean companies had built up huge debt loads as they invested heavily in new industrial capacity. Now they found they had too much industrial capacity and could not generate the income required to service the debt that they had taken on to build the capacity. South Korean banks and companies had also made the mistake of borrowing in dollars, much of it in the form of short-term loans that would come due within a year. Thus, when the South Korean won started to decline in the fall of 1997, companies saw their debt obligations balloon. Several large companies defaulted on their debt service obligations and filed for bankruptcy. This triggered a decline in the South Korean currency and stock market that was difficult to halt. The South Korean central bank tried to keep the dollar/won exchange rate above $1=W1,000, but found that this only depleted its foreign exchange reserves. On November 17 the South Korean central bank gave up the defense of the won, which quickly fell to $1=W1,500.

With its economy on the verge of collapse, on November 21 the South Korean government requested $20 billion in standby loans from the IMF. As the negotiations progressed, it soon became apparent that South Korea was going to need far more than $20 billion. The country's short-term foreign debt was found to be twice as large as previously thought at close to $100 billion, while its foreign exchange reserves were down to less than $6 billion. On December 3 the IMF and South Korean government reached a deal to lend $55 billion to the country.

Answer the following questions:

1. What are the factors that lead to the Asian Crisis?
2. What was the added factor behind the investment boom in most Southeast Asian economies? Why?
3. Why did the investments create excess capacity?
4. Why was it becoming increasingly difficult for these governments to maintain the peg of their currencies against the US dollar?
5. When and where did the Asian crisis begin first?
6. What did foreign investors do when they sensed the beginning of the crisis in Thailand?
7. How did the IMF help the Thai government and what did it require the Thai government to do?
8. What did the IMF do to help Indonesia with the devaluation of the Indonesian rupiah?
9. Which country was the final domino to fall?
10. When did the IMF and South Korean government reach a deal to lend $55 billion to the country?

Unit 12

Securities Market

Learning Objectives

Text A
- to learn the major economic functions of securities markets in modern societies
- to examine their providing modes to realize the benefits

Text B
- to learn the constant evolution of the types of securities traded as well as the way in which they are traded with the change of technology, social needs and political conditions

Text A

Why Do Securities Markets Exist

Securities markets play a vital role in modern societies. They increase investment opportunities and standards of living, provide diversification opportunities, and allow opportunities to shift one's investment risk level.[1] In this section we examine the roles and benefits provided by (1) primary markets, (2) secondary markets, and (3) professional security management.

Primary Market Benefits

Recall that the primary market refers to trades in which a user of capital issues a security to a capital supplier in return for cash. The security issuer then uses the cash to acquire (hopefully) profitable real assets. Benefits provided by primary markets are twofold: (1) wealth of a society is increased; (2) consumption and investment flexibility is increased.

Wealth of Society Consider individuals such as Thomas Edison, Henry Ford, and William Gates. During their career, these people created new industries that led to significant employment and increased standards of living. Each had a unique idea that resulted in a value to society. But none had (initially) enough personal capital needed to implement their ideas. Society benefited by improved productivity, these entrepreneurs benefited by increased wealth, and purchasers of the securities also benefited from

increases in the value of securities they bought.

The story of these individuals is an obvious extreme. But the point that financial markets help increase the future wealth of society also relates to everyday life. For example, how many college readers of this text would be able to personally afford their education costs if they had to rely solely on personally assets? Students who borrow to help finance their education costs are using the financial markets to make an investment in their personal human capital.[2] The ability to borrow improves their future wealth as well as their value to society.

Consumption and Investment Flexibility The presence of financial markets also increases consumption and investment flexibility. If a primary market (which issues a financial claim in return for cash) did not exist, people could consume no more than the market value of any real assets that they owned. Automobiles and houses could not be purchased until people had sufficient real assets to do so. But with the presence of a primary market, individuals can borrow and spend today using a promise to repay with future income.[3]

From the investment perspective, without the existence of securities created in a primary market, people accumulating savings would be forced to save by acquiring real assets (which they might not have the skill and time to manage or are more risky than they desire). The presence of financial securities created in the primary market provides such savers with an easy and inexpensive way to accumulate wealth through financial investment.

In short, primary markets increase the wealth of society and provide an improvement in consumption and investment flexibility.

Securities created in the primary market can either be held by the security buyer or traded in secondary markets. Securities that are held by the buyer are referred to as private placements. A loan made by a bank to a business or individual is an example of a private placement. The bank intends to hold the security for the full life of the security with no intention of selling it to another party. Securities that are to be traded in secondary markets are referred to as public placements. A mortgage loan made by a bank becomes part of a public placement when it is pooled with other mortgage loans and sold in secondary markets as mortgage-backed debt obligation.[4]

Secondary Market Benefits

Recall that the term secondary market refers to trades between a buyer and a seller after the original security issue. Consider these benefits created by the existence of a secondary market:

- price discovery
- reduced transaction costs
- diversification improvements
- liquidity

Price Discovery By knowing the market price at which market participants are willing to currently trade the security, we can infer the rate of return that investors who own a given security require. For example, the rate of return that investors require on a bond issue of AT&T can be calculated by knowledge of the bond's maturity, promised interest payments, and current market price. Similarly, knowledge of AT&T's current stock price helps in estimating the required return on the firm's common stock. Knowledge of current capital costs helps financial managers decide whether new projects are likely to cover the required financing costs. This is of considerable value to society, since it allocates resources to business ventures that are expected to create wealth for society.

Reduced Transaction Costs Significant economies of scale are possible from creating network that brings together potential buyers and sellers.[5] For example, having a central location at which a large number of different stocks can be traded makes it much less costly for buyers and sellers to find each other. Many developments in the way in which securities are traded have occurred simply in an effort to reduce trading costs. Examples included methods by which large quantities of stock are traded, the growth of discount brokerage houses, and the recent markets is driven by desire to minimize trading costs.

Diversification Improvements Diversification consists of owning a large number of different securities. It is a principal way in which portfolio risk can be minimized. Although diversification can be achieved via primary market purchases, small investors find it much easier to achieve a reasonable level of diversification by trading in secondary markets, simply because smaller quantity of securities may be traded.

For example, a $100 million portfolio conceivably could obtain sufficient diversification by purchasing a large number of new issues in primary market transactions. But an individual with only $25,000 to invest would find such an approach almost impossible.

Liquidity A commonly cited reason for the existence of secondary markets is the improved liquidity they provide. A perfectly liquid security could be sold immediately and at no cost (commissions, taxes, effects on price, etc.). To the extent that time and costs arise in a trade, liquidity decreases.

The benefits of having liquid markets are obvious: they allow one to trade when there is a need for cash or when excess cash is available. As an example, consider the shares of Fictitious Corporation. Assume that when you purchase a share of this firm's common stock you have the rights to any dividends the company will pay in the future. But you are not allowed to ever sell the shares (perhaps because there is no secondary market available). Would you be willing to purchase the shares? Probably, if the share price was low enough! Now let's say that a market is created in which you are allowed to trade the shares at low cost and rapidly at any time you wish. Would you be willing to purchase the shares at a higher price than without the secondary market? Certainly. The option to trade has a value that is created by secondary markets.

While no secondary market is perfectly liquid, most markets provide relatively rapid and low-cost opportunities to trade.

Professional Security Management Benefits

Ownership interests in professionally managed security portfolios have become such an important element of security market transactions that they must be considered a vital component of the overall security market structure. In fact, individual and institutional investors could conduct all of their investment activities through such security management firms, never having to go directly to either the primary or the secondary markets.[6]

Many variants of professionally managed portfolios exist, each appealing to the needs of a group of investors. For example, in the case of mutual funds, investors place cash into the portfolio and in return receive an ownership claim equal to the proportion their investment represents of total assets.[7] So, if the market value of a portfolio was $9 million at the close of trading on a particular day and a college foundation contributed $1 million to the portfolio at that time, the foundation would receive a 10% ownership claim.

Professionally managed portfolios provide three potential advantages: (1) diversification, (2) lower cost of portfolio management, and (3) professional management.

Diversification By pooling their capital, individual investors are able to purchase a larger number of different securities than if they had simply invested on their own. This is an important advantage for individual investors with small amounts to be invested.

Lower Cost of Portfolio Management The percentage cost of managing a portfolio is inversely related to the dollar amount being managed.[8] For example, the manager of a large portfolio can negotiate trading commissions with brokers to levels not available to smaller investors. And accounting costs can be spread over all investors in the portfolio. In addition, there is the cost associated with selecting securities to be held in the portfolio. For a given research effort, security analysis costs are the same whether the portfolio has $10,000 in assets, $100 million in assets, or $1 billion. Notice the words "for a given research effort." It is likely that greater research effort would go into a $100 million portfolio than for a $10,000 portfolio. But even then, economies of scale result in lower selection cost per $1 of managed assets.

Professional Management Many investment companies claim that an advantage of using their services is the portfolio will be managed by a full-time experienced portfolio management group. Although the answer is not clear, by turning the management of a security portfolio over to professionals, investors might be less likely to make poor decisions about the types of securities purchased.

New Words

shift	/ʃɪft/	v.	转换
issue	/'ɪsjuː/	v. & n.	发行；证券
issuer	/'ɪsjuːə/	n.	发行人
cash	/kæʃ/	n.	现金
asset	/'æset/	n.	资产
productivity	/ˌprɒdʌk'tɪvɪti/	n.	生产力
entrepreneur	/ˌɒntrəprə'nɜː/	n.	企业家
finance	/faɪ'næns/	v.	供给……经费，负担经费
claim	/kleɪm/	n.	要求而得到的东西
real asset			不动产
promise	/'prɒmɪs/	n.	承诺
accumulate	/ə'kjuːmjʊleɪt/	v.	积聚
saving	/'seɪvɪŋ/	n.	存款
pool	/puːl/	v.	共享；集中(钱、力量等)
obligation	/ˌɒblɪ'geɪʃən/	n.	债务
infer	/ɪn'fɜː/	v.	推断
maturity	/mə'tʃʊərɪti/	n.	成熟期；到期日
payment	/'peɪmənt/	n.	付款，支付，报酬
return	/rɪ'tɜːn/	n.	利润
cover	/'kʌvə/	v.	包含；够支付
allocate	/'æləkeɪt/	v.	分配
venture	/'ventʃə/	n.	企业
network	/'netwɜːk/	n.	网络
improvement	/ɪm'pruːvmənt/	n.	进展
conceivably	/kən'siːvəbli/	adv.	令人信服地
excess	/ɪk'ses/	adj.	额外的
dividend	/'dɪvɪdend/	n.	股息或红利
variant	/'veərɪənt/	n.	变量
close	/kləʊz/	n.	收盘，交易结束

Phrases

in return for	作为……的报答
result in	导致
by knowledge of	依据，根据

at no cost   不花钱
appeal to   对……有吸引力
turn over   移交给

Special Terms

securities market	证券市场
primary market	一级市场
secondary market	二级市场
financial market	金融市场
private placement	私募,非公开发行
public placement	公募,公开发行
mortgage loan	抵押贷款
price discovery	价格发现
transaction cost	交易成本
rate of return	回报率
common stock	普通股
discount brokerage house	贴现经济公司
institutional investor	机构投资者
mutual fund	共同基金,互助基金

Notes

1. They increase investment opportunities and standards of living, provide diversification opportunities, and allow opportunities to shift one's investment risk level.
   它们(证券市场)增加投资渠道,提高生活水平,提供多样化的投资机会,还允许投资人转换投资风险水平。
   句中 diversification 表示多样化,指投资者买不同资产的组合,以实现在一定条件下组合资产的风险最小,这一过程称为多样化或分散化。

2. Students who borrow to help finance their education costs are using the financial markets to make an investment in their personal human capital.
   那些通过贷款来支付教育费用的学生正在使用金融市场来对他们个人的人力资本进行投资。

3. Automobiles and houses could not be purchased until people had sufficient real assets to do so. But with the presence of a primary market, individuals can borrow and spend today using a promise to repay with future income.
   (如果一级市场不存在)人们只有等到拥有足够的不动资产的时候才能购买汽车和住

房。但是随着一级市场的出现,个人只需一个用将来的收入偿还贷款的承诺就可以借贷和消费当前的钱款。

句中 not... until 表示"直到……才"。

句中 primary market 表示一级市场、初级市场,指新发行的证券首次公开出手的市场。一级市场的销售收益归证券的发行者所有。一级市场也指政府证券的拍卖和期权、期货合约首次出售的场所。

4. A mortgage loan made by a bank becomes part of a public placement when it is pooled with other mortgage loans and sold in secondary markets as mortgage-backed debt obligation.

当一项抵押贷款和其他抵押贷款集中在一起并在二级市场中作为抵押债务销售时,它就成为向公众新发行或增发行的一部分。

句中 secondary market 表示二级市场,指证券在一级市场上发行之后,又在投资者之间再次进行买卖的市场,包括交易所(exchange)和场外(柜台)(over-the-counter market)。二级市场的销售收益由出售证券的交易商或投资者获得,而不归最初发行证券的公司所有。二级市场也指货币市场工具在投资者之间进行交易的场所。

5. Significant economies of scale are possible from creating network that brings together potential buyers and sellers.

把潜在的买卖双方集合到一起形成网络,在创造这种网络的过程中就可能出现重大的规模经济。

句中 economy of scale 表示规模经济,指当生产和交易的规模增大时,其成本以更大的比例减少,也就是经济活动的规模越大,单位成本越低。反之则为规模不经济。

6. In fact, individual and institutional investors could conduct all of their investment activities through such security management firms, never having to go directly to either the primary or the secondary markets.

事实上,个体和机构的投资者可通过这样的证券管理公司来从事他们所有的投资活动,而不必直接进入一级或二级市场。

句中 institutional investor 表示机构投资者,指买卖证券的数量或金额足以使他们享有优惠待遇或较低佣金的非银行人士或机构。由于市场假设机构投资者具备较佳的专业知识,因而可以更好地保护自己,因此需要遵守的保护性限制较少。

7. For example, in the case of mutual funds, investors place cash into the portfolio and in return receive an ownership claim equal to the proportion their investment represents of total assets.

例如,在共同基金的情况下,投资者把现金放置在投资组合中,作为回报,他们得到了与他们的投资在总资产中所占比例相当的所有权。

句中 mutual fund 表示共同基金,指一种集体投资的工具,其基金来源于股东,由投资公司经营,投资于股票、债券、期权、商品或货币市场证券。这些基金提供给投资者多样化和专业管理的好处,并为此收取一定的管理费用,通常是每年收取资金总额的 1% 或更少。

句中 portfolio 表示投资组合，指一名投资者持有的资产组合，例如股票、债券及共同基金。为减低风险，投资者倾向持有超过一种的股票及其他资产。

8. The percentage cost of managing a portfolio is inversely related to the dollar amount being managed.

经营投资组合的百分比成本与所经营的资金量成反比。

句中 is inversely related to... 表示"与……成反比"。

Exercises

I. Discuss the following questions.

1. How is savings transferred to consumption and investment through the primary market?
2. Which function of a secondary market helps to transfer economic resources over industries? How is this function executed?
3. What is the driving force of development of secondary markets? Please explain the reason.
4. What is liquidity? Why do we say it is very important to security markets?
5. What are the benefits of diversification? How do common investors achieve diversification via different ways?
6. What are the benefits of securitization of mortgage loans to the commercial banks and other institutions?

II. Analyze the case below and discuss the questions.

We all have something to say about NYSE.

Questions:
1. Discover how the NYSE (New York Stock Exchange) grows to become the global marketplace of today.
2. Can you enumerate some world famous stock exchanges around the globe? Do you know what is the major criteria to evaluate the scope of the exchanges?

III. Match the terms in column A with the explanations in column B.

A	B
1. diversification	A. anything that an individual or a corporation owns that has economic value to its owner
2. issuer	B. investments, including dividends, interest, royalties, and capital gains
3. promise	C. to demand or ask for as one's due
4. claim	D. to commit oneself to do
5. liquidity	E. A risk management technique that mixes a wide variety of investments within a portfolio. It is designed to minimize the impact of any one security on overall portfolio performance.
6. asset	F. to set apart for a special purpose; designate
7. allocate	G. the degree to which an asset or security can be bought or sold in the market without affecting the asset's price
8. portfolio	H. a share of profits received by a stockholder or by a policyholder in a mutual insurance society
9. dividend	I. a non-bank person or organization that trades securities in large enough share quantities or dollar amounts that they qualify for preferential treatment and lower commissions
10. institutional investor	J. the entity, such as a corporation or municipality, that offers (or proposes to offer) its securities for sale

IV. Fill in the blanks of the following sentences with the words or phrases given below. Make changes when necessary.

issue	implement	finance	accumulate	pool
maturity	cover	variant	broker	infer

1. The committee's suggestions will be _____ immediately.
2. His brother is an insurance _____.
3. The repairs to the school will be _____ by the education department.
4. Will $17 _____ the cost of the damage?
5. Banknotes of this design were first _____ 20 years ago.
6. "Behavior" is the American _____ of the British "Behaviour."
7. What can we _____ from his refusal to see us?
8. He gradually _____ an impressive collection of paintings.
9. When did the stock market reach its _____?
10. None of us can manage to do this task separately, so let's _____ our resources to accomplish it successfully.

V. Put the following into English.

1. 发行和买卖股票和债券的场所
2. 作为公募一部分的抵押贷款
3. 减少交易成本
4. 投资者需要的回报率
5. 购买公司的一股普通股票
6. 贴现经济公司提供的服务
7. 共同基金是一种集体投资的工具
8. 和经纪人商议交易佣金
9. 持有投资组合中4%的资产净值
10. 通过证券管理公司来从事所有的投资活动

VI. Translate the following sentences into English.

1. 没有任何一个二级市场是永远流动的。
2. 大多数金融市场为贸易提供迅速而低成本的机会。
3. 被购买者持有的股票称为私募,而在二级市场上交易的股票称为公募。
4. 投资者对AT&T公司发行的债券所要求的回报率可以根据债券的成熟期、持有期间获得的红利以及当前市场价格进行计算来获得。
5. 追求收益的人们正在日益关注有抵押和资产作支持的文件,因而市场的流动性在增长。

VII. Translate the following passage into Chinese.

A commonly cited reason for the existence of secondary markets is the improved liquidity they provide. A perfectly liquid security could be sold immediately and at no cost (commissions, taxes, effects on price, etc.). To the extent that time and costs arise in a trade, liquidity decreases.

The benefits of having liquid markets are obvious: they allow one to trade when there is a need for cash or when excess cash is available. As an example, consider the shares of Fictitious Corporation. Assume that when you purchase a share of this firm's common stock you have the rights to any dividends the company will pay in the future. But you are not allowed to ever sell the shares (perhaps because there is no secondary market available). Would you be willing to purchase the shares? Probably, if the share price was low enough! Now let's say that a market is created in which you are allowed to trade the shares at low cost and rapidly at any time you wish. Would you be willing to purchase the shares at a higher price than without the secondary market? Certainly. The option to trade has a value that is created by secondary markets.

Text

Investment Management in the 1990s

The types of securities traded as well as the way in which they are traded are constantly evolving as technology, society's needs, and political conditions change. The pace of change seems to be accelerating, driven both by increasing numbers of investors and competition. Most professionals agree that the major areas of change are in (1) globalization, (2) securitization, (3) derivatives, and (4) technology.

Globalization

Perhaps the most significant long-term development of recent years has been the creation of a truly global security market. Users of capital compete around the world for sources of money, and investors recognize the diversification and return advantages of investing beyond their own political borders. Security firms that had previously conducted business solely within their local country have created alliances with firms in other countries which give both a global presence.

Global investing has become the "thing to do." One significant reason is the growth of free market capitalism and democratic institutions. For example, Pacific Rim countries (known as the Pac-Rim) have experienced dramatic growth in both real economics and financial markets. In some of these countries, equity returns of 500% in a year are common. (It goes both ways; large negative returns also occur.) Eastern Europe is seeing a rebirth in real asset growth and the financial markets needed to supply the capital and liquidity to support such growth. And the growth potential of China is almost unimaginable.

Even in well-developed economics, international competition has forced a reduction in the regulation of security market transactions and led to significant growth of trading. In England, for example, fixed commission rates were eliminated during the 1980s and created a growth in trading and repositioning of securities firms, referred to as the "Big Bang."

Advances in technology have made global integration physically possible. Satellite communications allow markets to be continuously linked so prices in foreign markets can be accurately monitored and orders can be executed within minutes on the major world exchanges.

The growth of institutional investors has also spurred the movement to global investing. Institutions were among the first to recognize the value of global investment and they had a large enough asset base to motivate investment firms to make any changes necessary to allow them to do so. For example, without pressure from pension funds and endowment funds, banks (which hold custody of the international securities owned) would probably not have improved their international custodial services as rapidly as they did.

The history of financial markets has entered a new era, which brings with it both opportunities and risks. Serious investment students must become more aware of differences in world cultures, be attentive to potential political risk, and learn about currency risk.

Securitization

The term "securitization" refers to taking a pool of loans and using them as collateral for a bond issue that is sold in the primary markets and later traded in secondary markets. Securitized issues are often called "assets backs" because they are backed by a specific pool of loans. Another term applied to them is "pass-throughs," since both principal and interest are passed through to the security holder when paid.

The most common form of asset-backed security is the mortgage-backed obligation. The mortgage-backed market is principally in the United States. During the past 25 years, the mortgage pass-through market has grown from virtually zero to almost 20% of the value of all U.S. bond issues. A smaller market also exists in securities backed by credit card and automobile loans.

We noted earlier that the growth of the asset-backed market is an illustration of how financial markets react to a societal need. In this case, banks did not wish to hold long-term mortgage obligations during periods of rapid changing interest rates. Securitization of the mortgage allowed them to be held by security market participants who were more willing to accept their interest rate risk.

But managing the risks of these securities requires new investment concepts and tools. Among these are new forms of financial derivatives.

Derivatives

Although active markets in options and futures were created earlier, it is in the decade of the 1990s that they came to their maturity. They are now widely used by sophisticated investors to manage various forms of investment risk. For example, during the period when a bank is putting together a mortgage pass-through that will be sold in the primary market, the bank has an investment in loans which bears interest rate risk. To offset this risk, the bank can take an appropriate position in mortgage futures.

Although futures and options represent useful risk management tools, they should not be used unless one has a full understanding of them. Like a powerful medicine, unless they are used properly, they can cause serious harm.

Technology

Recent advances in technology have had profound effects on the types of information available, the way in which securities are traded, and the techniques used to select securities.

A few decades ago information about individual stocks and bonds was usually obtained from paper documents that were often updated only once a year. For example, if you wished to obtain information on a common stock, you would write the company for a copy of its annual report, copy security registration documents filed with governmental bodies such as the Securities and Exchange Commission, and examine investment information manuals printed by firms such as Moody's and Standard & Poor's. Information about stock prices was available on only current prices via a phone call to one's broker.

Today a wealth of information is available via computer-based products. Computer networks, such as the Bloomberg System, provide extensive data on virtually all actively traded securities in the United States plus analytic programs that aid in evaluating a particular trading strategy. Standard & Poor's provides a CD-ROM that has 20 years of financial statement data as well as past prices and dividends on virtually all actively traded stocks in the world. Morning Star has a CD-ROM that furnishes past returns and portfolio holdings on more than 4,000 investment company portfolios. Compact Disclosure supplies full copies of recent corporate annual reports. The list continues to grow.

The way in which securities are traded has also been permanently changed by new technologies. Numerous computer-based networks link security traders so they can find current prices at which they can buy or sell and actually execute orders. Many discount brokerage houses now provide individual investors with the ability to buy and sell securities without ever contacting a broker. Even the Internet provides ways of buying and selling securities (as well as extensive databases such as access to corporate document files with the Security Exchange Commission).

Finally, analytic techniques used in security selection have changed significantly with advances in computer use. This has led to the creation of new approaches such as "qualitative investing," "high-tech investing," "factor model selection," and so on.

Answer the following questions:

1. Give the main reasons for global investing.
2. Why do we say that securitization has made the connection between borrowers and investors more efficient?
3. What kind of changes has the wide use of derivatives brought to investment management?
4. What are the effects that the advances in technology have had on investment management?

Unit 13

Monetary Policy and Fiscal Policy

Learning Objectives

Text A
- to learn what are monetary policy and fiscal policy
- to understand the functioning of the two policies

Text B
- to understand the active elements of a sound monetary policy
- to know the focus of reforms of wholly state-owned commercial banks

Text A

The Basic Idea of Monetary and Fiscal Policy

In the past, when America embraced a philosophy of Laissez Faire, the government did little to monitor and control the economy. After the depression, however, that philosophy changed radically. Today we all have come to understand that one of the federal government's most important roles is regulating and ensuring the stability of the economy.

The government has two major ways of doing this. The government can enact fiscal policy changes or it can enact monetary policy changes:

❖ *Fiscal Policy*—The power of the federal government to tax and spend in order to achieve its goals for the economy.

❖ *Monetary Policy*—Programs that try to increase or decrease the nation's level of business by regulating the supply of money and credit.

In order to understand the functioning of these two policies we must again revisit the concept of inflation. Remember, inflation is when the value of money goes down. This means that it costs more money to buy products. Think of the economy in terms of supply and demand; the more money there is out there being spent, the less the money is worth. The supply is high, thus the value is comparatively low. What this also means is that people are spending, and this is good. So what we have to do is to find the proper balance between the amount of spending and money in circulation and an acceptable level of inflation.[1] Economists have placed "healthy" inflation at 2–3%.

Fiscal Policy

Taxes

Fiscal Policies include raising or lowering of taxes. If we raise taxes we are taking money out of circulation. When one considers the impact of taxes one must look at the sector of society being impacted by the tax hike. Does it impact the middle class, working class or upper class? There are differing philosophies on who should shoulder the tax burden. Some feel it should be the wealthy while other look to the middle class. The reality is that the middle class pay the largest amount of taxes overall. Raising taxes to the middle class will limit consumer spending, so if you are going to do that you had better have a good reason. Clearly raising taxes will slow down spending, economic growth as well as inflation.

The question then comes to tax cuts. Who do you want to cut taxes too? Who do you want to encourage to spend? Again, recent economic history proves that cutting taxes to the middle class is the only effective way to encourage growth and spending.

Spending Programs

The grand daddy of all fiscal policy spending programs was FDR's New Deal. Knowledge of the New Deal is essential to understand the importance of government spending, as well as its shortfalls.[2] As any student of American History knows, the New Deal did not end the Depression, W.W. II did. It did, however, help to move the economy along and did help millions of people. Spending programs pump money into an economy and increase spending and growth. They also have the potential impact of increasing inflation as more money circulates in the economy.

Again, when determining what spending programs to initiate depends on where you want the impact to be. If you build highways you will create jobs for the working class, same with housing projects, etc. These types of jobs employ many workers. If you build B2 bombers, however, less workers are employed at a much higher cost. Who gets the money here? The large corporation that builds them does, that's who. So you see, how you spend the money means as much as how much money you spend.

Spending cuts have the same impact. If you cut homeless shelter there are people out on the streets. From an economic impact perspective that may not seem like much but now you

have a human-interest issue.[3] If you close military bases, you may well shut down the town that thrives off of the existence of the base. Some bases employ up to an over 20,000 townspeople with no other viable means of support. You have to consider the impact and the location of the base. When the federal government cut funding for the F-14 Tomcat Fighter built by Grumman on Long Island it had a terrible impact on the Long Island economy as those highly technical workers sought to find jobs. Long Island is a wealthy suburb of New

York City, however, those workers were more likely to find work then if the factory had been located in a more rural area.

Monetary Policy

Monetary policies are enacted by the Federal Reserve Board of Governors who run the Federal Reserve System. The Fed has several policies they can take through the Board of Governors and the Open Market Committee. Most often they are led in their actions by the Chairman of the Federal Reserve Board, a post currently held by Alan Greenspan. The powers of monetary policies often have immediate and forceful impact so what the Fed does is closely watched. Every word that comes out of Greenspan's mouth is seen as a sign for what he thinks of the economy. Entire businesses exist just to watch the Fed and Mr. Greenspan. The Fed's basic monetary policy tools are:

- ❖ Reserve Requirements
- ❖ Discount Rate
- ❖ Open Market Operations
- ❖ Printing Money

Each policy has one basic goal—impact the money supply. All of these policy actions work using the laws of supply and demand. The more money in circulation, the more spending there is and the higher inflation is. The less money there is in circulation, the less spending there is, and inflation decreases. Those policies that restrict the money supply are known as "tight" and those that put more money into circulation are known as "loose."[4] Let's examine each of the policy actions and their possible results.

Change in Reserve Requirements

The Federal Reserve System has the power to set an amount, or percentage, of deposits that its member banks must keep in reserve at the Fed.[5] If the Fed raises its reserve requirements then banks have less money on hand and thus have less to lend. This lowers the amount of money in circulation and could have the impact of slowing the economy and inflation. Conversely if the Fed lowers the reserve requirements, banks have more money on hand, more to lend and more money goes into circulation, thus increasing spending and possibly inflation.

Changing the Discount Rate

One of the most important and publicly watched Fed actions, the discount rate is the interest rate that the Fed charges banks on money the banks borrow from the Fed[6]. Member banks borrow money from the Fed to pay out loans and other investments but they must pay a fee, the discount rate. The reason this can be done is that the Fed acts as the central bank and makes loans to other depository institutions. These institutions may borrow money from the Fed because they either have an unexpected drop in their member bank reserves or because they are faced with seasonal demands for loans.[7] The discount window is a teller's window at the Fed that depository institutions use to borrow member bank reserves. For a bank to obtain a loan, it must agree on the terms of the loan in advance. Next, the depository institution delivers collateral to the window. Then the loan is granted and appears as an increase in the institution's member account. Currently the Fed charges 5.3% and the banks charge 8.5%—10%. The Prime Lending Rate is the lowest rates banks are allowed to charge their customers. The Prime, as of December 31, is 8.5%.

If the Fed lowers the discount rate, banks are charged less for the money they borrow and thus more people borrow.[8] This increases the amount of money in circulation, speeds up the economy and increases inflation. Conversely, if the Fed raises the discount rate, this lowers the amount of money in circulation because fewer loans are extended as the Prime goes up. This slows the economy and lowers inflation.

Open Market Operations

Open Market Operations are the Fed's power to buy and sell government securities like T-Bills. The Fed uses Open Market Operations more than any other tool to regulate the economy. Most people do not pay attention to this less public action but it is very effective.

If the Fed buys back bonds it is putting money into circulation because the money is going from the government to the people. So if the government buys bonds it increases inflation. Selling bonds restricts the money supply. If we do this we can lower inflation rates.

Printing Money

Printing money is the simplest and most clear of all the Fed's operations. The government does not, as a matter of sound economic policy, print money or destroy money in order to effect changes in the economy. The power, however to do so, does exist. If the government prints money it increases the amount in circulation and if it destroys money it restricts the amount in circulation. This has a corresponding effect on inflation. To illustrate the possible negative effects of just printing more money to counter deflation, consider the case of the Weimar Republic in Germany during the Depression. To counter deflation and pay off reparations debts owed to France, Germany began to overprint money. This action caused hyperinflation. Germans saw the value of the Mark plummet as prices skyrocketed. Shoppers literally carried money in wheelbarrows. It was worthless.

New Words

depression	/dɪˈpreʃən/	n.	萧条，衰退
radically	/ˈrædɪkəli/	adv.	激进的
enact	/ɪˈnækt/	v.	制定，颁布
regulate	/ˈreɡjʊleɪt/	v.	管制
inflation	/ɪnˈfleɪʃən/	n.	通货膨胀
supply	/səˈplaɪ/	n.	供给
demand	/dɪˈmɑːnd/	n.	需求

circulation	/ˌsɜːkjʊˈleɪʃən/	n.	流通,循环
hike	/haɪk/	n.	大幅度增加,提高
shortfall	/ˈʃɔːtfɔːl/	n.	缺点,不足之处
pump	/pʌmp/	v.	抽出(注入)液体、气体等
circulate	/ˈsɜːkjʊleɪt/	v.	流通,循环
reserve	/rɪˈzɜːv/	n.	储备
tight	/taɪt/	adj.	紧缩的;严格的
loose	/luːs/	adj.	宽松的
conversely	/kənˈvɜːsli/	adv.	相反地
depository	/dɪˈpɒzɪtəri/	adj.	存款的,存储性的
teller	/ˈtelə/	n.	(银行)出纳员
collateral	/kəˈlætərəl/	n.	担保物,抵押品
sound	/saʊnd/	adj.	合理的
effect	/ɪˈfekt/	v.	引起,产生
hyperinflation	/ˌhaɪpərɪnˈfleɪʃən/	n.	极度通货膨胀,恶性通货膨胀
plummet	/ˈplʌmɪt/	v.	突然下降,大跌
wheelbarrow	/ˈwiːlˌbærəʊ/	n.	独轮手推车

Phrases

pump... into...	把……注入
shut down	关闭,停工,停业
thrive off	蓬勃发展
in circulation	在流通中
pay out	付出大笔款项,支付
pay off	还清,付清

Special Terms

Laissez Faire	自由放任
tax hike	税收大幅上升
tax cuts	税收降低
the New Deal	新政
government spending	政府支出
the Depression	大衰退
Federal Reserve System	联邦储备体制
reserve requirements	存款准备金要求
discount rate	贴现率

interest rate   利率
open market operations   公开市场操作
prime lending rate   基本利率
T-Bills (treasury bills)   国库券

Notes

1. So what we have to do is to find the proper balance between the amount of spending and money in circulation and an acceptable level of inflation.
   因此,我们应该在支出额和流通中的货币量与可接受的通货膨胀水平之间寻求一种适当的平衡。
   句中 find the proper balance between... 表示"在……与……之间寻求平衡"。

2. Knowledge of the New Deal is essential to understand the importance of government spending, as well as its shortfalls.
   对新政的了解对于理解政府支出的重要性和缺点至关重要。
   句中的 knowledge of... 表示"对……的了解,掌握"。

3. From an economic impact perspective that may not seem like much but now you have a human-interest issue.
   从经济影响的角度看,这也许不会产生什么大的影响,但是(减少为无家可归的人提供避难所)会成为一个有关人类权益的问题。

4. Those policies that restrict the money supply are known as "tight" and those that put more money into circulation are known as "loose."
   限制货币供应的政策是紧缩的货币政策,而将更多的货币投入到流通中的政策是宽松的货币政策。

5. The Federal Reserve System has the power to set an amount, or percentage, of deposits that its member banks must keep in reserve at the Fed.
   联邦储备体制有权设定其成员银行在联邦储备局储备的存款量或存款比例。

6. ... the discount rate is the interest rate that the Fed charges banks on money the banks borrow from the Fed.
   贴现率就是指银行向联邦储备局借款时,联邦储备局收取的利息率。

7. These institutions may borrow money from the Fed because they either have an unexpected drop in their member bank reserves or because they are faced with seasonal demands for loans.
   这些机构从联邦储备局贷款,或许是因为他们的成员银行中出现了意想不到的存款储备的下降,或许是因为他们面临着季节性的贷款需求。

8. If the Fed lowers the discount rate, banks are charged less for the money they borrow and thus more people borrow.

如果联邦储备局降低了贴现率,那么银行向联邦储备局支付的利息就会降低,因此会有更多的人从银行贷款。(由于银行向联邦储备局支付的利息减少,银行也会降低为他人提供贷款的利息率,因此会有更多的人向银行贷款。)

Exercises

I. Discuss the following questions.

1. For the government, what are the two major ways of regulating and ensuring the stability of the economy?
2. What are the effects of raising or lowering the taxes?
3. What are the effects of spending programs?
4. What are the possible results of changing reserve requirements?
5. What are open market operations? And what are the effects of open market operations?

II. Analyze the case below and discuss the question.

Applying Monetary and Fiscal Policies

When East Germany and West Germany were reunited in 1990, the West German government accepted the obligation to attempt to raise living standards in the eastern part of Germany rapidly. This required an immediate increase in government spending, in East German infrastructure, and in transfer payments to the residents of the former East Germany.

For political reasons, the German government did not want to raise taxes much.

Question:
Could you give some suggestions to the German government to increase its government spending without raising taxes much?

III. Match the terms in column A with the explanations in column B.

A	B
1. Laissez Faire	A. a bank regulation that sets the minimum reserves each bank must hold to customer deposits and notes
2. government spending	B. the lowest rate banks are allowed to charge their customers
3. discount rate	C. the cost of borrowing money expressed as a percentage of the capital borrowed
4. interest rate	D. government purchases financed by taxes or government borrowing

5. prime lending rate   E. the buying and selling of government securities in the open market in order to expand or contract the amount of money in banking systems

6. treasury bills   F. the rate of interest that the Fed charges banks on the money they borrow from the Fed

7. open market operations   G. an increase in the price of a basket of goods and services that is representative of the economy as a whole

8. inflation   H. a person who serves customers, keeps accounts and does other administrative work in a bank

9. bank teller   I. a bill of exchange issued by the central bank, to be repaid within a certain period of time

10. reserve requirements   J. policy of freedom from government control, especially for private commercial interests

IV. Fill in the blanks of the following sentences with the words or phrases given below. Make changes when necessary.

| regulate | plummet | pump | loose | circulate |
| enact | conversely | sound | collateral | initiate |

1. Although it is expected to rise, the price of crude oil will decline on the prospect of more oil _____ from Iraq.

2. In _____ the money supply, the Federal Reserve System uses the reserve requirements, open market operations and the discount rate.

3. An increase in government spending will increase aggregate demand and reduce the level of unemployment. _____, a decrease in government expenditure will work in a different way.

4. Buying securities will put more money into _____ and start to speed up the economy.

5. The bank is holding the deeds of our house as _____ for the loan.

6. It is hoped that the Board's _____ will bring the strike to an end and quell the employees' anxiety.

7. Thanks to the imports from China, the prices of household appliances have _____ in this area.

8. Because of the _____ of the new bill, the company expanded successfully into the food industry.

9. Low level of budget deficit and public debt or _____ public finance refers to a budget deficit no bigger than 3% of GDP and public debts no bigger than 60% of GDP.

10. The restrictions on imports from China have been _____ by the Parliament because of the huge potential of the Chinese market.

V. Put the following into English.

1. 控制货币供给的第二大政策工具
2. 充分就业和价格稳定
3. 扩张性货币政策
4. 紧缩性财政政策
5. 降低税率或提高公共投资
6. 使更多的货币进入流通领域
7. 对政府债券的买卖
8. 监督和管理商业银行
9. 制定并执行货币政策和财政政策
10. 发行债券以减少流通中的货币

VI. Translate the following sentences into English.

1. 如果一个国家不注意不断地改善自己的财政政策,就会招来许多麻烦,最终甚至会导致经济危机的发生。
2. 政府支出的增加会增加总需求并降低失业水平,相反地,政府支出的减少会减少总需求并因此降低就业水平。
3. 与政府支出不同的是,政府可以迅速调整税率,因此税率成为了短期内政府稳定财政政策的主要工具。
4. 由于贴现率的变化对货币供给造成的影响小于准备金率变化所产生的影响,因此,联储经常会运用这一工具来调整货币供给。
5. 中国政府执行稳健的货币政策和积极的财政政策,保证了中国经济健康、稳定的发展。

VII. Translate the following passage into Chinese.

The Federal Reserve has three main tools for maintaining control over the supply of money and credit in the economy. The most important is known as open market operations, or the buying and selling of government securities. To increase the supply of money, the Federal Reserve buys government securities from banks, other businesses, or individuals, paying for them with a check (a new source of money that it prints); when the Fed's checks are deposited in banks, they create new reserves—a portion of which banks can lend or invest, thereby increasing the amount of money in circulation. On the other hand, if the Fed wishes to reduce the money supply, it sells government securities to banks, collecting reserves from them. Because they have lower reserves, banks must reduce their lending, and the money supply drops accordingly.

Text

China's Monetary Policy in the Coming Years

Prevention and dissolution of financial risks and financial support to economic development have been the basic principles in the formulation of China's monetary policy. The moderately tight monetary policy pursued since 1993 was effective in containing inflation and bringing the economy to a soft landing. Responding to the deflationary tendency in the wake of 1997 Asian financial crisis, China adopted a proactive fiscal policy. On the monetary front, we have chosen a sound monetary policy, instead of a proactive one. There are several reasons for this choice. The state-owned enterprises were highly indebted and demand for lending was sluggish; commercial banks, weak in self-discipline, already had high NPLs ratios; moreover, the root cause of deflation was structural imbalances within the economy, not insufficient money supply. An overly expansionary policy against such a backdrop would do no good in addressing deflation, rather it would harm the soundness of economy.

A sound monetary policy is neither a conservative policy nor contraction in money supply. It includes the following active elements. First, there has been a moderate increase in money supply. In recent years, money growth has been 5 percentage points higher than the sum of economic growth rate and price changes. Second, the central bank has given guidance to commercial banks in loan portfolio adjustment. Since 1998, a total of 500 billion has been provided as house mortgage and other forms of consumer loan and more than one trillion *yuan*'s bank loan has been provided for fixed assets investment. Third, exchange rate stability has been maintained. Fourth, monetary policy transmission mechanism has been improved. The PBC abolished credit ceiling and switched to indirect monetary policy tools. Practices in past years have proved the correctness of sound monetary policy.

In the coming years, the PBC will strengthen regulations and supervision with a view to reducing NPLs ratio by 2–3 percentage points every year. At the same time, we will continue to support the economy to grow at 7% annually while preserving the value of RMB. Thus, the current monetary stance will not change. Our goal in the sound monetary policy is to prevent financial risks and provide greater financing support to the real economy.

As a macroeconomic policy, monetary policy deals with aggregate indicators. The current problem of commercial banks rich with deposit savings while small and medium enterprises complaining of no access to bank loans was caused by the deficiencies in enterprise operational mechanism. The solution to this problem lies in enterprise restructuring. The enterprises should improve their creditworthiness while banks should be more aggressive in marketing. We have set the monetary and credit objectives as the following. M2 and M1 are expected to grow by 13%, M0 within RMB150 billion *yuan*, and loan incremental of all financial institutions above RMB1.3 trillion *yuan*.

Improving Monetary Policy Mechanism

Looking ahead, market forces will be more effective in China and the financial sector will open up further. How to improve monetary policy mechanism to respond to these changes has become a pressing task.

First of all, what should be the intermediary objective? Like in many other countries, the goal of monetary policy in China is to preserve stability of the value of our currency and promote economic growth. In the past, we relied on credit ceiling as the major monetary policy tool. In 1996, money supply became the intermediary objective. As financial reform progresses, there has been more discussions on the choice of intermediary objective. Some people have questioned the fitness of money supply as such an objective. Since money supply is still closely related to output and price changes and can be adjusted through interest rates movements, central bank lending and open market operations, it is a proper intermediary objective for China at the current stage. Meanwhile, we shall also look at other indicators and make a study on the choice of intermediary objective in light of new developments, especially the leverage role of interest rates in macroeconomic adjustment.

Second, how should we coordinate local currency and foreign currency interest rates? The volume of capital inflow and outflow will grow as a result of China's WTO accession, hence, the interaction between foreign currency and RMB interest rates will be stronger. Nevertheless, RMB is yet fully convertible, and domestic consumption and investment remain the driving force in economic growth in China. There is, more often than not, a cyclical discrepancy between China and major industrial countries. In 1998, China cut interest rates in order to contain deflation while the US raised interest rates to reign in inflation. Therefore, China needs to have an independent interest rate policy for a rather long time to come. While foreign currency rates shall move along with international market rates, the RMB interest rates will have to follow domestic economic developments. This may give rise to arbitrage. But giving up an independent policy in RMB interest will clearly do a greater harm than arbitrage.

We shall proceed steadily with interest rates liberalization. The first step is to increase the band by setting a minimum lending rate or a ceiling for deposit rates. Secondly, open market operation will have a larger role to play. By the end of 2001, the total of treasury bonds, financial bonds, commercial bank papers and corporate bonds issuance almost reached 4 trillion *yuan*. The central bank is better placed to engage in bond transactions to make adjustments in money supply and affect market interest rates.

Third, keep a close eye on asset prices fluctuations and support the healthy development of capital market. With their real asset liability ratio being around 75%, a large number of Chinese industrial enterprises are not qualified to get loans. Between 1992 and now, capital raised in stock market since 1992 by industrial and commercial enterprises amounted to RMB770 billion *yuan*, while bank loans reached RMB8.6 trillion *yuan*, reflecting a heavy reliance on bank financing by the enterprises. Household savings are deposited in commercial banks due to lack of direct investment tools. Commercial banks, however, have difficulties in finding qualified customers in enterprises. Such a financing structure is not only wasting fund to some extend, but also making it difficult for monetary policy to be transmitted from commercial banks to industrial and commercial enterprises. Therefore, it is necessary for the central bank to give special consideration to stock market development in the formulation of monetary policy, give qualified institutional investors access to inter-bank lending market and allow securities firms to get securities collateralized loans.

Strengthening Financial Supervision and Promoting Bank Reforms

Efficient mobilization of savings in the form of deposits and reallocation thereof among regions, sectors and enterprises are made possible through bank intermediation. In 1998, the PBC replaced credit ceiling with indirect monetary policy instruments such as interest rates. However, due to multi-levels in management and operation, branches of wholly state-owned commercial banks are not so efficient to respond to supply and demand changes in fund allocation, thus blocking the transmission of monetary policy. The domestic commercial banks will face great challenges when foreign banks are granted national treatment in 2006.

Reforms of wholly state-owned commercial banks must be further accelerated. The focus here is how to transform wholly state-owned commercial banks into financial institutions that operate on a truly commercial basis and improve their liquidity, safety and profitability. Efforts should be made in improving corporate governance and enhancing internal control and performance. Prudential accounting, five-category loan classification standard as well as loan loss provisioning and writing-off will be implemented. NPLs ratio of wholly state-owned commercial banks shall be reduced by three percentage points every year. Capital adequacy will be increased to international standards through government funds injection and ownership reform on the basis of lowering risky assets and internal control. Commercial banks will be also urged to disclose their 2001 operational information in June this year. Overall, efforts have to be taken in recent years to increase the competitiveness of wholly state-owned commercial banks and create a favorable environment for the conduct of monetary policy.

Maintaining RMB Exchange Rate Stability and Gradually Promoting RMB Convertibility

China adopted the managed floating exchange rate regime in 1994. The nominal RMB to dollar exchange rate appreciated five percent, and real exchange rate appreciated 30 percent in the past seven years. Long-term stability of RMB exchange rate is conducive to stability and economic growth in China, in Asia and the world at large. China's official foreign exchange reserves have grown to USD223.5 billion by the end of February this year, an increase of USD11.2 billion compared with the end of 2001. At present, the over supply in China's foreign exchange market is based on foreign exchange control. The RMB is not likely to come under excessive upward pressure if the pent-up demand for foreign exchange is gradually released. Confronted with the challenges of our WTO membership, we will improve the RMB exchange rate mechanism and increase the floating band appropriately.

Foreign Direct Investment (FDI), total external debts and external financing by enterprises totaled USD600 billion by the end of 2001. At the same time, the sum of official foreign exchange reserves, net foreign assets of financial institutions and corporate sector overseas investment topped USD350 billion. We are in a new stage of foreign capital utilization. Overseas investment is increasing while massive capital inflow continues. As a result of WTO accession, intensified international capital movement will increase the pressure on capital account convertibility.

China has made RMB convertibility an objective since 1993. In recent years, the RMB has been accepted not only in Hong Kong and Macau of China but also in neighboring countries. Some money exchanges in developed countries handle RMB exchange too. In addition to solid national economic strength, full convertibility of the Chinese currency will require a strong macroeconomic management capacity, a sound banking system and a viable real sector. China is yet to achieve these. Recent financial crises have manifested the importance of a prudent approach in capital account liberalization. We will follow a gradual and prudent approach.

Answer the following questions:
1. What are the active elements of a sound monetary policy?
2. What should be the intermediary objective of monetary policy in China?
3. How should we coordinate local currency and foreign currency interest rates?
4. How will China proceed steadily with interest rate liberalization?
5. What is the focus of reforms of wholly state-owned commercial banks?

Unit 14

International Corporate Governance

Learning Objectives

Text A
- to learn the function and composition of corporate governance
- to understand the elements that make good corporate governance

Text B
- to understand the efforts of the Chinese government to establish a modern corporate governance system
- to learn the strategic transformation of SOEs during the process of China's bid to establish a modern corporate governance

Text A

International Corporate Governance

Corporate governance is the set of mechanisms—both institutional and market-based—that induce the self-interested controllers of a company (those that make decisions regarding how the company will be operated) to make decisions that maximize the value of the company to its owners (the suppliers of capital). Or, to put it another way: "Corporate governance deals with the ways in which suppliers of finance to corporations assure themselves of getting a return on their investment."[1]

The governance mechanisms that have been most extensively studied in the US can be broadly characterized as being either internal or external to the firm. The internal mechanisms of primary interest are the board of directors and the equity ownership structure of the firm. The primary external mechanisms are the external market for corporate control (the takeover market) and the legal/regulatory system.

Internal Governance Mechanisms

Boards of Directors

Corporations in most countries of the world have boards of directors. In the U.S., the board of directors is specifically charged with representing the interests of shareholders. The board exists primarily to hire, fire, monitor, and compensate management, all with an eye towards maximizing shareholder value.[2] While the board is an effective corporate governance mechanism in theory, in practice its value is less clear. Boards of directors in the US include some of the very insiders who are to be monitored; in some cases they (or parties sympathetic to them) represent a majority of the board. In addition, it is not uncommon that the CEO is also the chairperson of the board. Finally, the nature of the selection process for board members is such that management often has a strong hand in determining who the other members will be.[3] The primary board-related issues that have been studied in the US are board composition and executive compensation. Board composition characteristics of interest include the size and structure of the board: the number of directors that comprise the board, the fraction of these directors that are outsiders, and whether the CEO and chairperson positions are held by the same individual.[4] Executive compensation research is fundamentally concerned with the degree to which managers are compensated in ways that align their interests with those of their companies' shareholders.

Ownership Structure

Ownership and control are rarely completely separated within any firm. The controllers frequently have some degree of ownership of the equity of the firms they control; while some owners, by virtue of the size of their equity positions, effectively have some control over the firms they own. Thus, ownership structure (i.e. the identities of a firm's equity holders and the sizes of their positions) is a potentially important element of corporate governance.[5]

It is reasonable to presume that greater overlap between ownership and control should lead to a reduction in conflicts of interests and, therefore, to higher firm value. The relationships between ownership, control, and firm value are more complicated than that, however. Ownership by a company's management, for example, can serve to better align managers' interests with those of the company's shareholders. However, to the extent that managers' and shareholders' interests are not fully aligned, higher equity ownership can provide managers with greater freedom to pursue their own objectives without fear of reprisal; i.e, it can entrench managers.[6] Thus, the ultimate effect of managerial ownership on firm value depends upon the trade-off between the alignment and entrenchment effects.

Shareholders other than management can potentially influence the actions taken by management. The problem in the typical US corporation, with its widely-dispersed share ownership, is that individual shareholders own very small fractions of an individual firm's shares and, therefore, have little or no incentive to expend significant resources to monitor managers or seek to influence decision-making within the firm. Moreover, the free-rider problem reduces the incentives for these disparate shareholders to coordinate their actions. However, individual shareholders who have more significant ownership positions have greater incentives to expend resources to monitor and influence managers.

As with ownership by managers, ownership by outside blockholders is not an unequivocally positive force from the perspective of the other shareholders. Blockholders can use their influence such that management is more likely to make decisions that increase overall shareholder value. These are the shared benefits of control, i.e, blockholders exercise them but all shareholders benefit from them. However, there are private benefits of control as well—benefits available only to blockholders.

These private benefits can be innocuous from the perspective of other shareholders, e.g., a blockholder may simply enjoy the access to powerful people that comes from being a major shareholder. However, if blockholders use their control to extract corporate resources, the private benefits they receive will lead to reductions in the value of the firm to the other shareholders. Thus, the ultimate effect of blockholder ownership on measured firm value depends upon the trade-off between the shared benefits of blockholder control and any private extraction of firm value by blockholders.

In many countries of the world, the government is a significant owner of corporations. Government ownership represents an interesting hybrid of dispersed and concentrated ownership. If we view the government as a single entity, state-owned corporations have very concentrated ownership.[7] Unlike private blockholders, however, government ownership is funded with money that ultimately belongs to the state as a whole and not to the individuals within the government that influence the actions of the firm. In this regard, the ultimate ownership of state-owned companies is, in fact, quite dispersed. Over time, there has been a trend away from state ownership of corporate assets. The conversion from state to private ownership, termed privatization, provides an interesting setting in which to examine the effects of ownership on firm performance.

External Governance Mechanisms

The Takeover Market

When internal control mechanisms fail to a large enough degree—i.e., when the gap between the actual value of a firm and its potential value is sufficiently negative—there is an incentive for outside parties to seek control of the firm. The market for corporate control in the US has been very active. Changes in the control of firms virtually always occur at a premium, thereby creating value for the target firm's shareholders.[8] Furthermore, the mere threat of a change in control can provide management with incentives to keep firm value high, so that the value gap is not large enough to warrant an attack from the outside. Thus, the takeover market has been an important governance mechanism in the US.

As with other potential corporate governance mechanisms, however, the takeover market has its dark side for shareholders. In addition to being a potential solution to the manager/shareholder agency problem, it can be a manifestation of this problem.

Managers interested in maximizing the size of their business empires can waste corporate resources by overpaying for acquisitions rather than returning cash to the shareholders.

The Legal/Regulatory System

In "Law and Finance" (1998) LaPorta, Lopez-de-Silanes, Shleifer, and Vishny (LLSV), they hypothesize that the extent to which a country's laws protect investor rights—and the extent to which those laws are enforced—are fundamental determinants of the ways in which corporate finance and corporate governance evolve in that country. Their empirical evidence indicates that there are significant differences across countries in the degree of investor protection, and that countries with low investor protection are generally characterized by high concentration of equity ownership within firms and a lack of significant public equity markets. That highly concentrated ownership as LLSV suggested, leads to an equity agency conflict between dominant shareholders and minority shareholders.

Based on the above, the elements of effective corporate governance will include the following:

The board and management of companies should, as a mark of good corporate management, take into account the realities of the contemporary multilateral governance relationships between firms, state and civil society and as such, pilot the affairs of the company within the legal corporate framework prevalent in any particular state and promote accountability to the shareholders but "properly address the concerns of other legitimate stakeholders." By so doing, companies will avert the destructive campaigns and demonstrations of a civil society. However, it is not intended to suggest that companies will engage in all social and political responsibilities, but since their products are directed at civil society (customers), companies should engage in legitimate social responsibilities, such as ensuring that the health and safety of their employees and customers are "respected and not recklessly jeopardised." It is in this direction that the OECD principles of corporate governance provide that good corporate governance is a matter of concern of and for the people.[9] It is vital to the wellbeing and the welfare of not only the "owners" and "shareholders" of the companies, but the workers and the people of the society as a whole.

Secondly, transparency, effective communication and accountability should be the underlying value within the strategies of corporate governance. Board and management should ensure the confidence of investors without which the reputation of the corporation will soil, and promote external takeover bidders. As Sheriden, T and Kendall, N succinctly describe, that "effective governance for Mr... involves him improving communications between himself, the investors, and the managers, so to gain a better understanding of management's strategy and business aims... [thereby] making a better fist of building long-term shareholder value than the bidding company."

It is therefore suggested that good corporate governance should be that which the management structure is designed to run in a transparent way to enhance the trust of the stakeholders. There should be an open and equitable relationship between the management, the board and the shareholders. All shareholders of the same share-weight must be accorded the same treatment. Much as well, as emphasised by the OECD principle, the corporation should be run to support society, it must be geared toward the heart and mind of society. So the system whereby the shareholders' interest and profit maximisation are the primary concern of the company and keeps everybody else out, cannot, it is considered, withstand the present global civil society volatility. There should be a way of enhancing good corporate practice, ensuring moderation between the company corporate objectives with the "necessary" social realities of the community. This has been the bane of social unrest of civil society against most companies of developed countries' origin operating in developing countries.[10] Corporate governance should not be run to exploit the community.

New Words

accord	/əˈkɔːd/	v.	给予
accountability	/əˌkaʊntəˈbɪlɪti/	n.	责任
agency	/ˈeɪdʒənsi/	n.	代理处,经销处
align	/əˈlaɪn/	v.	联合,与……一致
alignment	/əˈlaɪnmənt/	n.	联合
avert	/əˈvɜːt/	v.	转移
bane	/beɪn/	n.	毒药,祸害
blockholder	/ˈblɒkhəʊldə/	n.	大股东
CEO	/ˌsiːiːˈəʊ/	n.	首席执行官
chairperson	/ˈtʃeəˌpɜːsən/	n.	董事长
compensate	/ˈkɒmpənseɪt/	v.	酬报
conversion	/kənˈvɜːʃən/	n.	转换,转变
corporate	/ˈkɔːpərɪt/	adj.	公司的,法人的
determinant	/dɪˈtɜːmɪnənt/	n.	决定性因素
disparate	/ˈdɪspərɪt/	adj.	不同的,异类的
disperse	/dɪˈspɜːs/	v.	(使)分散
empirical	/ɪmˈpɪrɪkəl/	adj.	完全根据经验的,经验主义的
entrench	/ɪnˈtrentʃt/	v.	确立,是处于牢固地位
entrenchment	/ɪnˈtrentʃmənt/	n.	确立
equitable	/ˈekwɪtəbəl/	adj.	公平的,公正的
exercise	/ˈeksəsaɪz/	v.	运用,行使
expend	/ɪkˈspend/	v.	花费,消费

extract	/ɪkˈstrækt/	v.	得到，提取
fist	/fɪst/	n.	抓住，抓牢
fraction	/ˈfrækʃən/	n.	（小）部分
free-rider	/ˈfriːˌraɪdə/	n.	免费搭乘的人，不劳而获者，无本获利者
governance	/ˈɡʌvənəns/	n.	管理，统治
hybrid	/ˈhaɪbrɪd/	n.	杂交种，混合物，合成物
hypothesize	/haɪˈpɒθəsaɪz/	v.	假设，假定，猜测
innocuous	/ɪˈnɒkjuəs/	adj.	无害的，不得罪人的
insider	/ɪnˈsaɪdə/	n.	内部人士
institutional	/ˌɪnstɪˈtjuːʃənəl/	adj.	机构的
jeopardise	/ˈdʒepədaɪz/	v.	使受危险，危及
manifestation	/ˌmænɪfeˈsteɪʃən/	n.	表现，表明
maximize	/ˈmæksɪmaɪz/	v.	使……最大化
moderation	/ˌmɒdəˈreɪʃən/	n.	适度
monitor	/ˈmɒnɪtə/	v.	监管
overlap	/ˈəʊvəˈlæp/	n.	（两个或两个以上东西的）重叠，互搭
performance	/pəˈfɔːməns/	n.	表现，业绩
pilot	/ˈpaɪlət/	v.	引导
privatization	/ˌpraɪvətaɪˈzeɪʃən/	n.	私有化
regulatory	/ˌreɡjʊˈleɪtəri/	adj.	规范的
reprisal	/rɪˈpraɪzəl/	n.	报复
set	/set/	n.	（一）套
setting	/ˈsetɪŋ/	n.	环境，背景
share-weight	/ʃeə weɪt/		股份比重
soil	/sɔɪl/	v.	损坏，玷污
succinctly	/səkˈsɪŋktli/	adv.	简洁地，简便地
takeover	/ˈteɪkˌəʊvə/	n.	接管
term	/tɜːm/	v.	把……称为
trade-off	/treɪd ɒf/	n.	平衡，协调
transparency	/trænˈspærənsi/	n.	透明度
underlying	/ˌʌndəˈlaɪɪŋ/	adj.	根本的，潜在的
unequivocally	/ˌʌnɪˈkwɪvəkəli/	adv.	意思明确地
volatility	/ˌvɒləˈtɪlɪti/	n.	不稳定性，多变性
warrant	/ˈwɒrənt/	v.	使……有正当理由

Phrases

at a premium	（股票）溢价，超过面值的价格
be charged with	对……负有责任

by virtue of	因为，由于，凭借
from the perspective of	从……角度来看
to align... with...	把……与……联合起来
to have a strong hand in	对……有很大的支配权
with an eye towards	目的是……

Special Terms

board of directors	董事会
corporate governance	公司治理
OECD	经合，经济合作与发展组织
equity ownership	股权所有
ownership structure	所有权结构

Notes

1. Corporate governance deals with the ways in which suppliers of finance to corporations assure themselves of getting a return on their investment.
   公司治理是有关公司的资金供应方为保证其投资回报所采用的方法。

2. The board exists primarily to hire, fire, monitor, and compensate management, all with an eye towards maximizing shareholder value.
   董事会的职责主要是：聘任、解雇、监管和补偿管理人员，以期股东价值的最大化。

3. Finally, the nature of the selection process for board members is such that management often has a strong hand in determining who the other members will be.
   最终，董事会成员的遴选程序就导致管理层经常能极大地掌控其他董事会成员的任命权。

4. Board composition characteristics of interest include the size and structure of the board: the number of directors that comprise the board, the fraction of these directors that are outsiders, and whether the CEO and chairperson positions are held by the same individual.
   我们所关注的董事会构成特性包括董事会的大小与结构，即：组成董事会的董事数量、董事为局外人的比例，以及首席执行官和董事长是否由同一人担当。

5. Thus, ownership structure (i.e. the identities of a firm's equity holders and the sizes of their positions) is a potentially important element of corporate governance.
   因此，所有权结构（即：公司股权所有者的身份和职务高低）就成为公司治理的一个潜在重要的因素。

6. However, to the extent that managers' and shareholders' interests are not fully aligned, higher equity ownership can provide managers with greater freedom to pursue their own objectives without fear of reprisal; i.e. it can entrench managers.

   但是,如果经理和股东的利益没有充分联合起来,股权所有越大,经理就有更大的自由去达到他们的目标,无需担心报复,也就是说,更大的股权所有会确立经理的牢固地位。

7. If we view the government as a single entity, state-owned corporations have very concentrated ownership.

   如果我们把政府看作是一个独立的实体,那么国有企业的所有权就非常集中了。

8. Changes in the control of firms virtually always occur at a premium, thereby creating value for the target firm's shareholders.

   企业的管控变更通常发生在企业的股价超出面值时,因此给目标企业的股东创造了价值。

9. It is in this direction that the OECD principles of corporate governance provide that good corporate governance is a matter of concern of and for the people.

   为此目标,OECD(经合组织)关于公司治理的原则中就规定:好的公司治理就是要关注民生,服务民意。

   句中 in... direction 表示"为了……的目的",provide 意为"规定"。

10. This has been the bane of social unrest of civil society against most companies of developed countries' origin operating in developing countries.

    这已造成了民间社会动荡的恶果,不利于大多数发达国家在发展中国家建立的公司的运作。

    句中 social unrest 指的是"社会动荡";句中 civil society 意为"民间社会"。

Exercises

I. Discuss the following questions.

1. What is corporate governance?
2. What are the major responsibilities of the board of directors?
3. What are the common problems with the board of directors in the US?
4. What is the trend in the ownership structure?
5. What comprises good corporate governance?

II. Analyze the case below and discuss the question.

In the US, deficiencies in governance structures often resulted in extreme battles for corporate control, battles that, more often than not, proved destructive—for companies, employees and shareholders. This degree of conflict led to loss of jobs and misallocation of capital, and forced sacrifices in vital areas such as R&D. Many takeover attempts were warded off by tactical means that were even worse—poison pills and scorched earth defenses, and loading up on too much debt, putting the corporation's very survival at risk. The best way we can avoid coming to such a pass is to pre-empt it, by having an adequate corporate governance framework in the first place.

> **Question:**
> Based on the knowledge you get from the text, analyze the above US case and state its implication for sound corporate governance.

III. Match the terms in column A with the explanations in column B.

A	B
1. corporate	A. an act of gaining control of a company, by buying most of its shares
2. finance	B. having the power to make and carry out decisions, especially in business
3. equity	C. belonging to or related to a corporation
4. takeover	D. something that has a single, separate and independent existence
5. executive	E. responsibility
6. management	F. money provided by a bank or other organizations to help run a business
7. incentive	G. the equal parts into which the ownership of a company is divided, on which no fixed interest is paid
8. entity	H. the people in charge of a firm or organization
9. accountability	I. a person's general comfort, good health, and happiness
10. welfare	J. an encouragement to do something

IV. Fill in the blanks of the following sentences with the words or phrases given below. Make changes when necessary.

charge	assessment	outsider	election	setting
commitment	enhance	characteristics	manager	represent

1. Jensen (1993) acknowledges the legal system as a corporate governance mechanism but _____ it as being too blunt an instrument to deal effectively with the agency problems between managers and shareholders.
2. Our company recognizes the importance of corporate governance for the effective management of the company and is _____ to leadership in corporate governance.
3. Corporate governance is the system by which companies are _____ and directed.

4. The Board takes an active role in setting policies for the company and overseeing the management of the company's business and affairs. Board members are _____ by the company's shareholders each year at the annual general meeting of shareholders.

5. In _____ their responsibilities, the directors owe some fiduciary duties to the company.

6. The Board has adopted a Board Charter that, among other things, _____ out the responsibilities of the Board.

7. The company provides continuing education opportunities for all directors so that they can maintain or _____ their knowledge and understanding of the business of the company.

8. The Board regularly _____ its own effectiveness and the contribution of each Board committee and director.

9. The Corporate Governance Committee assists the Board in fulfilling its responsibilities with respect to the composition and _____ of the Board and Board committees as well as corporate governance standards and practice.

10. Higher proportion of _____ directors are not associated with superior firm performance, but are associated with better decisions concerning such issues as acquisitions, executive compensation, and CEO turnover.

V. Put the following into English.

1. 股东、公司董事、管理人员及当地的利益相关者
2. 将国有产业的所有权从政府手里转给普通民众
3. 公司治理中透明、负责、问责及公正的价值观
4. 政府决策人员具体参与公司治理
5. 董事会的职责是管理或指导公司业务
6. 首席执行官协调和主持公司管理工作
7. 董事必须具有独立性
8. 改善董事会的运作质量
9. 投资者保护
10. 股权分散

VI. Translate the following sentences into English.

1. 一国的公司治理制度包括正式和非正式的规章、惯例以及民营和政府的执法机制等。
2. 很多国家今天面临的主要挑战不是如何制定更完善的公司治理法律和规定——很多国家现在已有成文的规定——而是如何有效地执行这些法规。
3. 建立一个有法律授权、政治上独立和经费充足的司法体系对于加强公司治理、提高公司业绩和国家长期经济增长至关重要。
4. 公司治理框架应该促进市场的透明度和有效性,与法律规定相协调,并阐明监管、规范和实施权力的责任分工。

5. 公司治理框架应确保对公司的战略性指导、董事会对管理层的有效监督以及公司和股东对董事会的问责权。

VII. Translate the following passage into Chinese.

The board of supervisors is an indispensable corporate body in the Chinese corporate governance structure. Pursuant to the Corporate Law, supervisors shall perform the following duties: (1) examine corporate financial affairs; (2) supervise directors and executives' breaches of statutes or memorandum of associations in performing their duties; (3) demand that directors and executives redress their misconduct damaging the corporate interest; (4) propose special meetings of the shareholders; and (5) other duties as stipulated in the memorandum of associations. Supervisors also have the power to audit the board of directors' meeting. The board of supervisors includes shareholder representatives and certain employee representatives, with the percentage of representation of each group to be stipulated in the memorandum of association. The employee representatives are elected by the corporate employees in democratic elections. In order to secure the impartiality of supervisors, "directors, executives or financial officers may not concurrently serve as supervisors."

Text B

Corporate Governance in China

Overview

After 20 years of exploring gradual reform, Chinese enterprises have come to realize that the corporate governance is the center of the enterprise reform in China. The Fourth Plenum of the Chinese Communist Party's 15th Central Committee held in September 1999 adopted a decision that calls for "strategic adjustment" of the state sector by withdrawing what should be withdrawn. This decision identifies corporate governance as the core of the modern enterprise system. Since then, China has made significant progress in developing the foundations of a modern corporate governance system. More than 1200 companies have diversified their ownership through public listing. 80 percent of small and medium sized firms have been transformed into non-state-owned enterprises. A basic legal framework has been established. However, there is vast scope for further institution building to improve the corporate governance practice of Chinese enterprises.

Most listed companies in China were reformed state-owned enterprises in which holding shareholders control the shareholders' general meeting and the board of directors is an outstanding problem, with the board serving basically as the agency of major shareholders. Directors are mainly nominated by major shareholders and elected to the board by the shareholders' general meeting. The board highly overlaps management, and "control by insiders" is a widespread problem among China's listed companies. This governance structure enables holding shareholders to cause large numbers of connected deals to take place between a listed company and themselves by manipulating the shareholders general meeting and the board, at the expense of the interests of the company and medium-sized and small shareholders. The host of problems exposed in the process of development of the securities market prompted Chinese authorities to put revamping the juristic-person governance structure of listed companies on the agenda.

The first Chinese Corporation Law was enacted in January 1904, during the late Qing Dynasty. When the new China was founded in 1949, business corporations gradually disappeared. This was due to importation of the highly centralized economy model from the former Soviet Union. In the late 1970s, China started to introduce a market economy, SOEs were redefined as business corporations, and private corporations were incorporated.

Among other things, the traditional Chinese SOE governance system was one of the major built-in institutional obstacles hindering profit-maximization at enterprise levels. In the period of the planned economy, SOEs were treated as a branch of government, and enterprise governance was nothing more than a part of the general system of government. The purpose of SOEs was thus to fulfill the production plans of the government agencies, not profit-maximization. SOE managers became accountable to government agencies rather than to the market. The SOE leaders were in essence government officials in terms of their responsibility toward their supervising government agencies, their official ranking and their promotion.

SOE Governance Reform

The traditional enterprise governance regime is not compatible with the market economy that China is in the midst of developing. For instance, most traditional SOE leaders are likely to be loyal to their supervising government agencies and lack the expertise and experience needed to operate the SOE business in a competitive environment. The transition from the planned economy to a market economy requires reformation of the composition and function of SOE governance.

Chinese policy and law makers have been struggling in their efforts to determine the optimal corporate governance model for Chinese SOEs. At first, Chinese SOEs were granted more autonomous powers, and SOE leaders were given more authority to manage SOEs with a view toward profit maximization. These legislative objectives are reflected in the SOEs Law of 1988 and the implementing regulations of 1992. However, with general managers lacking any meaningful checks and balances from other interest groups within the SOE governance structure, it is not surprising that these leaders began to misuse their power. Compared with the traditional governance structure of SOEs in the period of the planned economy, the transitional governance structure of SOEs was even worse. The transitional SOE leaders had more managerial powers than their predecessors, as well as more resources, thereby facilitating embezzlement and misuse. Moreover, this period also included unnecessary and excessive government interventions. In addition, government agencies did not understand that their role as a shareholder of a business corporation was different than their role as a government agency. There were also no predictable or feasible institutional norms established to govern the relationship among government agencies, SOE leaders and other constituencies, such as employees. In short, the transitional governance structure represented a creative yet unsuccessful effort to restructure the SOE governance regime.

In addition to frequently reported managerial corruption, the SOE governance regime was also marked by unsatisfactory financial performance. As indicated in a report of the China Enterprise Evaluation Association, the efficiency of China's top 500 industrial enterprises was much lower than the top 500 global companies. The average ratio of profits to assets of the Chinese enterprises was 2.78%, compared to 11.29% for global companies in 1988. The per capita income for Chinese enterprises was $27,456 (in USD) while their global counterparts enjoyed a per capita income of $288,855 (in USD) during the same period. In another example, the average total assets and sales revenues of China's top 500 industrial enterprises in 1998 was $711.6 million and $398.1 million (in USD), respectively, accounting for a mere 0.88% and 1.74% of the top 500 global companies. Although there are other factors contributing to this poor financial performance of SOEs, unsuccessful SOE governance played a substantially negative role.

In light of the shortcomings within both its traditional and transitional governance structures, China has begun to look to the successful corporate governance role models in market economies and has begun implementing some common corporate governance norms (including general meeting of shareholders, board of directors and board of supervisors). In his government working report before the NPC on March 5, 2000, Premier Zhu Rongji promised that the "Chinese government will actively encourage multinational corporations to participate [in] the restructuring and transformation of SOEs." Multinational corporations will be able to acquire State shares in the future. More liberalized policies are expected to attract foreign investors to enter the Chinese securities market after China enters the WTO.

Regulatory System

Since the beginning of 2000, the China Securities Regulatory Commission (CSRC) has adopted serials of measures with regard to the improvement of the corporate governance structure of listed companies.

First, CSRC has formulated the basic norms of corporate governance so that listed companies can follow the rules; secondly, CSRC issued "Guide to the Establishment of Independent Directors System" with the aim of standardizing the operations of the board of directors. Each listed company should at least have one-third independent directors, who will play their role in related trading, nomination of directors, remuneration and appointment and dismissal. With regards to standardizing the relations between controlling shareholders and listed companies, the CSRC has promoted the separation of listed companies from controlling shareholders in personnel, assets and financial affairs.

In addition to that, the CSRC has formulated a "Guide to Articles of Association of Listed Companies," "Standardization of Shareholders' Meeting" in an attempt to standardize the operation of the shareholders' meeting, the boards of directors and the boards of supervisors. The CSRC has also adopted a series of measures concerning the accounting norms and accounting services and standardizing the operations of listed companies. For companies that cannot realize internationalization in accounting norms due to legal problems, the CSRC has raised the standards for information disclosure. In 2000, the CSRC formulated the standards for the listing of financial institutions, according to the international standards, as well as strengthened regulation of accountants and accountants' offices engaging in securities business and made open criticisms of accountants and accountants' offices that violated the law and regulation and punished them more severely.

In order to improve the quality of listed companies, CSRC has strengthened examination at the time of listing and provided advance demand and guidance concerning standard operations and strengthened regulation after they are listed. Special measures that have been adopted are:

Establishing an examination system of listed companies. In 2001, CSRC issued the rules on the examination of listed companies, which provide that one-third of the newly listed companies would be checked every year, chiefly on their governance structure, financial affairs, the use of money raised and the operation of information disclosure. At the same time, it has carried out special checks on major risks reflected in complaints from investors and exposed by the media and the problems discovered during routine operations. The companies subject to checks are required to submit correction reports and reveal them openly. The commissioned organizations are required to review the correction results of the companies subject to checkups. It has introduced the system of talks with chairman of the board of listed companies. If serious problems are found during checkups, the companies concerned would receive internal criticism or open criticism according to the seriousness of the cases. If any company is found to have violated the regulations, CSRC will put it on file for investigation. If a case is serious enough, it would be handed over to the judicial organs for criminal investigation.

Introducing the classified management of listed companies. CSRC is introducing the classified management system, that is, to carry out classified regulation on the basis of making a comprehensive analysis and assessment of the operational risks and information disclosure risks. The dispatched organizations are required to fix the responsibilities on every person to monitor the listed companies in their respective jurisdiction.

Establishing a quick response mechanism. CSRC has introduced a quick response information regulation system, which will review the information from various media or submitted by dispatched organizations so as to discover problems and handle them timely.

The withdrawal system for listed companies. In March 2001, CSRC promulgated the rules on the implementation of suspending and terminating the listed companies that suffer losses. In April 23 and June 23, 2001, CSRC terminated the trading of the stocks of PT Shuixian and PT Jinman. Rules on the delisting of companies that committed major irregularities are also in the works.

Corporatization reform will not, however, be successful without sound corporate governance. It is necessary for Chinese policy makers to consider the corporate governance structure as the core of the corporate system and clarify the duties of the various corporate actors, such as the shareholders, the board of directors, the board of supervisors and the executives. It is hoped that by eliminating excessive governmental control, ensuring the government's interest as an investor, and effectively holding the management accountable, Chinese SOEs will become more successful and attractive to foreign investors.

Good corporate governance in China, however, will not result from mere changes in the Corporate or Securities Laws. Good corporate governance will also depend heavily upon the successful reform of government agencies and the legal system.

Answer the following questions:
1. When did China begin to identify corporate governance as the core of the modern enterprise system?
2. What is the widespread problem among China's listed companies?
3. How did China's enterprises evolve through history?
4. What are the gradual changes of governance regime in China's SOEs?
5. What are the efforts of China's CSRC to improve corporate governance of the listed companies?

Unit 15

Human Resources Management

Learning Objectives

Text A
- to know the definition of human resources management and learn the whole process of the human resources management and the possible challenges that the human resources management may face in the future

Text B
- to understand how the job is terminated and the kinds of job termination

Text A

Human Resources Management

The last two decades have seen a marked change in human resources management, the process of acquiring, deploying, and developing people for organizational success. Each of the three words in this key term reflects a separate change in the field. No longer can companies afford to look at people as a commodity to be exploited to exhaustion and then discarded.[1] In today's organizations employees are viewed as human resources that need to be carefully nurtured, accommodated and developed. Human resources management involves the following process:

- ❖ human resources planning
- ❖ the employment process
- ❖ evaluating and developing job performance
- ❖ compensation and benefits

Human Resources Planning

Imagine you had the task of finding 3,000 employees for a brand-new automobile assembly plant. That is precisely the challenge Toyota motor Company faced in 1987 while its new factory was being built in Georgetown, Kentucky. This situation dramatizes the need for human resources planning, the systematic process of forecasting the future demand for employees and estimating the supply available to meet that demand.[2] Employees represent a substantial investment, and their employment and redeployment requires as much planning as for other assets.

Forecasting demand Human resources planners consider both internal and external factors when forecasting a firm's demand for workers. Internal factors include possible shifts in goods or services, planned expansions or contractions in operations, purchases of new equipment, and likely personnel changes such as retirements and leaves of absence.[3] Perhaps the most important external factor to consider in planning for workers is the state of the nation's economy. Rising or falling interest rates, for example, can affect a firm's sales and hence its demand for human resources. Other important external factors include government regulations, technological changes, and the level of competition a firm faces.

Estimating the supply of workers Forecasting the supply of workers available from within a company requires estimating how many current workers are qualified to move into anticipated vacancies.[4] The human resources department also needs to assess production schedules and budgets. Equal Employment Opportunity goals, and possible relations, plant choosing, turnover and absenteeism rates, and transfers within a firm.

Planning to meet needs After the human resources specialists have forecast the demand and supply of personnel, they develop a plan to assure a work force appropriate for the company. If they anticipate a greater demand than the supply available, their plan will focus on attracting new employees. If, on the other hand, they see supply exceeding demand, they will plan for a reduction of the work force.

Job analysis Hiring, training, and evaluating employees is a lot easier when both the employer and the prospective employee know precisely what a job entails. The information should come from a job analysis, a systematic study of each employee's duties, tasks and work environment.

The Employment Process

The procedure by which a firm matches its hiring needs with the available human resources is the employment process. It includes recruitment, the process of attracting qualified people to apply for the job; selection, the identification of appropriate candidates; and orientation, the systematic introduction of new employees to their new organization, job,

and coworkers. At any point in this procedure, the employer may determine that its needs and the job applicant's do not match and reject the application. Applicant may also withdraw at any point.

Recruiting The objective or recruiting is to attract a pool of qualified applicants from which to choose the most appropriate person for a particular job. If recruiting produces only as many as candidates as there are jobs, the employer cannot be selective. If, on the other hand, the efforts to recruit result in a flood of applicants, the firm needs to have a systematic screening apparatus in place.[5]

Selection Employee selection may be described as a screening or sifting process that identifies applicants who should be extended a job offer.[6] It is constrained by Equal Employment Opportunity regulations and historically has been plagued by haphazard practices and outright abuses. Various types of testing, interviews, physical examinations, and reference checks are all part of this sometimes lengthy sorting-out process.

Orientation Soon after a new employee joins a firm, he or she should receive an orientation, the process of introducing new employees to their new organization and job. During the orientation the human resources representative commonly covers background like the company's history, organizational structure, product or service lines, and key managers. Other topics may include the company's employee policies and procedures like the sick leave and vacations, the availability of health and life insurance and safety regulations.

Evaluating and Developing Job Performance

Once people have been hired, constructive steps must be taken to keep them productive, relatively content, and up to date. This is where performance appraisal, employee assistance programs, and training and development come into play. We examine each of these important human resources management activities in the section along with a look at promotion, transfer, and discharge.

Performance appraisal Most public and private organizations big enough to have a formalized management system conduct some type of performance appraisal. A performance appraisal is a formal assessment of how well employees are doing their jobs. Performance appraisal serves two kinds of purposes. First, it helps evaluate employees, including determining eligibility for pay rises and promotion and deciding which employees to retain. Second, it helps develop employees because it is future oriented and aimed at improving the employees' career potential.

Employee assistance program People do not leave their personal problems on the doorstep when they go to work. Drug and alcohol, domestic, financial, and emotional problems accompany employees into the workplace. Employee drug and alcohol abuse alone cost U.S. economy an estimated $60 to $100 billion a year. As a result, many companies have developed employee assistance programs (EAPs) that offer help and counseling for employees with personal problems. EAPs, in the long run, save rather than cost the company money. The nature and extent of a company's EAP is limited only by management's imagination and willingness to help troubled employees get back on the right track.

Training and development programs Workplace training today is an immense undertaking. In 1987, according to one study, U.S. public and private organizations budgeted $32 billion for training and development. The term training and development refers here to the process of changing employee attitudes and/or behavior through some type of structured experience. A recent training trend of great importance is an emphasis on remedial education. In view of the fact that 29 percent of American high school students drop out before graduation, companies are having to take up educational slack through remedial courses in reading, writing, math and interpersonal relations. America's competitiveness is tied directly to the quality of its new workers.

Promotion, transfer and discharge A promotion is an advancement granted to an employee to a higher position, greater responsibility, or more prestige. Sometimes a promotion includes a transfer, a shift from one job to another or in an organization that may or may not require a change in the employee's place or work. Transfer can also be a horizontal change that does not involve a promotion. A discharge, or termination is a permanent separation initiated by the employer, usually for causes such as absenteeism or poor job performance.

Compensation and Benefits

Employees work for compensation, the money or benefits or both for which an employee exchanges work.

A business compensation system has three main purposes: attracting qualified employees, retaining those employees, and motivating higher levels of performance from them. A firm achieves each of these goals through the various aspects of the compensation system.

A compensation system includes base pay (refers to the basic wages or salaries that workers receive), incentives (refer to bonus and other plans designed to encourage employees to produce work beyond the minimum acceptable levels), and benefits (refer to services that employees receive that are paid for by the employer, like health insurance, pension, and vacations). A good system motivates effective performance by establishing fair individual rates of compensation and by effectively linking performance to compensation.[7]

Today's Human Resources Challenges

At no other time in history has business faced so many and such complex human resources challenges as it does today. It worths summarizing them:

- ❖ How to establish and maintain equal employment opportunities for women and minority group members
- ❖ How to cope with the increasingly complex legal requirements related to employee compensation and benefit plans
- ❖ What to do about the skyrocketing costs of health care, which directly affect the cost of medical insurance
- ❖ How to set up equitable rates of pay to reflect female and male employees' comparable worth to the firm
- ❖ What businesses can use to motivate employees when labor market conditions

dictate that entry-level salaries must nearly match those being paid to senior employees in the same job classification
- ❖ How to motivate new hires in two-tier system who will never achieve the base pay of senior employees in the same job[8]
- ❖ Seek out solutions to curb on-the-job use of alcohol plaguing entry-level employees
- ❖ How to balance the employee's right to privacy with the employer's right to know in the areas of drug and AIDS testing
- ❖ How to deal with AIDS and fear of AIDS in the workplace

New Words

exploit	/ɪkˈsplɔɪt/	v.	开拓,开发
exhaustion	/ɪgˈzɔːstʃən/	n.	疲惫,竭尽
discard	/dɪsˈkɑːd/	v.	丢弃,抛弃
nurture	/ˈnɜːtʃə/	v.	养育,教育
evaluate	/ɪˈvæljueɪt/	v.	评估,评价
dramatize	/ˈdræmətaɪz/	v.	加剧,使激烈
systematic	/ˌsɪstɪˈmætɪk/	adj.	系统的,体系的
personnel	/ˌpɜːsəˈnel/	n.	人员,职员,人事
regulation	/ˌregjʊˈleɪʃən/	n.	规章,规则
forecast	/ˈfɔːkɑːst/	v.	预测,预见
anticipate	/ænˈtɪsɪpeɪt/	v.	预期,预见
prospective	/prəˈspektɪv/	adj.	预期的
screen	/skriːn/	v.	筛选
sift	/sɪft/	v.	详审;挑选
outright	/ˈaʊtraɪt/	adj.	彻底的,完全的
appraisal	/əˈpreɪzəl/	n.	评价,评估
eligibility	/ˌelɪdʒɪˈbɪlɪti/	n.	适任,合格
interpersonal	/ˌɪntəˈpɜːsənəl/	adj.	人与人之间的,人际的
slack	/slæk/	v.	松懈,减弱
remedial	/rɪˈmiːdiəl/	adj.	治疗的,补救的
horizontal	/ˌhɒrɪˈzɒntl/	adj.	水平的
termination	/ˌtɜːmɪˈneɪʃən/	n.	终止
minority	/maɪˈnɒrɪti/	n.	少数民族
contraction	/kənˈtrækʃən/	n.	收缩
expansion	/ɪkˈspænʃən/	n.	扩充,开展
privacy	/ˈprɪvəsi/	n.	隐私,秘密

vacancy	/ˈveɪkənsɪ/	n.	空缺,空白
haphazard	/ˌhæpˈhæzəd/	adj.	偶然的,偶尔的
immense	/ɪˈmens/	adj.	巨大的
exchange	/ɪksˈtʃeɪndʒ/	v.	交换
retain	/rɪˈteɪn/	v.	保留
comparable	/ˈkɒmpərəbəl/	adj.	可比较的
plague	/pleɪg/	v.	折磨,使苦恼

Phrases

focus on	将注意力集中于
a reduction of	减少……
tied directly to	直接与……有联系
move into	进入;就职
appropriate for	适合于
get back on	回归于
up to date	更新
relate to	与……有关
come into play	开始活动;起作用
cope with	处理,对付
afford to	供应得起;经受得起

Special Terms

deploy	展开,配置
training	培训
turnover	流通量,营业额
promotion	晋升
employment	雇佣人员
redeployment	调遣;调换
work force	职工总数
job analysis	职业分析
recruitment	招募人员,补充人手
orientation	情况介绍
job performance	业绩,绩效
performance appraisal	绩效评估
discharge	解雇
transfer	调任

compensation	薪酬
base pay	基本工资
incentive	红利
bonus	奖金
benefit	待遇
absenteeism	旷工
pension	养老金

Notes

1. No longer can companies afford to look at people as a commodity to be exploited to exhaustion and then discarded.
   公司已经无法承担将雇员只是看作商品，在使用到无法再使用时便弃置不理了。
   句中 to be exploited to exhaustion 表示"将……用到极致"。

2. This situation dramatizes the need for human resources planning, the systematic process of forecasting the future demand for employees and estimating the supply available to meet that demand.
   这种情形加剧了人力资源计划的必要性。人力资源计划是指对未来员工的需求量进行预测，并对为满足此需求所需要的员工进行估计的系统化程序。
   句中 dramatizes the need 表示"加剧……的必要性"；meet that demand 表示"满足需要"。

3. Internal factors include possible shifts in goods or services, planned expansions or contractions in operations, purchases of new equipment, and likely personnel changes such as retirements and leaves of absence.
   内在的因素包括在货物和服务上有可能出现的变化，运营计划中公司的扩展或是收缩，购买新的设备，以及有可能出现的诸如退休或是空缺所造成的人员变化。
   句中 possible shifts 表示"可能的变化"。

4. Forecasting the supply of workers available from within a company requires estimating how many current workers are qualified to move into anticipated vacancies.
   要预测一个公司内部可能提供的职员，需要估计在现有员工当中有多少人具备进入预期空缺的资格。
   句中 current workers 可译为"现有的职员"；are qualified to 表示"具备资格做某事"。

5. If, on the other hand, the efforts to recruit result in a flood of applicants, the firm needs to have a systematic screening apparatus in place.
   然而，另一方面，如果招募员工导致了申请者过多，那么公司就得适当地采取系统的筛选措施。
   a flood of 意为"许多，泛滥"，而 in place 在这里是"相应地"。

6. Employee selection may be described as a screening or sifting process that identifies applicants who should be extended a job offer.

雇员选拔可被称为是对工作申请者进行筛选或是甄选从而确定谁能获得工作的机会。

7. A good system motivates effective performance by establishing fair individual rates of compensation and by effectively linking performance to compensation.

一个好的体系通过建立公平的个人薪酬比例,并将业绩与薪酬有效联系起来,从而激励有效的业绩。

8. How to motivate new hires in two-tier system who will never achieve the base pay of senior employees in the same job

在双重体系中,新员工从事同样的工作,却得不到与资深员工同样的基本工资,如何激励这些员工

Exercises

I. Discuss the following questions.

1. According to the article, what is human resources management and what factors have contributed to its importance?
2. What is the human resources planning process?
3. What are the steps in the employment process? Explain each step.
4. Why is human resources management especially important today?
5. Why are employee orientations important?
6. What should a good compensation system accomplish?

II. Analyze the case below and discuss the questions.

> Hi, Ray, I think it's sort of ironical that we end up like this. I asked for leniency for my family, remember, well, I got none and you'll get none.
>
> —A note purported to be written by US Air employee David Burke to his former supervisor Raymond Thomson

The above note, which was reprinted in the December, 12, 1987 edition of *The San Diego Union*, was found at the crash site of Pacific Southeast Airlines Flight #1771. Forty-three people died in the crash—including David Burke and Raymond Thomson.

This tragic scenario, while extreme in the sense of desperation that it conveys, highlights the chaos that can follow an employee's termination. In this case, Burke was fired for allegedly stealing $69,000 in beverage receipt from US Air, Inc. (which owns Pacific Southeast Airlines) and for drinking on the job. According to newspaper accounts, however, the feud between Burke and Thomson had apparently started at least five months before the tragedy when Burke stated in an informal complaint to California Department of Fair Employment and Housing that he had twice been passed over for promotion because of his race and had accused Thomson of discrimination. While we may never know all the details of the meetings between the two men, one thing is clear. An employee was fired, and in the aftermath, of that firing he carried out a vengeful act against his former boss that left 43 dead and their families devastated.

Questions:
1. Should managers who read this account be afraid to fire anyone for it will be creating a mass murderer? Explain the reasons.
2. What role could an employee assistance program (EPA) have played in this situation?

III. Match the terms in column A with the explanations in column B.

A	B
1. performance appraisal	A. the systematic introduction of new employees to their new organization, job, and coworkers
2. employee assistance program	B. a standardized screening device intended to predict the applicants' potential for successful job performance
3. discharge	C. a formal assessment of how well employees are doing their jobs
4. compensation	D. the systematic process of forecasting the future demand for employees and estimating the supply available to meet that demand
5. employment test	E. a written summary of the duties, tasks, and responsibilities associated with a job
6. orientation	F. the process of attracting qualified people to apply for the job
7. recruitment	G. a systematic study of each employee's duties, tasks, and work environment
8. job description	H. the money or benefits or both for which an employee exchanges work
9. job analysis	I. a permanent separation initiated by the employer, usually for causes such as absenteeism or poor job performance
10. human resources planning	J. a program that offers constructive help and counseling for employees with personal problems

IV. Fill in the blanks of the following sentences with the words or phrases given below. Make changes when necessary.

| initiate | personnel | participate | sift | termination |
| discharge | exchange | deploy | forecast | appraisal |

1. He was anxious to _____ out of that department in the branch company for a promotion and better pay.
2. After his _____ from the company, he went to China to be an English teacher.
3. This company will spend a large sum of money to _____ the new employee into the management and the regulation of the company.
4. In order to expand the sales of the company, the manager has to actively _____ in all kinds of international meetings.
5. It wouldn't be wise to buy the company before having it _____.
6. After several rounds of talk, both sides cannot reach the agreement so they decided to _____ their contract.
7. To be a good human resources manager, it is necessary to _____ the future need of the employees of the company.
8. An interviewee will become an employee of a company only after _____ for several times.
9. Airline _____ can purchase flight tickets at reduced prices, which is also a kind of welfare.
10. One of the important steps of human resources management is to _____ people.

V. Put the following into English.

1. 职业发展咨询
2. 协调企业目标与员工个人目标
3. 影响员工职业生涯的因素
4. 企业培训工作
5. 人员调配
6. 人力资源需求预测
7. 绩效考核
8. 较大的工作自由权
9. 平等就业的机会
10. 接受职业技能培训

VI. Translate the following sentences into English.

1. 人力资源管理的目的就在于合理地使用人力资源,最大限度地提高人力资源的使用效益。

2. 人员调配指经主管部门决定而改变人员的工作岗位、职务、工作单位或隶属关系的人事变动。
3. 企业招聘既是一个获得人才的过程，也是一个宣传企业的过程。
4. 法律禁止在雇佣过程中出现在性别、种族、肤色、国籍、地区以及年龄等方面的歧视。
5. 晋升和调动是员工职业发展的直接表现和主要途径。

VII. Translate the following passage into Chinese.

Bill Wilson was attracted to the secretarial field because he felt that office automation would offer jobs with increased responsibility, technical expertise, and higher pay. He reasoned that new technology would increase office productivity and eliminate some of the more tedious secretarial tasks, and this would allow secretaries, such as himself, to take on more administrative and decision-making tasks. He felt this would be especially true in decentralized setups with the computers and word processors dispersed throughout the organization, and with secretary-executive teams grouped around departments or projects.

Wilson was disappointed to find that many of the executives in the organization, including his boss, saw things quite differently. For example, his boss saw no need to share administrative and decision-making tasks with the secretaries. Instead, she saw them working in centralized work areas where they would move into specialized work processing or technical positions.

Then, what should Wilson do to make in defense of a decentralized setup?

Text B

Job Termination and Retirement

As the story goes, when Henry Ford wanted to fire someone, he did it quickly and absolutely. The terminated person would return from a vacation to find the office furniture stacked in the hall and a note on the door informing this person that he was fired! Today, however, firing a subordinate is probably one of the most unpleasant tasks a superior must face. The pattern of firing managers differs from that of terminating lower-echelon employees. Managers may be dehired, often because of their closeness to the colleagues who hired them, while lower-level employees are subject to some form of involuntary termination.

Dehiring

The process of getting an employee to quit voluntarily so that it is unnecessary to fire that person is called dehiring. Other terms used in place of dehiring are *selecting-out* and *outplacing*. When a firm wants to help a dehired executive get a job elsewhere, it may retain an outplacement counselor to help the executive with his or her self-appraisal, resume, job-search strategy, and interviewing techniques. On the other hand, if the firm wants to keep an executive but cannot correct his or her failings, it may turn to mid-career counseling. Such counseling should help the executive understand what the problem is, how his or her behavior affects other people on the job, and how to correct the problem.

Involuntary Termination

The involuntary termination of an employee's services may take either of the two forms: a discharge and a layoff.

A discharge is permanent and a layoff may be either permanent or temporary, but it usually does not reflect on the employee's character or competence. Management's right to fire employees comes from the position that employees serve entirely at the employer's will. This is known as the employment-will doctrine that has prevailed in the U.S. since the late 1800s. Although still entrenched, this doctrine is being challenged by individual employees who feel they have been fired without reasonable cause. This is true of blue and white-collar employees alike. Employees are pointing especially to two factors: the promise of job security in employee handbooks and the lack of effective job performance evaluations.

In addition to individual court actions, pressure is being put on state legislature to pass laws prohibiting firings except for just cause such as criminal acts, drunkenness, and incompetence. Wrongful discharge suits are a hot topic in the law field, and this is forcing human resources managers to rewrite handbooks and to design new systems to document their cases.

Alternatives to Job Dehiring and Termination

When companies cut payrolls, they usually fire employees on the basis of seniority, not performance—with the last hired being the first fired. But in the face of severe competitive pressures, some companies and industries also are trying new ways to keep a stable, yet flexible and productive, work force. In addition to early retirements, other approaches include retaining, loaning employees to other divisions, use of temporary workers or part-time contractors as buffers to fluctuations, reduced workweeks during business down cycles, and work sharing.

Under work sharing, a firm's employees take reductions in hours and pay. In some states, workers on a work-sharing program are eligible for partial employment benefits for the days they don't work. This program has been used by the state of Arizona, as well as Motorola, its largest employer. These efforts to provide employment security take the place of the usual hire-and-fire cycles and are contributing to the competitiveness of many American firms by maintaining a vigorous, productive, and stable work force.

Retirement

In 1950 about 27 percent of women and men aged 65 or older stayed in the labor force. This was true even though about half the employers in the United States had policies requiring employees to step down at 65. The amendments in 1978 to the Age Discrimination Act, however, raised the mandatory retirement age to 70. And some states are beginning to revoke any mandatory retirement legislation. But now, despite the higher age limits, fewer than 15 percent of women and men remain in the labor force after age 65. A major reason for this is the increase in early-retirement plans. But in another 30 years or so, another trend will become evident: innovative programs to keep workers on the job rather than pushing early retirement. Let's take a quick look at these two opposing trends in retirement.

Early-retirement programs When Michael Blumenthal became CEO of Burroughs Corps. in 1981, he gave almost 300 middle managers at least 55 years old a chance to take an early retirement. Burroughs paid out nearly $16 million in early-retirement benefits. In 1983, Eastman Kodak paid over $140 million to more than 5,000 employees who left. Many companies these days consider early-retirement incentives whenever an economic downturn or technological change requires cutbacks in the work force. Known as open windows or golden handshakes, voluntary early-retirement plans usually are aimed at people over 50 with at least 10 years of service. Typically, the "carrot" is some combination of a pension bonus, medical insurance benefits, and severance payment based on salary and years at the company. Probably the most serious complaint about the early-retirement plans is that the employees may not be as voluntary as they are supposed to be. Thus, an employee in a shaky company may have to decide whether to stay and face the risk or being laid off or take what she or he can get and leave. If an early-retirement program is shoved down a person's throat, it may be, in effect, a way of firing that person. In all, Americans now have a preference for early retirement, and management often is glad to offer this.

Down the road: Keeping older employees Looking ahead about 30 years, we see demographics turning around. Today's baby boomers will reach retirement age, and a shortage of skilled workers is likely. Some experts feel that tomorrow's retirement policies must persuade at least some employees to work to age 65 and beyond. According to James W. Walker, a human resources management consultant, "... I see a gradual trend toward the use of part-timers, creative ways of employing older workers through various methods of flexible employment, the encouragement of lateral moves or downward moves." For some time into the future, human resources management will face increasing challenges in matching attitudes toward retirement with the human resources needs of the company. More and more companies are taking at least two basic steps. The first step is offering preretirement

planning programs to encourage employees to think about the problems and benefits of retirement before they actually stop working. The second is to develop career continuation, or career extension, programs for senior executives. Such programs provide for the senior executives to leave the executive suite at age 65, but to continue working for the company in some other professional capacity, sometimes with reduced hours.

Answer the following questions:

1. When might it not be to the advantage of a 55-year-old executive, who is outplaced, to accept the company's offer to provide an outplacement counselor's help, say, six months?
2. What is dehiring?
3. What may early-retirement programs have in common with firing or dehiring a person?
4. What does employment-at-will doctrine mean?
5. What are the alternatives to job dehiring and termination?

Unit 16

Global Logistics

Learning Objectives

Text A
- to learn several global integrated logistics strategic options
- to understand several global logistics activity management

Text B
- to understand the requirement of logistics in German recycling economy
- to learn logistics process tasks in recycling economy

Text A

Global Integrated Logistics

The need to maintain or increase profits and sales sends many firms into global markets. International trade is growing rapidly worldwide than domestic economies. In 1998, world trade was about $6.5 trillion. With the information of NAFTA (North American Free Trade Agreement), APEC (Asian-Pacific Economic Cooperation), and numerous other trade blocks in recent years, the message is clear: international trade will continue to increase at an even faster rate. As global trade increases, so does the pressure on companies to develop integrated logistics systems to move their products. Logistics is defined as a business planning framework for the management of material, service, information and capital flows.[1] Worldwide integrated logistics expenditure was approximately $1.3 trillion in 1980 and $2.8 trillion in 1999.

Global Integrated Logistics Strategic Options

Global operating strategies center around four elements: technology, manufacturing, marketing and integrated logistics. In this context, integrated logistics becomes a strategic weapon to open and protect markets. In developing integrated logistics as a strategic weapon, four options are available to a global company:
- proprietary system
- third parties

- general trading companies
- export trading companies

Proprietary System

The most common option is to develop a proprietary system. Companies invest large sums in logistics for specific markets. This system offers a lower overall integrated logistics cost, lets the company participate in the local economy through investment in distribution facilities, and provides tight integrated logistics control. The downsides of this system include huge investment, risk from nationalization, complex management requirements and lower economic scale than intermediaries.[2]

Third Parties

Using third parties reduces investment, increases responsiveness to changing customer needs, and allows more flexibility in evaluating new integrated logistics technology.[3] However, third parties usually provide only fixed services, generate high per unit variable costs, and allow for little participation in the local economy.

General Trading Companies

General trading companies (GTCs) are a third option. GTCs are common in Japan and R. O. Korea. They assist in marketing and financing, and handle overseas product logistics requirements such as packaging, warehousing, transportation, and customer service. GTCs assume the roles of brokers, shippers, and financial intermediaries. GTCs provide access to many global markets through established integrated logistics systems. Their primary disadvantage is size. GTCs are usually very large organizations and unfortunately are sometimes unaware of the needs of smaller companies.

Export Trading Companies

The last option, the export trading company (ETC), is an adaptation of GTC. ETCs normally take title to the goods; arrange for financing, documentation and shipping; sell the goods through their own distributors or outlets. They can offer lower integrated logistics costs and better service than other options.

Which option is best for a company depends on a number of factors. A large, protected market with high logistics costs suggests a proprietary system if the exporting or importing company has a global strategy.[4] To penetrate smaller, free trade markets without a large investment in a logistics system, a GTC or ETC is recommended. The third-party option may suit companies just beginning global distribution and lacking knowledge of distribution operations. Global companies not wanting to use trade companies can also use a third party.

Global Integrated Logistics Management

Compared with domestic logistics, which is hard enough to coordinate, global logistics brings a more difficult challenge. All integrated logistics activities are more involved and more complex. Packaging requirements vary, labeling differs, lead times lengthen, inventory management becomes more complex, intermediaries multiply, carrier selection and pricing increase in difficulty, and the list goes on.[5] But almost every company in the world is involved in international trade to some extent. This means that it must coordinate the movement of products across national boundaries.

Among global integrated logistics activities, the following deserve special attention:
- transportation
- warehouse management
- packaging
- inventory management
- material handling
- information systems

Transportation

Global transportation includes ocean freight, airfreight, motor and railroad services to and from the seaports and airports, as well as a limited amount of transborder pipeline transportation. And the two major means of transportation are global ocean freight and global airfreight.

Global Ocean Freight

High-density, lower-valued products normally move by ocean carrier. Water carriers haul large quantities of bulk commodities at relatively low prices. For example, much of aluminum processed in the eastern United States comes from Australia, not from the western United States, where substantial bauxite reserves exist. Moving bauxite 10,000 miles by ocean freight costs less than moving it 2,000 miles by train.

Ocean carriers operate as either liners or tramps. Liners operate on a fixed schedule, while tramps move when full.[6]

Global Airfreight

For most international moves, air is the only alternative to ocean freight. In terms of weight, air moves less than one-tenth of 1 percent. Yet it represents a much higher percentage of revenue because of the high value of products moving by air. However, airfreight is unlikely to make great dents in ocean freight market share due to the huge differences in rates.[7] When total integrated logistics costs are considered, airfreight movement can be cheaper than water due to reduced inventory carrying and customer service costs. Air responds quickly to customers, reducing warehousing needs, inventory levels, insurance costs, loss and damage claims, and the capital cost of inventory.

Warehouse Management

Global warehousing serves the purposes of receiving, transferring, picking, and shipping. Rapid movement of products through the warehouse deserves great emphasis.

Global integrated logistics employs a number of storage options. A manufacturer can store products in its own warehouses, public warehouses, transit sheds at a port, intransit storage areas where other tasks are performed, hold-on-dock storage with a carrier, or bonded warehouses where goods may be stored for up to three years without paying duties or tariffs. Which of these options a firm actually uses depends on global logistics system design, available facilities, countries involved in the movement, shipper and receiver preferences, and the terms of trade.

Packaging

Protective packing takes on special importance in global logistics. The product is handled more and is more susceptible to adverse weather. Packaging requirements add substantial costs to global integrated logistics. Packing adds material and labor costs, and other factors may add still more. Labeling and marking requirements vary from country to country. Labeling informs the parties involved in the movement of exactly the nature and quantity of the package contents.[8] Labeling regulations generally attempt to (1) force shippers to adhere to the existing product standards, (2) restrict and control the use of additives, (3) prohibit the use of misleading information, and (4) establish standard descriptions of products.

Marking is the use of letters, numbers, and symbols on the package to facilitate identification.[9] Markings could include gross weights, heights, invoice numbers, and transit instructions. Marking also provides information on how to handle the product.

Inventory Management

Inventory is the life of integrated logistics. Without it, there is nothing to do in physical supply—nothing to store, nothing to carry, and nothing to package. Inventory management on a global scale becomes even more difficult and more important. Distance, port delays, customs delays, and transit times encourage higher inventories. This, of course, increases the costs of inventory. Political decisions such as closing borders to trade or increasing trade tariffs and duties also add to the inventory problems. Companies may be forced to carry additional inventory to offset stockouts. Stockouts are much more common globally than would be acceptable domestically.

It is not unusual to find global companies carrying up to 50 percent or more of their assets in inventory, compared with 25 or 30 percent domestically. Currency exchange fluctuations also make valuation of inventory more difficult.

Material Handling

Material handling systems vary globally. In countries and regions like the United States, Canada, Australia, New Zealand, Hong Kong, Singapore, and most of Western Europe, these systems will be among the World's best, usually highly mechanized or automated. In developing countries, the majority of systems are manual. The flow of products throughout the entire warehouse and plants tends to be much slower in manual system. Also, some products require more sophisticated handling equipment, so some countries or ports may not be able to receive them. For example, some ports can handle only twenty-fit containers, while others cannot handle containers at all.[10]

Information Systems

Information systems are critical for decision-making. While developed countries have very sophisticated integrated logistics information systems, not all countries do. Many third-world countries use pencil and paper. Technologies such as automated data collection, and radio frequency systems are useless. Communications may be poor, and available information may be inaccurate. The defect of information systems may seriously damage efficiency.

With the rapid development of technology and global markets as well as the increasing emphasis on quality and customer satisfaction, a larger number of companies start operations worldwide. Logistics is essential for a company's competitive strategy and survival, especially for global manufacturing firms. Logistics helps improve a firm's competitive position by providing competitive advantage through competence in delivery speed, reliability, responsiveness, and low cost distribution.

New Words

integrated	/'ɪntɪgreɪtɪd/	adj.	综合的,完整的
logistics	/lə'dʒɪstɪks/	n.	物流,后勤
trillion	/'trɪljən/	num.	万亿
framework	/'freɪmwɜːk/	n.	框架,结构
proprietary	/prə'praɪətəri/	adj. & n.	所有的;所有权,所有者
approximately	/ə'prɒksɪmɪtli/	adv.	近似地,大约
facility	/fə'sɪlɪti/	n.	设备,机构
downside	/'daʊnsaɪd/	n.	底侧;缺点;下降趋势
nationalization	/ˌnæʃənəlaɪ'zeɪʃən/	n.	国有化
responsiveness	/rɪ'spɒnsɪvnɪs/	n.	响应
assume	/ə'sjuːm/	v.	承担;假设
adaptation	/ˌædæp'teɪʃən/	n.	适应;改制(物)
strategy	/'strætɪdʒi/	n.	战略
penetrate	/'penɪtreɪt/	v.	穿透,渗透
coordinate	/kəʊ'ɔːdɪneɪt/	v.	协调,调整
pipeline	/'paɪp-laɪn/	n.	管道
haul	/hɔːl/	v.	拖,拉
aluminum	/ə'ljuːmɪnəm/	n.	铝
bauxite	/'bɔːksaɪt/	n.	矾土,铁铝矿石
liner	/'laɪnə/	n.	班轮
tramp	/træmp/	n	不定期货船
alternative	/ɔːl'tɜːnətɪv/	adj. & n.	可供选择的;可供选择的事物

dent	/dent/	n. & v.	凹痕；削弱，削减
employ	/ɪm'plɔɪ/	v.	雇佣；使用
transit	/'trænsɪt/	n.	运输；中转
intransit	/ɪn'trænsɪt/	adj.	在旅途中的
carrier	/'kærɪə/	n.	运输船；搬运人
shipper	/'ʃɪpə/	n.	托运人，发货人
receiver	/rɪ'siːvə/	n.	收货人
preference	/'prefərəns/	n.	偏好
susceptible	/sə'septəbəl/	adj.	易受影响的
marking	/'mɑːkɪŋ/	n.	唛头
additive	/'ædɪtɪv/	n.	添加剂，附加物
identification	/aɪˌdentɪfɪ'keɪʃən/	n.	辨认，识别
offset	/'ɒfset/	v.	抵消，弥补
stockout	/stɒkaʊt/	n.	无存货
mechanized	/'mekənaɪzd/	adj.	机械化的
frequency	/'friːkwənsi/	n.	频率

Phrases

center around	围绕着……
be unaware of	没意识到……
take title to	对……有所有权
compared with	与……相比
to some extent	在一定程度上
take on	具有(特征等)，呈现
up to	将近
depend on	依靠，取决于
adhere to	坚持；符合
on a…scale	在……规模上

Special Terms

NAFTA	北美自由贸易协定
APEC	亚太经合组织
trade block	贸易区域
capital flow	现金流
variable cost	可变成本
lead time	从定货到交货的时间

inventory management	存货管理
bulk commodity	大宗商品;散装货
transit shed	中转货棚
bonded warehouse	保税仓库
terms of trade	贸易条款
gross weight	毛重
invoice number	发票号码
transit instructions	搬运指示

Notes

1. Logistics is defined as a business planning framework for the management of material, service, information and capital flows.
   物流被定义为企业管理物资、服务、信息及现金流的规划框架。

2. The downsides of this system include huge investment, risk from nationalization, complex management requirements and lower economic scale than intermediaries.
   这个体系的缺点包括投入高、存在国有化风险、对管理的要求复杂,而且经济规模不抵中间商。

3. Using third parties reduces investment, increases responsiveness to changing customer needs, and allows more flexibility in evaluating new integrated logistics technology.
   利用第三方可以减少投入,更好地回应顾客多变的要求,更加灵活地评测新的物流技术。

4. A large, protected market with high logistics costs suggests a proprietary system if the exporting or importing company has a global strategy.
   具有全球战略的出口公司或进口公司,在物流成本高、保护性的大规模市场可建立自有物流体系。

5. Packaging requirements vary, labeling differs, lead times lengthen, inventory management becomes more complex, intermediaries multiply, carrier selection and pricing increase in difficulty, and the list goes on.
   包装要求各不相同,标签千差万别,交货时间延长,存货管理更加复杂,中间商数量增多,租船和定价的难度增加,如此等等。

6. Ocean carriers operate as either liners or tramps. Liners operate on a fixed schedule, while tramps move when full.
   海运船只可选班轮或不定期船。班轮有固定的船期,不定期船则是货满起航。

7. However, airfreight is unlikely to make great dents in ocean freight market share due to the huge differences in rates.
   然而,由于运费的巨大差价,空运不可能大量削减海运的市场份额。

8. Labeling and marking requirements vary from country to country. Labeling informs the parties involved in the movement of exactly the nature and quantity of the package contents.

不同的国家对标签和唛头的要求有所不同。标签可以告知运输中各相关方包装内货物的性质和数量。

9. Marking is the use of letters, numbers, and symbols on the package to facilitate identification.

唛头是包装上用来帮助识别的字母、数字和符号。

10. For example, some ports can handle only twenty-fit containers, while others cannot handle containers at all.

比如,有些港口只能装卸 20 英尺的标准集装箱,还有些港口根本无法装卸集装箱。

Exercises

I. Discuss the following questions.

1. Why is logistics important? Briefly explain from the view of macro-economy and individual company respectively.
2. In what way is global logistics more complex than domestic logistics?
3. Compared with ocean freight, what are the advantages and disadvantages of airfreight?
4. What storage options can global integrated logistics employ?
5. What is marking and what is its function?

II. Analyze the case below and discuss the question.

Case One

GR is an air-conditioner manufacturer with fixed assets of 2 billion *yuan*. The annual sales revenue in the latest three years is 16 billion *yuan*. It attempts to enter Brazilian market.

Case Two

WF is a carpet company with assets about 2.5 million *yuan*. It has no experience of international trade before. There is ready market for carpets in Britain these years. It plans to get their carpets sold there.

Question:

Discuss the advantage and disadvantage of each global logistics strategic option and choose a suitable one for each company.

III. Match the terms in column A with the explanations in column B.

A	B
1. invoice	A. a large ship for carrying passengers or goods on long journeys
2. liner	B. a list of items provided or worked done together with their cost, for payment at a later time
3. bonded warehouse	C. a building where large quantities of goods are stored without paying tariffs
4. lead time	D. a person who buys and sells things for other people
5. strategy	E. the time needed to produce goods before they can be delivered
6. broker	F. a supply of something that is available to be used in the future or when it is needed
7. reserve	G. a shop that is one of many owned by a particular company and that sells the goods which the company has produced
8. outlet	H. the amount of money moving into and out of a business
9. gross weight	I. the process of planning something or putting a plan into operation in a skillful way
10. capital flow	J. weight including the container or wrapping

IV. Fill in the blanks of the following sentences with the words or phrases given below. Make changes when necessary.

integrated	approximately	coordinate	assume	alternative
preference	susceptible	distribution	offset	downside

1. Because of financial trouble, their project of setting up Shanghai branch will be delayed _____ another one year.
2. For most people Pepsi and Coca Cola are very similar in taste, but some people do have great _____ for one or the other.
3. Petrol price had risen twice by the end of last year to _____ the increased cost of crude oil.
4. Unemployment, inflation and wide gap between the rich and the poor are often the _____ of a market economy.
5. Small enterprises are usually more _____ to economic crisis than large international enterprises.
6. The marketing plans turned out to be a failure. And the general manager should _____ the major responsibility.
7. Apple is one of the few _____ businesses in the IT sector. The company makes the computer hardware, accessories, operating system and much of the software itself.

8. To improve efficiency, they appointed a new manager to _____ the work of the team.
9. Nokia, as the largest mobile phone manufacturer in the world, has established worldwide _____ systems.
10. For some unknown reason, our original solution doesn't work. Do you have an _____ solution?

V. Put the following into English.
1. 主要交通方式
2. 充足的黄金储备
3. 外汇浮动
4. 削减市场份额
5. 增强竞争优势
6. 全球综合物流体系
7. 提高产品质量和顾客满意度
8. 跨国管道运输
9. 符合现有的产品标准
10. 密度大、价值低的产品

VI. Translate the following sentences into English.
1. 物流对一个公司的生存和发展至关重要,对全球性的生产商尤其如此。
2. 运输是物流中的重要因素,因为任何公司,无论生产什么、销售什么,都需要将货物从一个地方运送到另一个地方。
3. 随着企业间的竞争日趋激烈,企业必须提高物流效率,降低物流成本,以提高整体竞争力。
4. 技术的快速进步、全球市场的不断发展以及对服务质量和消费者满意度的重视,是全球物流业高速发展的主要原因。
5. 物流业不应该是一个保护性的行业,只有开放才能健康发展。

VII. Translate the following passage into Chinese.
Manufacturers have long realized that carrying a larger inventory of parts or components than they absolutely need is a waste of time, space, and resources—and it ties up cash that could otherwise be earning interest. But in recent years, this mentality has increasingly spread from car manufacturers to service companies: retailers, hospitals, grocery stores. This means businesses today increasingly rely on systems, companies and people who make sure that precise amounts of materials get to where they need to be at precisely the right time. In industries where margins are thin and competition is intense, the ability to handle logistics effectively is a huge competitive advantage. For titans like

Wal-Mart and Dell, logistics isn't just a necessary back-office function; it's the heart of the business and the root of their competitive advantage.

Text B

Logistics in Creating a Recycling Economy

The German recycling industry has experienced dramatic changes. The focus is no longer on simple waste disposal that is organized and carried out by many small regional firms directed or financed by communities. These firms have been replaced by large, autonomous companies that contribute to an entirely new sector of the German economy. The market volume of this new recycling sector is estimated to be approximately 75 billion Deutsche marks (DM), or almost $50 billion, annually. More and more attention is paid to recycling consumer items, which is growing faster than the disposal of production waste and packaging materials. In Germany a total of 338.5 million tons of waste are generated annually with approximately 43.5 million tons by private households. The goal is to recover 29 percent (or 13 million tons) of household waste.

Logistics effectiveness is very important in recycling industry. According to statistics, logistics processes make up about 40–60 percent of the total disposal cost. By restructuring and developing intelligent logistics networks, companies engaged in waste disposal and redistribution of recycled products can reduce costs and gain strategic, competitive advantages.

Fifteen years ago the primary logistics task was to collect waste from every household, trade and industrial institution. Waste streams were not differentiated, and no distinction was made about how to treat the waste. The final destination was generally the community disposal area. Waste transportation was primarily many short trips. However, things are quite different now. With new laws implemented and technological progress, logistics tasks have been undergoing great changes.

Laws and Logistics Implications

New Changes in Laws

During the last 10 years Germany has seen much innovation in environmental legislation. There are three important new changes.

First, waste is now defined as "all removable items that an owner discards, wants to discard, or has to discard."

Second, based on the new definition, the law provides priorities for treating waste. The preferred option is to prevent any waste completely. The next option is to recycle or recover the material to make it less harmful to the environment, or to reuse certain components. Only if recycling is technically impossible can waste be burned as a means to produce energy. The final option, legal only if the other options are not feasible, is the mere disposal of waste.

The third major innovation significantly affects producers, retailers and consumers, and introduces the idea of product responsibility. Everyone who develops, produces, processes or sells a product has full responsibility for minimizing waste during its use and disposing of it in an environmentally friendly manner.

The main reason for the emphasis on recycling is the decreasing space at public disposal areas and increasing awareness of environmental protection.

Logistics Implications

As a result of the changes in laws, logistics tasks become more complex than 15 years ago.

First, transportation pressure is on the rise.

New laws require that material being recycled be categorized. That means, every type of waste must be treated differently. To meet the demand, a variety of processing facilities with advanced technology has developed. Since processing facilities can only achieve high productivity when they have large quantities, there are only a few facilities in Germany for each waste type. Large amounts of materials are transported to a variety of processing plants and recycled in different waste channels throughout Germany. Usually long distances are involved. Also, production plants receiving material to be recycled need to receive the right quantity and quality at the right time.

A good example of the complexity that logisticians have to confront is the typical household. A household can create up to six different waste streams: glass, paper, bulky items, plastic materials, biodegradable (可生物分解的) waste, and the "rest" — including complex consumer goods. These different types have to be collected separately and brought to a related processing plant or disassembly facility. The result is more trips, more vehicles required.

Second, logistics also assumes the responsibility of dealing with redistribution.

New laws encourage disassembly activities. On one hand, disassembly makes it possible to extract and process high-quality secondary materials. On the other hand, disassembly permits the recovery of complete products and components that can be reused as replacement parts or in new products. Therefore, disassembly represents the best way to achieve a recycling economy.

Consider household appliances. They represent refrigerators, washing machines, drying machines, freezers, dishwashers and ovens. About 12 million used household appliances (with a total weight of 650,000 tons) are discarded annually in Germany. This amount is derived by considering the number of households in Germany, the average number of appliances each household has, and the average service life of an appliance. (Appliances generally have a service life of 15 years.) Household appliances contain a great variety of valuable as well as harmful materials. They contain components suitable for product and material recycling. Every disassembled component or material has to be treated separately.

The market can be divided into two parts: the first one is the market for reusable products and components. The second is a market for recycled materials.

The following estimates for a washing machine are only an example; however, they reveal a potential of salvage value. Based on the market price for secondary materials, recycling certain materials in a washing machine can generate up to 16 DM (or $10). In addition, reusable components, such as the engine and pump, can earn up to 106 DM (or more than $60) in the spare parts market. The total salvage value of about 120 DM (or $75) per washing machine shows the importance of efficient redistribution and disassembly.

Logistics Process Tasks

Logistics e-distribution is a holistic system requiring strategic planning. The redistribution process, however, includes dynamic activities, such as registration and collection, transportation, and handling processes.

Registration and Collection

Collection is physically picking up used consumer products. Before collection is made, a flow of information—defined as registration—from the consumer to the service provider is needed. New information technology has to be used in registering and identifying used products. This will most likely increase the number of appliances registered because owners will have a convenient, fast and cheap way to dispose of used products. Logistics information about all products and processes—product development, procurement, production and finally distribution—is vital. Only with a complete information system can effective collection routes and transportation means be planned and control of redistribution be guaranteed. Disassembly facilities work best with advance knowledge of the type, quality, quantity and location of used material.

Transportation

Redistribution requires effective transportation in two aspects. First, transportation routes have to take into account population density and collection points. Second, transportation has to be economic and ecologically efficient. "Breakeven" points (保本点) must be calculated for trucks, railcars and ships. Given the legal restrictions on dangerous and contaminated goods, special logistics technologies are needed.

The distances between disassembly facilities and collection points are usually very far, so transportation costs are high. Depending on the quantity of used products and the location of the final destination, trains or ships could be used for long-distance movements. Because the time to transport used household appliances is not critical, more ecological transportation choices, such as by ship, should be chosen.

Handling

Handling presents another challenge. Redistribution handling occurs twice—first when collection trucks unload at interim storage areas and again when products are unloaded at their final destination. There is no automation. Handling operations are extremely slow and labor intensive.

Another problem is that products are frequently damaged. Appliances are usually loaded on top of each other in a container. This procedure has several weaknesses. Container loading is not automated. The potential for damaging or destroying an appliance during transportation is very high. Also containers are not usually filled to capacity, thus reducing efficiency (sometimes causing empty trips) and increasing costs. In this respect, automation must be closely linked with the development of a container specially designed for the transportation of household appliances.

The potential of future waste logistics lies in the development of redistribution processes for used consumer products. The intent is to reduce energy and resource consumption through product and material recycling to meet ecological goals. A step toward achieving these goals is the integration of waste logistics processes into existing logistical structures. Distribution and redistribution processes must be coordinated. Deliveries of new and collection of old products from consumers should be simultaneous.

Efficient collection and redistribution of used products open a new world for logistics service providers to increase their market share even in an extremely competitive environment. The market is characterized by many small disassembly businesses; all are competing for larger quantities of used products.

The successful competitors will have a strong customer orientation and will provide quick and reliable disposal of used household appliances. They will use environmentally friendly methods to deal with wastes on the way and will have guaranteed transportation to provide superior service for their clients. These strategies are the key to achieve a strong market position and realize a functioning recycling economy.

Answer the following questions:

1. What changes has German recycling economy experienced?
2. What is the difference between present logistics and 15 years ago in recycling economy?
3. What innovation has been made in environmental legislation in the past ten years?
4. Why is registration important?
5. What problems have been found with the handling of household appliances in transportation?

Unit 17

E-commerce

Learning Objectives

Text A
- to learn what is E-commerce
- to know the types of E-commerce
- to understand the advantages of E-commerce

Text B
- to know the problems in E-commerce in China
- to learn what is the best way out

Text A

Understanding E-commerce

What Is E-commerce?

Electronic commerce (or E-commerce) encompasses all business conducted by means of computer networks. It reflects a paradigm shift driven by two primary factors:

❖ a wide range of converging technological developments and
❖ the emergence of the so-called "knowledge economy."¹

When communications networks first became available, entrepreneurs were quick to recognize their value and use them to create business opportunities. Recent advances in telecommunications and computer technologies have moved computer networks to the centre of the international economic infrastructure. Most prominently, the meteoric rise of the Internet and the World Wide Web has transformed global commerce by facilitating instantaneous, inexpensive contact among sellers, buyers, investors, advertisers and financiers anywhere in the world.² The rapid integration of Internet and other telecommunications-based functions into nearly every sphere of business has led to an international focus on the new world of E-commerce.³

These technological developments have gone hand in hand with a trend, predominantly in the developed world, towards a post-industrial knowledge economy. This new paradigm, which is already having a significant impact on the way in which people lead their lives, is

227

difficult to define but is characterized by—
- an emphasis on the human mind, rather than merely physical automation;
- being information—rather than energy intensive;
- sustainability through networks, not single organizations;
- supporting distributed rather than centralized intelligence;
- requiring multiple skills and continuous learning;
- replacing lifetime employment with labor market flexibility;
- customized rather than standardized products; and
- being enabled by information and communications technologies (ICTs), whilst simultaneously driving the development of new ICTs.

Just as the industrial society built on and then dominated the agricultural society, the knowledge society is now building on the platform provided by the industrial society.[4] It can be argued that E-commerce, along with the technologies and knowledge required to effect it, is the first real manifestation of the knowledge society. The question for the less industrialized developing countries is whether they can use appropriate technologies to leapfrog into the knowledge society, by-passing some of the stages of the industrial paradigm.[5]

Among the principal activities that can be identified as contributing to global E-commerce are—
- government services and information;
- business-to-business wholesale and retail services and sales;
- business-to-consumer (and consumer-to-consumer) retail sales and transactions;
- financial services and transactions;
- subscription and usage-based telephony, online and Internet access services;
- subscription or transaction-based information services and software sales;
- advertising and marketing services; and
- ancillary functions contributing to business/commercial activities.

Types of E-commerce

There are a number of different types of E-commerce:

B2B—Business to Business

Business to Business E-commerce has been in use for quite a few years and is more commonly known as EDI (electronic data interchange). In the past EDI was conducted on a direct link of some form between the two businesses whereas today the most popular connection is the Internet. The two businesses pass information electronically to each other. B2B E-commerce currently makes up about 94% of all E-commerce transactions.

B2C—Business to Consumer

Business to Consumer E-commerce is relatively new. This is where the consumer accesses the system of the supplier. It is still a two-way function but is usually done solely through the Internet.

7. Why may radio be the least expensive of all media?
8. Why is radio sometimes called the theatre of the mind?
9. Why does radio have high level of acceptance at the local level?
10. What are the disadvantages of radio advertising?

Unit 10

International Payment

Learning Objectives

Text A
- to learn some methods of international payments and settlements

Text B
- to understand the importance of payment currency in international payments and settlements

Text A

Basic Methods of International Payments and Settlements

Key Factors Determining the Payment Method

International payments and settlements are financial activities conducted among different countries in which payments are effected or funds are transferred from one country to another in order to settle accounts, debts, claims, etc, emerged in the course of political, economic or cultural contracts among them. The specific payment method is generally influenced by the following factors:

- ❖ the business relationship between the seller and the buyer
- ❖ the nature of the merchandise
- ❖ industry norms
- ❖ the distance between the buyer and the seller
- ❖ the potential for currency fluctuation
- ❖ political and economic stability in both the buyer and the seller's country

Relative Security of Payment Methods

In international business, the seller and the buyer are far from each other. It is, of course, the desire of all parties for a transaction to have absolute security. The seller wants to be absolutely sure that he gets paid, while the buyer wants to make absolutely certain he gets what he has ordered. In fact, there can't be absolutes of certainty for both parties to a transaction. If one has absolute security, the other party correspondingly loses a degree of security. Also, a buyer or seller who insists on having the transaction work only for himself will find that he is losing a great deal of business. International business, therefore, often requires a compromise on the part of the seller and the buyer that leads to relative security for both parties.

Settlement on Commercial Credit

The following categories are the usual methods of payment to settle international transactions on commercial credit. All have variations and permutations, and yet here is a brief description.

Payment in Advance

It is also called advance payment. The buyer places the funds at the disposal of the seller prior to shipment of the goods or provision of services.[1] While this method of payment is expensive and contains a degree of risk, it is quite common when the manufacturing process or services delivered are specialized and capital-intensive. In such circumstances the parties may agree to fund the operation by partial payment in advance or by progressive payment. It provides greatest security for the seller and involves greatest risk for the buyer.

Characteristics:

1. Provides greatest security for the seller and greatest risk for the buyer;
2. Requires that the buyer have a high level of confidence in the ability and willingness of the seller to deliver the goods as ordered.

Basic points to be considered in using advance payment:

1. The credit standing of the exporter must be exceedingly good;
2. The economic and political conditions in the exporter's country should be very stable;
3. The importer should have sufficient balance sheet liquidity or be confident of obtaining working capital by way of import financing;
4. The importer should have the knowledge that the exchange control authorities in his country will permit advance payment to be made.[2]

Open Account

An arrangement between the buyer and the seller whereby the goods are manufactured and delivered before payment is required. Open account provides for payment at some stated specific future date and without the buyer issuing any negotiable instrument evidencing his legal commitment.[3] The seller must have absolute trust that he will be paid at the agreed date. It provides the least risk for the buyer and the greatest risk for the seller.

Essential features of open account business are:

1. The credit standing of the importer must be very good;
2. The exporter is confident that the government of the importer's country will not impose regulations deferring or blocking the transfer

of funds;

3. The exporter has sufficient liquidity to extend any necessary credit to the importer or has access to export financing.[4]

Remittance

Remittance refers to the transfer of funds from one party to another among different countries. That is, a bank (the remitting bank), at the request of its customer (the remitter), transfers a certain sum of money to its overseas branch or correspondent bank (the paying bank) instructing them to pay to a named person or corporation (the payee or beneficiary) domiciled in the country.

Collection

An arrangement whereby the goods are shipped and the relevant bill of exchange is drawn by the seller on the buyer, and documents are sent to the seller's bank with clear instructions for collection through one of its correspondent banks located in the domicile of the buyer.

1. Documentary collection: Documentary collection may be described as collection on financial instruments being accompanied by commercial documents or collection on commercial documents without being accompanied by financial instruments, that is, commercial documents without a bill of exchange.

   - The seller ships the goods and obtains the shipping documents, and usually draws a draft, either at sight or with a tenor of xx days on the buyer for the value of the goods;
   - The seller submits the draft(s) and / or document(s) to his bank, which acts as his agent;
   - The bank acknowledges that all documents as noted by the seller are presented;
   - The seller's bank sends the draft and other documents along with a collection letter to a correspondent bank usually located in the same city as the buyer;
   - Acting as an agent for the Remitting Bank, the Collecting Bank notifies the buyer upon receipt of the draft and documents;
   - All the documents, and usually title to the goods, are released to the buyer upon his payment of the amount specified or his acceptance of the draft for payment at a specified later date.

2. Clean collection: Clean collection is collection on financial instruments without being accompanied by commercial documents, such as invoice, bill of lading, insurance policy, etc.[5]

   - An arrangement whereby the seller draws only a draft on the buyer for the value of the goods / services and presents the draft to his bank.
   - The seller's bank sends the draft along with a collection instruction letter to a correspondent bank usually in the same city as the buyer.

An essential feature of collection is that although it is safer than on open account for the

4. Just as the industrial society built on and then dominated the agricultural society, the knowledge society is now building on the platform provided by the industrial society.
正如工业社会建立在农业社会基础之上并支配着农业社会一般,知识型社会也正是建立在工业社会所提供的平台之上。

just as 做"正如……"解释。

5. The question for the less industrialized developing countries is whether they can use appropriate technologies to leapfrog into the knowledge society, by-passing some of the stages of the industrial paradigm.
工业欠发达国家所面临的问题是,是否可以使用适当的技术绕过工业模式的某些阶段,直接进入知识型社会。

6. Due to the global reach of the Internet, businesses and organizations are able to send messages worldwide, exploring new markets and opportunities.
因为互联网在全球的扩展,各种企业和组织能够在全世界范围内发布信息,开拓新的市场和商机。

这里 reach 用作名词,含有"范围、延展"之意。

7. E-commerce provides customers with a platform to search product information through global markets with a wider range of choices, which makes comparison and evaluation easier and more efficient.
电子商务为客户提供了一个平台,使他们可以在选择范围更加广泛的全球市场中搜索产品信息,这使比较和评估变得更为简单和有效。

which 在这里指代的是前面的主句。

Exercises

I. Discuss the following questions.

1. What are the two primary factors driving the paradigm shift to knowledge economy?
2. What is the first real manifestation of the knowledge society?
3. What are the principal activities that can be identified as contributing to global E-commerce?
4. Among all different types of E-commerce, which is growing in use and what can be done by using it?
5. In what ways do organizations benefit from E-commerce?

II. Work in groups and discuss the following question.

If you are given some money to open a store on-line, what products do you think are the most profitable and why?

III. Match the terms in column A with the explanations in column B.

A	B
1. auction	A. to offer or propose (an amount) as a price
2. ancillary	B. to produce as a result or to bring about
3. refund	C. being beyond what is required or sufficient
4. effect	D. something transacted, especially a business agreement or exchange
5. paradigm	E. the basic facilities and services needed for the functioning of a community or society
6. dispatch	F. subordinate, auxiliary, helping
7. bid	G. a repayment of funds
8. transaction	H. to relegate to a specific destination or send on specific business
9. superfluous	I. a public sale in which property or items of merchandise are sold to the highest bidder
10. infrastructure	J. an example that serves as a pattern or model

IV. Fill in the blanks of the following sentences with the words or phrases given below. Make changes when necessary.

auction	facilitate	sustainability	distribute	bid
flexibility	dispatch	retrieve	refund	purchase

1. At an _____ in Berlin on Saturday, Steffen bought the 5.5 metres, special long wheelbase French Citroen CX 25 Prestige limousine that was part of the car pool of former East German leader Erich Honecker.

2. As with other assets, investment in marketable equity securities is recorded, when acquired at cost, which includes the _____ price and incidental acquisition costs such as brokerage commissions and taxes.

3. In order to _____ tax administration, a copy of all contracts for the import of technology signed with foreigners shall be sent to the local tax authorities for reference.

4. You may not post, _____, or reproduce in any way any copyrighted material, trademarks, or other proprietary information without obtaining the prior written consent of the owner of such proprietary rights.

5. The Business Council believed that more _____ and facilitation measures offered by the Guangdong Government to outward processing enterprises would encourage more OPOs to enter the domestic market.

6. Following the _____ economic development and increasing population in China, the process of industrialization and urbanization is also accelerating.

7. If the product is in short supply relative to the demand, the price will be _____ up and some consumers will be eliminated from the market.

8. Copies of RD slips will be sent and buyer will have to sort out claims with post office and to _____ compensation up to ￡28.
9. Party A may at any time _____ its personnel to inspect Party B's equipment room and to check the operation of Party B in regard to the use, broadcasting or re-transmission of trading information, to which Party B shall not refuse or avoid.
10. If a product was not priced properly as determined by Kodak, Kodak has the right to correct the price on any previously placed orders and re-price the product or _____ any purchases on the product.

V. Put the following into English.

1. 认识到它们的价值并利用它们创造商业机会
2. 按照链接的地址直接在商家的商品目录系统中下订单
3. 技术和商业的迅速融合
4. 知识经济真实的体现
5. 提供一张返程机票
6. 在商业拍卖网站上列出要出售的商品名录
7. 在任何地点进行任何交易
8. 进入那些传统企业难以进入的市场
9. 廉价的产品和服务所带来的竞争上的优势
10. 降低在信息处理、存储上的成本消耗

VI. Translate the following sentences into English.

1. 计算机技术的最新发展使企业家认识到电子商务可能会改变现有的商业模式。
2. 新技术的出现将经济的发展引入了一片全新的天地,并对人们的生活产生了重大的影响。
3. 经济的快速发展建立在很多因素之上,比如完善的基础设施、充足的人力资源等。
4. 电子商务为厂商提供了展示他们产品的平台,也使买家有了更多的选择。
5. 通过网络人们可以在家里工作、购物,而不用再四处奔波。

VII. Translate the following passage into Chinese.

The delay in foreign banks entering the rapidly growing PRC online banking sector can partly be attributed to the fact that specific regulations on online banking services have only recently been issued. The *Interim Measures for the Administration of Online Banking Business* were promulgated by the People's Bank of China (PBOC) in July 2001 ("Online Banking Measures") and further information and procedural clarification was made available in April 2002 with the issuance of the *Notice of the People's Republic of China on Relevant Provisions Concerning Implementation of the Interim Measures for the Administration of Online Banking Business*. The Online Banking Measures require all banking institutions established in the PRC (including Chinese invested banks, joint venture banks, wholly foreign-owned banks and foreign bank branches) to obtain approval from the PBOC before offering online banking services in-country. In addition, offshore entities offering banking services via the Internet to customers in the PRC are also required to apply to the PBOC.

Text B

Understanding E-commerce in China

With the advent of Internet technology, profound historical transformation has brought about unprecedented changes to the human society covering every aspect of people's life, work and study. Today, more people become heavily dependent upon Internet and would be at a loss without it. Thus people say that "the time of E-commerce has come." But looking back upon the development and situation of E-commerce in China, we could clearly see that our E-commerce as an industry has problems and gaps both in application fields and transaction scale. The most accountable is the country's imperfect political environment for E-commerce, weak infrastructure, and people's consumption habits.

With E-commerce in the ascendant, market value rules are still the guideline for E-commerce development.

For over 20 years of reform in China, the country's information industry has witnessed fast development whose speed is rarely seen in the world. China's telephone and network users and scale are now second in the world only to that of the United States. According to survey data publicized on January 17 of this year by CNNIC, there are 8,920,000 Internet-accessing computers and around 22.5 million Internet users in China, which is above 2% of the total national population, a 33% increase in half a year's time compared with the number of 16.9 million people in July, 2000. With the increase of the number of Internet users, Internet-related environment is also developing rapidly. Bandwidth is increased by large extent. The total bandwidth of international lines has reached 1234Mbps, 4 times of 351Mbps in July of 2000. Wireless Internet applications are surfacing. Laws and ordinances pertaining to Internet management are coming into being. Rapid increase of Internet users and improving environment provide huge market potential and development prospects for E-commerce in China.

However, the development speed and scale of E-commerce is not in direct proportion to the increase of Internet users, and is affected and restricted by many factors including policy, goods flow, credit, and consumption habit. E-shopping and E-commerce covers 12.54% of most commonly used Internet services, much less than the 95.07% of e-mail use and also less than the 18.94% of Internet game entertainment. The reason why the slump of NASDAQ broke "network miracle" into "bubble economy" overnight is that E-commerce had deviated too far from the market value rules in its pursuit of "eye-ball economy" while ignoring the fact that the market value of E-commerce must be tested in practice over time. So let us look at some of the major problems and contradictions in the process of China's E-commerce development.

China's E-commerce is still at initial stage; there are no standard "rules of game." There needs to be a wholesome legal system as safeguard.

In spite of China's rapid development of Internet environment, sharp increase of Internet users, large increase of bandwidth, and promulgation of laws and regulations concerning Internet, up to date there is not a single piece of law or ordinance that truly aims at promoting E-commerce development. On one hand it is because E-commerce develops too fast for management stability; on the other hand, the emerging E-commerce threatens to impinge upon traditional industries, and it is hard to make "rules of game" that are satisfactory to both sides, so there is a lack of stable protective measures for E-commerce.

The monopoly of telecom industry, lack of uniform industry standards and interface disorder between industries hinder the development of infrastructure.

Internet application development is the basis for E-commerce development. Therefore Internet technology application and infrastructure construction should be reinforced. For historical reasons, there has been severe monopoly in telecom industry which is the foundation of Internet technology. Thus our Internet technology development lags far behind, and bandwidth for connection to international backbone has become a "bottleneck," causing slow transmission speed, small capacity, crowdedness, and high cost of Internet access. Meanwhile, uneven development of industries leads to different industry standards. Disorder and disputes between industries makes everyone a loser.

Low social information level, limited application fields and scale make E-commerce investment cost too high and unparallel to its output ratio.

The scale of Internet application directly influences the scale of E-commerce. But the fixed investment cost for building an E-commerce platform is quite high. According to market value rules, small scale causes high unit cost, and consumers will not purchase. Little proceeds lead to big loss which deprives enterprises of more capital for continuous and steady development. Thus a vicious cycle.

Traditional consumption behavior is deeply rooted; it takes time for people to accept E-commerce.

In daily life, people have formed rooted consuming habits, and they tend to carefully select and try before they buy. But the virtual nature of

Internet causes low trust and loyalty to E-commerce. Many people use Internet for information and communication but not purchase. According to CNNIC survey, of 22.5 Internet users, only 0.86% use Internet mostly for purchase of goods. So we can see it will take quite some time for people to accept E-commerce.

Improvement of macro policy environment and infrastructure will help promote national information level and build good atmosphere for E-commerce.

Today's China is in her historical stage of industrialization, and is now faced with the information tide. We must seize this opportunity to drive industrialization by computerization, bring our acquired advantage into play, and only in this way can we achieve leapfrog development of social productivity and double-fold push to the economic growth by industrialization and computerization. We should also consider China's economic structure, productivity level, computerization process and national cultural status quo to follow a path that is unique and most suitable to China.

Chain operation realizes integrated scale operation of E-commerce and solves many conflicts in E-commerce, which is an ideal way out for E-commerce.

The year 2000 witnessed ups and downs of Internet. People cherish "Internet miracle" one day, and hear "downs" the next. "Network miracle" became "network bubble" overnight, and people were at a loss! Everyone begins to look back upon the Internet "demon." From aforesaid we know that Internet is only an information carrier platform and tool, itself bringing no market value. Value is created when market activity is exercised on the platform. However, China's Internet characteristics lead to deficiencies in E-commerce, causing losses and bankruptcies of Internet enterprises.

On the basis of studying the status quo of China's E-commerce, Chinese.com initiated the model of "network chain operation." It utilizes the advantages of a unique domain name to build and perfect a network operation platform integrating brand, infrastructure, technology, product and market for alliance members to share. By scientific and rational division of labor and collaboration, a web alliance is developed to build a unified, wholesome resource information construction platform and market service system. This realizes integrated scale operation of E-commerce, provides customers with discreet, localized and professional service, perfects E-commerce platform construction, solves many deficiencies and conflicts in E-commerce, and paves a brand-new way for E-commerce development.

From the production management perspective of an Internet enterprise, the "chain operation" of Chinese.com mostly materializes on the following three levels:

Elements of enterprise production operation

Such elements of production management as brand, capital, technology, human resources, and market are basis for enterprise existence and development. Internet enterprises are no exception, and they must have these production business elements to operate and generate proceeds. As competition is fierce in Internet industry, investment cost of these elements are quite high, bringing upon relatively high business risks.

Information resource platform construction

One of Internet's main functions is its role as information hinge. So Internet enterprises must first build their information resource platform, ensuring accurate, timely, effective and abundant information resources to satisfy user demand for information.

Development and marketing of products or services

Another major function of Internet is market hinge. But it is only an information carrier and promulgation tool, itself not bringing any market value. Therefore Internet enterprises must develop and market products or services.

Answer the following questions:

1. What are the most accountable problems and gaps in the development and situation of E-commerce in China?
2. What is still the guideline for E-commerce development?
3. Why the development speed and scale of E-commerce is not in direct proportion to the increase of Internet users?
4. What are the major problems and contradictions in the process of China's E-commerce development?
5. What is the ideal way out for E-commerce in China?

Unit 18

International Business Organizations

Learning Objectives

Text A
- to get a brief and comprehensive understanding of the only global international organization—the WTO, its history, its objective, its structure, its policy and its outstanding achievements, etc.

Text B
- to know a lot of the Asia-Pacific Economic Cooperation, or APEC

Text A

World Trade Organization

The World Trade Organization (WTO) is the only global international organization dealing with the rules of trade between nations. At its heart are the WTO agreements, negotiated and signed by the bulk of the world's trading nations and ratified in their parliaments. The goal is to help producers of goods and services, exporters, and importers conduct their business.

The WTO's Past, Present and Future

The World Trade Organization came into being in 1995. One of the youngest of the international organizations, the WTO is the successor to the General Agreement on Tariffs and Trade (GATT) established in the wake of the Second World War. So while the WTO is still young, the multilateral trading system that was originally set up under GATT is well over 50 years old.

The past 50 years have seen an exceptional growth in world trade.[1] Merchandise exports grew on average by 6% annually. Total trade in 2000 was 22-times the level of 1950. GATT and the WTO have helped to create a strong and prosperous trading system contributing to unprecedented growth.

The system was developed through a series of trade negotiations, or rounds, held under GATT. The first rounds dealt mainly with tariff reductions but later negotiations included other areas such as anti-dumping and non-tariff measures. The last round—the 1986—1994 Uruguay Round[2]—led to the WTO's creation.

The negotiations did not end there. Some continued after the end of the Uruguay Round. In February 1997 agreement was reached on telecommunications services, with 69 governments agreeing to wide-ranging liberalization measures that went beyond those agreed in the Uruguay Round.

In the same year 40 governments successfully concluded negotiations for tariff-free trade in information technology products, and 70 members concluded a financial services deal covering more than 95% of trade in banking, insurance, securities and financial information.

In 2000, new talks started on agriculture and services. These have now been incorporated into a broader agenda launched at the fourth WTO Ministerial Conference in Doha, Qatar, in November 2001.

The work programme, the Doha Development Agenda (DDA)[3], adds negotiations and other work on non-agricultural tariffs, trade and environment, WTO rules such as anti-dumping and subsidies, investment, competition policy, trade facilitation, transparency in government procurement, intellectual property, and a range of issues raised by developing countries as difficulties they face in implementing the present WTO agreements.[4]

Therefore, it has been seen that the WTO was born because of negotiations; everything the WTO does is the result of negotiations.

The WTO's Objective in Brief

The WTO's overriding objective is to help trade flow smoothly, freely, fairly and predictably.

- ❖ Administering trade agreements
- ❖ Acting as a forum for trade negotiations
- ❖ Settling trade disputes
- ❖ Reviewing national trade policies
- ❖ Assisting developing countries in trade policy issues, through technical assistance and training programmes
- ❖ Cooperating with other international organizations

The WTO Agreements

How can the WTO ensure that trade is as fair as possible, and as free as is practical? By negotiating rules and abiding by them.

The WTO's rules—the agreements—are the result of negotiations between the members. The current set were the outcome of the 1986—1994 Uruguay Round negotiations which included a major revision of the original General Agreement on Tariffs and Trade (GATT).

GATT is now the WTO's principal rule-book for trade in goods. The Uruguay Round also created new rules for dealing with trade in services, relevant aspects of intellectual property, dispute settlement, and trade policy reviews. The complete set runs to some 30,000 pages consisting of about 30 agreements and separate commitments (called schedules) made by individual members in specific areas such as lower customs duty rates and services market-opening.

Through these agreements, WTO members operate a non-discriminatory trading system that spells out their rights and their obligations.[5] Each country receives guarantees that its exports will be treated fairly and consistently in other countries' markets. Each promises to do the same for imports into its own market. The system also gives developing countries some flexibility in implementing their commitments.

Dispute Settlement

The WTO's procedure for resolving trade quarrels under the Dispute Settlement Understanding is vital for enforcing the rules and therefore for ensuring that trade flows smoothly. Countries bring disputes to the WTO if they think their rights under the agreements are being infringed. Judgements by specially-appointed independent experts are based on interpretations of the agreements and individual countries' commitments.

The system encourages countries to settle their differences through consultation. Failing that, they can follow a carefully mapped out, stage-by-stage procedure that includes the possibility of a ruling by a panel of experts, and the chance to appeal the ruling on legal grounds. Confidence in the system is borne out by the number of cases brought to the WTO[6]—around 300 cases in eight years compared to the 300 disputes dealt with during the entire life of GATT (1947—1994).

Principles of the Trading System

The WTO agreements are lengthy and complex because they are legal texts covering a wide range of activities. They deal with: agriculture, textiles and clothing, banking, telecommunications, government purchases, industrial standards and product safety, food sanitation regulations, intellectual property, and much more. But a number of simple, fundamental principles run throughout all of these documents. These principles are the foundation of the multilateral trading system, of which the principle of trading without discrimination plays an important role.

A closer look at this principle—trade without discrimination:

Most-favored-nation (MFN): Treating other people equally

Under the WTO agreements, countries cannot normally discriminate between their trading partners. Grant someone a special favor (such as a lower customs duty rate for one of their products) and you have to do the same for all other WTO members.

This principle is known as most-favored-nation (MFN) treatment. It is so important that it is the first article of the General Agreement on Tariffs and Trade (GATT), which governs trade in goods. MFN is also a priority in the General Agreement on Trade in Services (GATS) (Article 2) and the Agreement on Trade-Related Aspects of Intellectual Property Rights (TRIPS) (Article 4), although in each agreement the principle is handled slightly differently. Together, those three agreements cover all three main areas of trade handled by the WTO.

Some exceptions are allowed. For example, countries can set up a free trade agreement that applies only to goods traded within the group—discriminating against goods from outside. Or they can give developing countries special access to their markets. Or a country can raise barriers against products that are considered to be traded unfairly from specific countries. And in services, countries are allowed, in limited circumstances, to discriminate. But the agreements only permit these exceptions under strict conditions. In general, MFN means that every time a country lowers a trade barrier or opens up a market, it has to do so for the same goods or services from all its trading partners—whether rich or poor, weak or strong.

National treatment: Treating foreigners and locals equally

Imported and locally-produced goods should be treated equally—at least after the foreign goods have entered the market. The same should apply to foreign and domestic services, and to foreign and local trademarks, copyrights and patents. This principle of "national treatment" (giving others the same treatment as one's own nationals) is also found in all the three main WTO agreements (Article 3 of GATT, Article 17 of GATS and Article 3 of TRIPS), although once again the principle is handled slightly differently in each of these.

National treatment only applies once a product, service or item of intellectual property has entered the market. Therefore, charging customs duty on an import is not a violation of national treatment even if locally-produced products are not charged an equivalent tax.

Secretariat

The WTO Secretariat, based in Geneva, has around 600 staff and is headed by a director-general. Its annual budget is roughly 160 million Swiss francs. It does not have branch offices outside Geneva. Since decisions are taken by the members themselves, the Secretariat does not have the decision-making role that other international bureaucracies are given.

The Secretariat's main duties are to supply technical support for the various councils and committees and the ministerial conferences, to provide technical assistance for developing countries, to analyze world trade, and to explain WTO affairs to the public and media.

The Secretariat also provides some forms of legal assistance in the dispute settlement process and advises governments wishing to become members of the WTO.

New Words

ratify	/ˈrætɪfaɪ/	v.	批准,认可
successor	/səkˈsesə/	n.	继承者,接任者
exceptional	/ɪkˈsepʃənəl/	adj.	杰出的,非凡的
tariff	/ˈtærɪf/	n.	关税
subsidy	/ˈsʌbsɪdi/	n.	(国家间的)财政援助
overriding	/ˌəʊvəˈraɪdɪŋ/	adj.	压倒一切的,首要的
resolve	/rɪˈzɒlv/	v.	解决
enforce	/ɪnˈfɔːs/	v.	推行,实施(法律等)
infringe	/ɪnˈfrɪndʒ/	v.	破坏,侵犯,侵害
appeal	/əˈpiːl/	v.	指控,控诉,为……提出上诉
confidence	/ˈkɒnfidəns/	n.	秘密(性);信任
sanitation	/sænɪˈteɪʃən/	n.	卫生;卫生设施
priority	/praɪˈɒrɪti/	n.	优先,优先权
barrier	/ˈbæriə/	n.	(贸易)壁垒;限制
violation	/ˌvaɪəˈleɪʃən/	n.	违反,违背
secretariat	/ˌsekrəˈteəriət/	n.	秘书处,尤指国际组织的
staff	/stɑːf/	n.	全体职员
bureaucracy	/bjʊəˈrɒkrəsi/	n.	行政系统,行政机构
council	/ˈkaʊnsəl/	n.	理事会,委员会
ministerial	/ˌmɪnɪˈstɪəriəl/	adj.	部长级的;行政(上)的

Phrases

deal with	涉及
the bulk of	大半,大多数
on average	平均起来
contributing to	对……有贡献的,起作用的
intellectual property	知识产权
abide by	坚持,遵守
run to	达到,发展到
non-discriminatory	一视同仁的,不歧视的
spell out	讲清楚,清楚地说明
map out	计划;绘制……的地图
a panel of	一专门小组
on legal ground	基于法律原由
be borne out	被证实了,被证明是理所当然的

charge on...	征收……
customs duty	关税
annual budget	年度预算

Special Terms

General Agreement on Tariffs and Trade (GATT)	关贸总协定
Dispute Settlement Understanding	《关于争议处理规则和程序的谅解》，简称《争端解决谅解》
anti-dumping	反倾销政策的
dispute settlement	争端解决
most-favored-nation treatment (MFN)	最惠国待遇

Notes

1. The past 50 years have seen an exceptional growth in world trade.
   在过去的 50 年里世界贸易经历了不同寻常的增长。

2. Uruguay Round：GATT 共主持了八轮多边贸易谈判，最近的持续时间最长的一轮叫乌拉圭回合谈判，该回合从 1986 年开始，前后长达 7 年半之久，其重要成果之一就是创立了 WTO。

3. Doha Development Agenda (DDA)："多哈发展议程"是新的一轮贸易谈判。这个回合的谈判于 2001 年 10 月在卡塔尔启动，预定 2004 年底完成。但谈判在 2003 年 9 月墨西哥坎昆（Cancun）会议期间破裂。从 2004 年初开始，美国副国务卿罗伯特·泽奥利克为打破多哈发展议程的僵局频频出访，与 40 多位贸易官员探讨推动谈判的最佳途径，行程达 32000 英里。7 月 25 日，泽奥利克又与贝宁、布基纳法索、乍德和马里这四个西非国家的部长开始商讨他们所关心的棉花贸易问题。

4. ...a range of issues raised by developing countries as difficulties they face in implementing the present WTO agreements.
   发展中国家提出了他们在履行世贸组织协议的过程中所面临的一系列有难度的问题。

5. Through these agreements, WTO members operate a non-discriminatory trading system that spells out their rights and their obligations.
   通过这些协议，世贸组织成员国运行着一个没有歧视的贸易体系，这一体系阐述清楚了他们的权利和义务。

6. Confidence in the system is borne out by the number of cases brought to the WTO.
   世贸组织所处理过的案例的数量证明了成员国对这一体系的信任程度。

Exercises

I. Discuss the following questions.
1. According to the article, what is the goal of the WTO in general?
2. What is the relationship between GATT and the WTO?
3. What role does negotiation play in the development and operation of the WTO?
4. How can the WTO ensure that trade is as fair as possible, and as free as is practical?
5. What is the most-favored-nation (MFN) policy?

II. Make a list of other international organizations besides the WTO to see what similarities and differences they have.

III. Match the terms in column A with the explanations in column B.

A	B
1. overriding	A. well above average; extraordinary; uncommon
2. priority	B. to approve and give formal sanction to; confirm
3. exceptional	C. financial assistance given by one person or government to another
4. enforce	D. first in priority; more important than all others
5. infringe	E. to make easy or easier
6. ratify	F. precedence, especially established by order of importance or urgency; an established right to precedence
7. facilitate	G. to bring to a usually successful conclusion; to make a determination
8. subsidy	H. the personnel who carry out a specific enterprise
9. resolve	I. to compel observance of or obedience to
10. staff	J. to transgress or exceed the limits of; violate; to encroach on someone or something

IV. Fill in the blanks of the following sentences with the words or phrases given below. Make changes when necessary.

unprecedented	map out	resolve	consult	enforce
spell out	bear out	appeal	ratify	infringe

1. Bars in Guangzhou will still be forced to close at 2 a.m. despite the late start times for World Cup soccer matches, police said yesterday. Police may be busy _____ the rule.

2. The men who had written and signed the Constitution became the leaders of the fight to _____ it.

3. The early 1990's finds an/a _____ tide of rural workers flooding into big cities in China.

4. The president will not make his reply to the ambassador until he has _____ with the cabinet.

5. What he has done really _____ the patent held by another company.

6. The contract _____ the two sides' rights and obligations, so it's not hard to find whose fault it is.

7. Confidence in the system is _____ by the number of cases brought to the WTO—around 300 cases in eight years compared to the 300 disputes dealt with during the entire life of GATT (1947—1994).

8. The board of the company thought the sentence of the local court was unfair; therefore, they decided to _____ to the Supreme Court for a new trial.

9. The WTO's procedure for _____ trade quarrels under the Dispute Settlement Understanding is vital for enforcing the rules and therefore for ensuring that trade flows smoothly.

10. The agency _____ an advertising campaign for the new product.

V. Put the following into English.

1. 制定和规范国际多边贸易规则
2. 组织多边贸易谈判
3. 解决成员之间的贸易争端
4. 提高政府采购透明度
5. 在国际贸易中消除歧视性待遇
6. 通过协商解决分歧
7. 启动新一轮多边贸易谈判
8. 达成电信服务协议
9. 部长级会议
10. 减少贸易壁垒并增加投资

VI. Translate the following sentences into English.

1. APEC 成立于 1989 年,其目的是为了进一步推进区域性经济繁荣并加强亚太地区国家间的经济合作。

2. WTO 的协议保证成员国的出口商品在其他成员国的市场上得到公平的待遇,如果成员国认为自己受到协议保护的权利受到了侵害,他可以把这一争端提请 WTO 来解决。

3. 1997 年 2 月 15 日,WTO 69 个成员国达成电信服务协议,此协议于 1998 年 2 月 15 日生效。

4. 1997年12月,70个国家达成一项多边金融协议,同意开放各自的金融服务业,它包括95%以上的有关银行、保险、证券和金融信息等方面的贸易。
5. 与其前身关贸总协定相比,WTO在调解成员间争端方面具有更高的权威性和有效性。

VII. *Translate the following passage into Chinese.*

In the WTO, when countries agree to open their markets for goods or services, they "bind" their commitments. For goods, these bindings amount to ceilings on customs tariff rates. Sometimes countries tax imports at rates that are lower than the bound rates. Frequently this is the case in developing countries. In developed countries the rates actually charged and the bound rates tend to be the same.

A country can change its bindings, but only after negotiating with its trading partners, which could mean compensating them for loss of trade. One of the achievements of the Uruguay Round of multilateral trade talks was to increase the amount of trade under binding commitments. In agriculture, 100% of products now have bound tariffs. The result of all this: a substantially higher degree of market security for traders and investors.

The system tries to improve predictability and stability in other ways as well. One way is to discourage the use of quotas and other measures used to set limits on quantities of imports—administering quotas can lead to more red-tape and accusations of unfair play. Another is to make countries' trade rules as clear and public ("transparent") as possible. Many WTO agreements require governments to disclose their policies and practices publicly within the country or by notifying the WTO. The regular surveillance of national trade policies through the Trade Policy Review Mechanism provides a further means of encouraging transparency both domestically and at the multilateral level.

Text B

Asia-Pacific Economic Cooperation

What is Asia-Pacific Economic Cooperation?

Asia-Pacific Economic Cooperation, or APEC, is the premier forum for facilitating economic growth, cooperation, trade and investment in the Asia-Pacific region.

APEC is the only inter-governmental grouping in the world operating on the basis of non-binding commitments, open dialogue and equal respect for the views of all participants. Unlike the WTO or other multilateral trade bodies, APEC has no treaty obligations required of its participants. Decisions made within APEC are reached by consensus and commitments are undertaken on a voluntary basis.

Asia-Pacific Economic Cooperation (APEC) operates as a cooperative, multilateral economic and trade forum. It is unique in that it represents the only inter-governmental grouping in the world committed to reducing trade barriers and increasing investments without requiring its members to enter into legally binding obligations. The forum succeeds by promoting dialogue and equal respect for the views of all participants and making decisions based on consensus to achieve its free and open trade and investment goals.

APEC has 21 members—referred to as "Member Economies"—which account for approximately 40% of the world's population, approximately 56% of world GDP and about 48% of world trade. It also proudly represents the most economically dynamic region in the world having generated nearly 70% of global economic growth in its first 10 years.

APEC's 21 Member Economies are Australia; Brunei Darussalam; Canada; Chile; People's Republic of China; Hong Kong, China; Indonesia; Japan; Republic of Korea; Malaysia; Mexico; New Zealand; Papua New Guinea; Peru; The Republic of the Philippines; The Russian Federation; Singapore; Chinese Taipei; Thailand; United States of America; Viet Nam.

Purpose and Goals

APEC was established in 1989 to further enhance economic growth and prosperity for the region and to strengthen the economic cooperation in the Asia-Pacific community.

Since its inception, APEC has worked to reduce tariffs and other trade barriers across the Asia-Pacific region, creating efficient domestic economies and dramatically increasing exports. Key to achieving APEC's vision are what are referred to as the "Bogor Goals" of free and open trade and investment in the Asia-Pacific by 2010 for industrialised economies and 2020 for developing economies. These goals were adopted by leaders at their 1994 meeting in Bogor, Indonesia.

Free and open trade and investment helps economies to grow, creates jobs and provides greater opportunities for international trade and investment. In contrast, protectionism keeps prices high and fosters inefficiencies in certain industries. Free and open trade helps to lower the costs of production and thus reduces the prices of goods and services—a direct benefit to all.

APEC also works to create an environment for the safe and efficient movement of goods, services and people across borders in the region through policy alignment and economic and technical cooperation.

APEC's Achievements

Since its inception in 1989, the APEC region has consistently been the most economically dynamic part of the world. In its first decade, APEC Member Economies generated nearly 70 percent of global economic growth and the APEC region consistently outperformed the rest of the world, even during the Asian financial crisis.

APEC Member Economies work together to sustain this economic growth through a commitment to open trade, investment and economic reform. By progressively reducing tariffs and other barriers to trade, APEC Member Economies have become more efficient and exports have expanded dramatically.

A highlight of APEC's achievements in the first 10 years:
- exports increased by 113% to over US$2.5 trillion;
- foreign direct investment grew by 210% overall, and by 475% in lower income APEC economies;
- real gross national product grew by about a third overall, and by 74% in lower income APEC economies;
- gross domestic product per person in lower income APEC economies grew by 61%.

Consumers in the Asia-Pacific have both directly and indirectly benefited from the collective and individual actions of APEC Member Economies. Some direct benefits include increased job opportunities, more training programmes, stronger social safety nets and poverty alleviation. More broadly however, APEC Member Economies on average enjoy lower cost of living because reduced trade barriers and a more economically competitive region lowers prices for goods and services that everyone needs on a daily basis, from food to clothes to mobile phones.

More importantly, economic growth leads to social advancement. In just the first decade of APEC's existence, we have seen:
- the United Nations Development Programme (UNDP) Human Development Index for lower income APEC economies improve by nearly 18 percent;
- poverty in East Asian APEC economies fall by about a third (165 million people), mostly as a result of strong economic growth;
- 195 million new jobs created in APEC Member Economies, including 174 million in lower income economies;
- infant mortality falling and life expectancy rising in lower income economies, which is linked to significant improvements in access to sanitation and safe water, and expanding public expenditure on health;
- heavy investments in human capital, with improving education enrolment ratios and growing expenditures in education.

APEC's Scope of Work

Asia-Pacific Economic Cooperation (APEC)

works in three broad areas to meet the Bogor Goals of free and open trade and investment in the Asia-Pacific by 2010 for developed economies and 2020 for developing economies.

Known as APEC's "Three Pillars," APEC focuses on three key areas:
- ❖ Trade and Investment Liberalisation
- ❖ Business Facilitation
- ❖ Economic and Technical Cooperation (ECOTECH)

The outcomes of these three areas enable APEC Member Economies to strengthen their economies by pooling resources within the region and achieving efficiencies. Tangible benefits are also delivered to consumers in the APEC region through increased training and employment opportunities, greater choices in the marketplace, cheaper goods and services and improved access to international markets.

Trade and Investment Liberalisation reduces and eventually eliminates tariff and non-tariff barriers to trade and investment. Protectionism is expensive because it raises prices for goods and services. Thus, Trade and Investment Liberation focuses on opening markets to increase trade and investment among economies, resulting in economic growth for APEC Member Economies and increased standard of living for all.

Business Facilitation focuses on reducing the costs of business transactions, improving access to trade information and aligning policy and business strategies to facilitate growth, and free and open trade. Essentially, Business Facilitation helps importers and exporters in the Asia-Pacific meet and conduct business more efficiently, thus reducing costs of production and leading to increased trade, cheaper goods and services and more employment opportunities due to an expanded economy.

ECOTECH is dedicated to providing training and cooperation to build capacities in all APEC Member Economies to take advantage of global trade and the New Economy. This area builds capacity at the institutional and personal level to assist APEC Member Economies and their people gain the necessary skills to meet their economic potential.

APEC's Operation

Every year one of the 21 APEC Member Economies plays host to APEC meetings and serves as the APEC Chair. The APEC host economy is responsible for chairing the annual Economic Leaders' Meeting, Selected Ministerial Meetings, Senior Officials Meetings, the APEC Business Advisory Council and the APEC Study Centres Consortium and also fills the Executive Director position at the APEC Secretariat. The Deputy Executive Director position is filled by a senior diplomat from the economy which will host in the next year.

APEC is not a donor organisation. Instead, APEC activities are centrally funded by small annual contributions from APEC Member Economies—since 1999 these have totalled US $3.38 million each year. These contributions are used to fund a small Secretariat in Singapore and various projects which support APEC's economic and trade goals. Since 1997

Japan has provided additional funds for projects (between US$2.7 and 4.2 million annually, depending on amount and exchange rates) which support APEC's trade and investment liberalisation and facilitation goals. Projects generally—
- relate to the priorities of APEC Economic Leaders and APEC Ministers,
- cover the interests of at least several APEC Member Economies,
- build capacity,
- improve economic efficiency, and
- encourage the participation of the business sector, non-governmental institutions and women.

APEC Member Economies also provide considerable resources to assist in the operations of APEC. These include the secondment of professional staff to the Secretariat; the hosting of meetings; and partial (or full) funding of some projects.

APEC Secretariat

The APEC Secretariat is based in Singapore and operates as the core support mechanism for the APEC process. It provides coordination, technical and advisory support as well as information management, communications and public outreach services.

The APEC Secretariat performs a central project management role, assisting APEC Member Economies and APEC fora with overseeing more than 230 APEC-funded projects. APEC's annual budget is also administered by the APEC Secretariat.

The APEC Secretariat is headed by an Executive Director and a Deputy Executive Director. These positions are filled by officers of ambassadorial rank from the current and incoming host economies respectively. The positions rotate annually. For 2006, the Executive Director is Ambassador Tran Trong Toan from Viet Nam and the Deputy Executive Director is Ambassador Colin Heseltine from Australia.

Answer the following questions:
1. How is APEC different from the WTO or other multilateral trade bodies?
2. What are the purposes and goals for APEC?
3. What are APEC's three key areas known as "Three Pillars"?
4. Compared with the WTO, what do you think of APEC's operation?
5. Please sum up APEC's outstanding achievements since its inception in 1989.

Unit 1

Text A

I. Discuss the following questions.
   (Omitted)

II. Analyze the case below and discuss the questions.
   (Omitted)

III. Match the terms in column A with the explanations in column B.
   1. —C   2. —F   3. —D   4. —H   5. —G
   6. —E   7. —J   8. —A   9. —I   10. —B

IV. Fill in the blanks of the following sentences with the words or phrases given below. Make changes when necessary.
   1. granted   2. crack into   3. assimilated   4. incorporate
   5. commitment   6. hamper   7. secure   8. withdrew
   9. exposes   10. exclusive

V. Put the following into English.
   1. firms specializing in export sales
   2. control a considerable share in manufacturing trade and investment
   3. enjoy relative competitive advantage in production and technology
   4. follow the operational strategy of the franchisers
   5. acquire an on-going firm in the host country
   6. lose control over the licensee on technology
   7. fully assimilate the latest technology offered by the headquarters
   8. engage in business on a global basis
   9. launch/introduce the new products to foreign markets
   10. hold the majority share of the joint venture

VI. Translate the following sentences into English.
   1. Wholly-owned subsidiaries may be started from the blueprint or by acquisition of a firm in the host country.
   2. Licensing can be used to enter and cultivate a foreign market that can't be tapped by export or some other entry mode.

3. Export is the easiest and most common approach for firms entering the international market because the risks of financial loss can be minimized.

4. A company's choice of entry mode to a foreign market depends on different factors, such as the ownership advantages, location advantages of the market, etc.

5. Many economists are constantly studying a variety of theoretical and practical issues arising from the expansion of international business activities.

VII. Translate the following passage into Chinese.

在合资企业的形成过程中，获得具有适当的教育背景和文化背景并且有价值的稀缺的人力资源是一个关键因素。欧洲和美国公司与日本企业进行合资的重要原因之一就是由于其"外来者"的身份，它们自身无法吸引本土的管理人员。实际上，大量合资企业成立的明显意图就是招纳具有管理能力的本土人士。本地合作伙伴参与合资企业的发展使合资企业在管理方面的负担小于独资公司。

资本是企业在进行合资时经常寻求的另一种资源。资本市场的特征是交易成本高昂，信贷市场对于那些没有或很少有信贷记录或信贷经验的年轻企业来说也并不完美。投资那些没有担保的高风险项目，比如研发，交易成本也非常高。规模小的技术型企业通常会在寻求资金进行扩张方面遇到巨大的困难，也因为如此，其合资的吸引力也很小。

Text B (Omitted)

Unit 2

Text A

I. Discuss the following questions.

(Omitted)

II. Analyze the case below and discuss the questions.

(Omitted)

III. Match the terms in column A with the explanations in column B.

1. —J   2. —I   3. —H   4. —G   5. —F
6. —E   7. —D   8. —C   9. —B   10. —A

IV. Fill in the blanks of the following sentences with the words or phrases given below. Make changes when necessary.

1. as   2. competitive   3. as well   4. such as
5. productivity   6. Except for   7. Nonetheless   8. likely
9. unlike   10. In addition

V. Put the following into English.

1. to impose restrictions on imports, and subsidize exports

2. to succeed in achieving a large trade surplus

3. natural advantage in endowment

4. acquired advantage in production

5. to export labor-intensive products and import capital-intensive products

6. to fail to distinguish human capital from physical capital

7. The markets within the industrial countries might overall have similar demands.

8. The occurrence of lags gives rise to technological-gap trade.

VI. Translate the following sentences into English.

1. If one country succeeds in achieving a large trade surplus, it can only do so if other countries run an equivalent trade deficit.

2. On the contrary, trade should benefit all countries by enabling them to enjoy more goods at lower cost than could be obtained in the absence of trade.

3. Countries in which labor is abundant will possess a comparative cost advantage in labor-intensive industries, while other countries in which capital is abundant will enjoy a comparative advantage in capital-intensive industries.

4. Evidence has shown that technological change and the international process of technological creation and diffusion exert a strong influence on patterns of trade.

5. It is indicated that the patterns of trade on durable consumer goods are in accordance with the theory of the International Product Life Cycle.

VII. Translate the following passage into Chinese.

　　自由贸易可以通过实现产业间和产业内两个层面上的专业化而获利。长期利益包括以下内容：(1)规模经济利益；(2)竞争加剧所带来的效率利益；(3)促进资本投资；(4)加快技术革新速度；(5)通胀缓和所带来的产出增加。自由贸易可以从总体上增加全球经济福利。

　　贸易保护主要有两种形式：关税和非关税壁垒。各国政府实行贸易保护主义的原因有很多：保护国内产业、平衡国际收支、征收更多税费，等等。贸易保护措施有：关税、进口配额、进口许可、禁运和自动出口限制等。

Text B (Omitted)

Unit 3

Text A

I. Discuss the following questions.
(Omitted)

II. Analyze the case below and discuss the questions.
(Omitted)

III. Match the terms in column A with the explanations in column B.

| 1.—J | 2.—F | 3.—C | 4.—G | 5.—B |
| 6.—H | 7.—A | 8.—E | 9.—I | 10.—D |

IV. Fill in the blanks of the following sentences with the words or phrases given below. Make changes when necessary.

1. consumption　　2. separately　　3. local, serve　　4. base

5. exported   6. merchandise   7. treatment   8. derived
9. presence, presence

V. Put the following into English.
1. service suppliers
2. to gain a share of the market
3. a firm based in another country
4. to make a bank loan to a firm
5. to be bound up with the movement of capital and labor across national borders
6. earnings from the export of services
7. domestically owned civil airlines
8. to absorb services supplied by another country
9. the relative importance of service inputs in manufacturing industry
10. greater investments of human capital

VI. Translate the following sentences into English.
1. Services with their nature distinct from that of industrial and consumer goods deserve special consideration.
2. The expansion of the world market has pulled the firms' demand for services and service agencies become market seekers for their prospective customers all over the world.
3. Accounting for a quarter of the volume of international trade, the international trade in services has a significant role to play in improving economic growth, employment expansion and international balance of trade of the countries that export and import services.
4. By exporting hi-tech services, the developed countries obtain high earnings; in addition, by employing low-cost labor from the developing countries, they can not only replenish labor resources but also gain bigger profits to make up for their trade deficit.
5. Taking advantage of their low-cost labor, some developing countries with abundant labor resources vigorously develop their export of services so as to gain foreign exchange.

VII. Translate the following passage into Chinese.

商品贸易在出口时需要填写报价单，而大多数服务贸易的出口不需要填报价单，也不需要在进入别国的时候通关。因此，要准确计算服务贸易的出口额并不容易做到。

如今，大多数业务服务公司开发国际业务的最重要的原因是寻找新的市场，但有些服务公司，像会计和广告公司就不是这样，他们开发国际业务的主要原因是一方面寻求新的市场，一方面还要跟踪客户。

Text B (Omitted)

Unit 4

Text A

I. Discuss the following questions.
(Omitted)

II. Analyze the case below and discuss the questions.
(Omitted)

III. Match the terms in column A with the explanations in column B.

1. —E   2. —H   3. —A   4. —F   5. —B
6. —J   7. —I   8. —C   9. —D   10. —G

IV. Fill in the blanks of the following sentences with the words or phrases given below. Make changes when necessary.

1. transitional   2. assimilate   3. licensing   4. address
5. equity   6. property   7. depreciate 8. capital
9. stake   10. subsidize

V. Put the following into English.

1. make scientific and technological developments accessible to all industries
2. seek international sales, market share, and cheaper production costs
3. migration of skilled personnel with knowledge of particular technologies
4. clear away barriers that impede technology transfers
5. improve the quality of the local environment via appropriate technologies
6. expand foreign markets for their national firms
7. enable private sector involvement
8. develop foreign trade in a reasonable sequence
9. purchase of stock or shares of foreign companies through investment funds
10. build and strengthen the system of innovation

VI. Translate the following sentences into English.

1. Developing countries, through the purchase of the core technology of foreign companies, may enhance their national strength or otherwise improve people's quality of life.
2. Local enterprises have laid a solid foundation for technologic innovation through bank loans, government subsidiaries, and so on.
3. Currently in China, some private-owned enterprises have been at the forefront of technology development.
4. The import of technology must be adjusted to local conditions, which will help to avoid unnecessary waste and minimize the risk.
5. Venture capital is characterized by being longer term and higher risk, with a greater degree of management control exerted by the investor.

VII. Translate the following passage into Chinese.

　　如果一家公司表示有兴趣获得一项试验室技术的许可，那么负责技术转让许可的人员就会对此公司是否有可能成功地开发这项技术并进行市场运作进行评估。一个合格的被许可人必须配置有必要的经济、研发、生产、销售以及管理能力并承担相应的责任。有能力、合格的被许可人能够保障试验室技术能够成功地商业化，并且使大众最终从中获益。一旦发现一个公司具有必要的能力，许可官员就会与之商谈许可协议。不同的发明需要不同的许可策略。例如，对于可能被广泛使用的科学工具的一般策略就是非专用许可（比如，可以许可数家公司）。相反，如果一项技术走向市场需要大量的投资，那么就只能许可给单独一家公司。由于特殊的使用领域或地理区域的不同，许可有可能是专用许可，也有可能是非专用许可。

Text B (Omitted)

Unit 5

Text A

I. Discuss the following questions.

(Omitted)

II. Calculation.

Specific tariff to be levied: $0.051 × 4,000 = $2,040

Ad valorem tariff to be levied: 6.25% × $5,000 × 4,000 = $1,250,000

Total tariff : $2,040 + $1,250,000 = $1,252,040

III. Match the terms in column A with the explanations in column B.

1. —J 2. —F 3. —D 4. —G 5. —C
6. —E 7. —H 8. —B 9. —I 10. —A

IV. Fill in the blanks of the following sentences with the words or phrases given below. Make changes when necessary.

1. artificially 2. implemented 3. detrimental 4. specifies
5. legitimate 6. precondition 7. stimulate 8. imposed
9. restraints 10. practice

V. Put the following into English.

1. resource allocation mechanism
2. distorted prices
3. trade protection policies
4. imports of raw materials and consumer goods
5. domestic enterprises with strong competitiveness
6. market access
7. favorable policies
8. domestic substitutes
9. a particular interest group
10. administrative procedures

VI. Translate the following sentences into English.

1. To some extent trade barriers can protect domestic enterprises, but overuse of this means is detrimental to national economic development.

2. Many countries in a free trade protocol with their neighboring countries still impose trade barriers on the rest countries in the world.

3. In the mediaeval times, tariffs were once levied by local governments, which is very rare now. Tariffs are usually levied by central governments.

4. For various reasons almost all countries impose trade barriers on certain goods crossing their borders. Trade barriers are mostly used to restrict imports, and two most frequently used import barriers are tariffs and quota.

5. Trade barriers, usually protective, are used to protect domestic manufacturers which are not rivals of foreign companies in free market.

VII. Translate the following passage into Chinese.

　　大多数经济学家认为,商品和服务在世界范围内的自由交换,可能对贸易各方都有益处。但实际上,世界上只有少数国家和地区实行自由贸易。香港是唯一一个真正意义上的贸易自由港。几乎其他所有的国家和地区,无论大小,都对外国进口商品实施某种形式的贸易壁垒。

　　多数贸易壁垒都有同样的宗旨:增加贸易成本,提高进口商品的价格。其目的不仅在于增加政府收入,也在于使进口商品价格相对高于国内替代品的价格,从而减少进口;将国外倾销商品的价格提高到市场水平,抵制倾销行为;报复别国对本国施加贸易壁垒的行为;保护本国的支柱产业,比如农业;扶植新兴产业的发展,使其具有国际竞争力。

Text B (Omitted)

Unit 6

Text A

I. **Discuss the following questions.**
(Omitted)

II. **Tell whether the following statements are True or False according to the text.**
1. F　　2. F　　3. F　　4. F　　5. T　　6. F

III. **Match the terms in column A with the explanations in column B.**
1.—E　　2.—F　　3.—A　　4.—H　　5.—I
6.—D　　7.—B　　8.—G　　9.—C

IV. **Fill in the blanks of the following sentences with the words or phrases given below. Make changes when necessary.**
1. embodies　　2. accelerated　　3. integrated　　4. penetration
5. consulted　　6. consecutive　　7. pervaded　　8. miscellaneous
9. unprecedented　　10. implication

V. **Put the following into English.**
1. products bearing the words "Made in China"
2. the largest country of labor-intensive products
3. foreign direct investment

4. to provide technology licensing and cooperative production

5. to conduct import and export trade on the Internet

6. processing trade as a leading trade form

7. rank the second in world's export trade

8. to acquire a larger share on the international market

9. an important export destination for other Asian countries

10. China accounts for over 11% of Japan's exports.

VI. **Translate the following sentences into English.**

1. China has increased its penetration into advanced country markets, and has simultaneously become a more important export destination, especially for regional economies.

2. The historical evidence, together with the still substantial development potential of the country, suggests that China could maintain relatively strong export growth for a number of years going forward.

3. A high share of imports for processing is embodied in China's exports as manufactured products.

4. China conducts various modes of trade such as processing with customer's materials, processing with consumer's samples, assembling with customer's parts, compensation trade, processing with imported materials in addition to general trade.

5. Since 1980s as enterprises in China experienced a rapid growth, business people started to develop processing trade in developing countries using mature technology, equipment and raw and processed materials.

VII. **Translate the following passage into Chinese.**

从20世纪90年代起,中国的进出口持续发展。中国贸易以比它的国内生产总值还快的速度增长。2001年它的贸易依存度是44%,是1990年的1.47倍还多。除1993年外,中国的出口量比它的进口量多,并在20世纪90年代经历了一个快速增长的贸易顺差。外贸成为20世纪90年代中国经济增长的主要引擎,平均占GDP增长的7.5%。比如,中国出口量增长10%,如果把直接和间接贡献作用都计算在内,那么在20世纪90年代它的GDP就会增长1%。

Text B (Omitted)

Unit 7

Text A

I. **Discuss the following questions.**

(Omitted)

II. **Analyze the case below and discuss the questions.**

(Omitted)

III. **Match the terms in column A with the explanations in column B.**

1. —F   2. —I   3. —A   4. —H   5. —J

6. —B   7. —C   8. —D   9. —G   10. —E

IV. Fill in the blanks of the following sentences with the words or phrases given below. Make changes when necessary.
1. standpoint   2. contact   3. concept   4. exclusive   5. integral
6. distribution 7. generated 8. convey   9. grip   10. eliminate

V. Put the following into English.
1. channel of distribution
2. market concept
3. development procedure of new products
4. competition-based pricing
5. market intermediaries
6. market coverage
7. independent retailer
8. trademark tactics
9. resources distribution
10. profit maximization

VI. Translate the following sentences into English.
1. A superb package plays an important part in the promotion of the product's sales.
2. The pricing strategy of a company should reflect the company's long-term development strategy, as well as the market goal in the near future.
3. Advertisement is one of the marketing strategies for the promotion of products. A product ad should demonstrate the product's quality, satisfying features and price.
4. Mainly dealing in the scope of stores and shops, most retailers store up goods in large quantity and variety.
5. The intensification of competition forced many factories to make products for professional markets, thus increasing the cost.

VII. Translate the following passage into Chinese.

　　报纸作为目前最为流行的广告媒介，具有成本和CPM（千次印象费）低的特点。目前主要都市报纸四分之一版面的CPM平均为4.64美元。

　　从地域角度来看，报纸具有很大的选择性。它们使得广告商可以准确地将广告投放到目的城市区域。从兴趣选择的角度来说，大多数报纸可以涵盖所有不同经济和社会阶层的读者，其影响力极为广泛。报纸广告具有一个得天独厚的条件，那就是它的机动灵活性。在大多数情况下，在印刷前数小时内都可以对广告样本做出改动。这使得广告商可以紧随全国性或地方性的事件、天气或者内部事务的变动。例如，《圣路易斯邮报》要求广告样本在报纸印刷前48小时送达即可。

　　因为80%的成人有读日报的习惯，报纸的覆盖面是非常高的。报纸使广告商可以迅速地传达到几乎所有的特定市场。报纸广告的频率同广告投入报纸的次数直接相关。广告投入的次数越多，读者阅读的频率就越高。

Text B　(Omitted)

Unit 8

Text A

I. **Discuss the following questions.**
   (Omitted)

II. **Analyze the case below and discuss the questions.**
   (Omitted)

III. **Match the terms in column A with the explanations in column B.**
   1. —H   2. —F   3. —A   4. —E
   5. —D   6. —C   7. —B   8. —G

IV. **Fill in the blanks of the following sentences with the words or phrases given below. Make changes when necessary.**
   1. vulnerable   2. curb   3. liability   4. skyrocket
   5. augur   6. play out   7. mandatory   8. promulgated
   9. quality   10. spot

V. **Put the following into English.**
   1. macroeconomic environment that influences marketing decision
   2. to realize the changes of people's buying behavior
   3. to consider the combination of economic variables to adapt to the purpose of marketing
   4. the overall indicator of evaluating market potential
   5. the huge income gap between the urban people and the rural people
   6. to hold a 90 percent share of the notebook computer market
   7. to keep a single-digit inflation rate
   8. to make strategic response to new marketing environment
   9. to keep long-term competitive advantages in the ever-changing market
   10. all the specific rules and regulations that restrict international marketing

VI. **Translate the following sentences into English.**
   1. In order to cultivate cultural sensitivity and accept new ways of acting within an organization, the management should formulate an internal training program.
   2. The evaluation of a country's market environment should start from the evaluation of economic variables related to the size and nature of the market.
   3. The complexity and vast changes of the Chinese market have always been the biggest challenges for Western marketers. Since the differences in cultural and economic background are so distinct that China is regarded as a combination of many small markets.
   4. Some governments opened their economy to foreign investors and only imposed the minimal constraints on them, hoping that these policies could promote the fast development of their economies.

5. WTO defines well-accepted economic practice in the international world for its member countries. Although it cannot have direct influences on individual enterprises, it does indirectly influence them through providing a more stable international market environment.

VII. **Translate the following passage into Chinese.**

中国市场的复杂性和巨大变化一直是西方营销者所面临的最大挑战。从地理区域上讲，中国的地区差异如此明显，以至于中国市场被认为是由许多小市场组成的。由于文化和经济背景不同，中国的沿海地区和中部地区，南方和北方的消费模式相差甚远。

为了更好地理解中国不同地区的消费者，盖洛普进行了大范围的调查。例如，中国北方地区的啤酒消费量远远高于其他地区。而在中国的东部地区，人们大多看报纸而不收听广播，这对于营销者如何为其产品做广告具有重要的意义。

Text B (Omitted)

Unit 9

Text A

I. **Discuss the following questions.**
   (Omitted)

II. **Analyze the case below and discuss the questions.**
   (Omitted)

III. **Match the terms in column A with the explanations in column B.**
   1. —C   2. —H   3. —A   4. —J   5. —B
   6. —G   7. —D   8. —I   9. —E   10. —F

IV. **Fill in the blanks of the following sentences with the words or phrases given below. Make changes when necessary.**
   1. advertiser   2. responses   3. interact   4. Sponsorship
   5. candidates   6. Brand image   7. commercial   8. sales promotion
   9. merchandise   10. awareness

V. **Put the following into English.**
   1. establish and develop a long-term brand identity and image
   2. sell their merchandise in a restricted area
   3. mirror fashion and design trends
   4. change the face of advertising completely
   5. send a consistent, persuasive message to target audience
   6. reach groups of consumers by using selective media
   7. conduct the necessary research that verifies facts about the messages of the advertisers and competitors
   8. affect the public's buying behavior

9. hope that the customers trust their products and advertising
10. determine the needs, wants and interests of target markets

VI. **Translate the following sentences into English.**

1. Advertising is a paid form of communication, although some forms of advertising, such as public service announcements, use donated space and time.
2. Advertising informs us about new and improved products and helps us compare different products and their features.
3. Advertisers are not objective and often slant or omit information to their benefit.
4. Advertisements should work with other forms of marketing communication to reach customers.
5. Only the advertiser (and the supporting ad agency) knows whether the ad campaign reaches its objectives, and whether the ad is truly worth the money.

VII. **Translate the following passage into Chinese.**

　　互联网广告之所以越来越流行的一个原因在于，它具有相对于其他广告媒体而言的明显优势。最明显的是，广告主可以在互联网上订制他们的信息。得益于营销数据库，广告主可以输入关键的人口统计和行为参数，使消费者觉得这个广告就是为他做的。以 classmates.com 这一网站为例，出现在同一网页上的广告产品通常是特定年龄群所感兴趣的。1960年高中毕业的人会看到一些宣传为提前退休而进行投资的旗帜广告。

　　将这些同样的数据库合并到一起，网络广告主就会对消费者的各方面行为习惯十分了解。广告主可以将各种数据库组合起来，形成相对全面的档案。如果广告主了解消费者的旅游行为、他们对特定媒体的偏好以及他们的信用卡使用情况，想想看广告主将会如何为这些消费者量身打造广告。

Text B　(Omitted)

Unit 10

Text A

I. **Discuss the following questions.**
(Omitted)

II. **Analyze the case below and discuss the question.**
(Omitted)

III. **Match the terms in column A with the explanations in column B.**

1. —J　　2. —I　　3. —H　　4. —G　　5. —F
6. —E　　7. —D　　8. —C　　9. —B　　10. —A

IV. **Fill in the blanks of the following sentences with the words or phrases given below. Make changes when necessary.**

1. in favor of　　2. accompanied　　3. exceedingly　　4. fluctuation
5. compromising　　6. undertaking　　7. commitments　　8. security
9. for the account of　　10. in a position

V. Put the following into English.

1. to settle international transactions on commercial credit
2. the credit standing of the exporter
3. prior to shipment of the goods or provision of services
4. to contain a certain degree of risk
5. to obtain working capital by way of import financing
6. to act as an agent for the Remitting Bank
7. upon receipt of the draft and documents
8. to present the draft to the bank
9. to contribute to the smooth conducting of international trade
10. an instrument for securing performance or payment

VI. Translate the following sentences into English.

1. There are some key factors determining the payment method such as the business relationship between the seller and the buyer, the nature of the merchandise and industry norms.
2. Collection on clean bill refers to the collection of the purchase price against the draft only, without any shipping documents attached thereto, such as invoice, bill of lading or insurance policy.
3. Under a bank guarantee, the bank shall assume irrevocable obligation to pay a sum of money in the event of non-performance of a contract by the principal.
4. A documentary Letter of Credit combines the payment and delivery date, acquiring a commercial compromising mode of balancing the interest conflicts between the buyer and the seller.
5. A Letter of Credit by its legal nature is a separate transaction from the sale or other contract on which it may be based. Banks deal with documents and not with goods.

VII. Translate the following passage into Chinese.

信用证是一种支付方式，一般用于国际货物买卖。从根本上说，信用证是一种机制，这种机制使得进口商/买方能够向出口商/卖方提供一种安全的付款方式，这种付款方式中有一家(或多家)银行的参与。信用证的专业术语是跟单信用证。我们首先必须清楚的是，信用证处理的对象是交易单证，而不是商品。国际贸易的理念是把风险从实际买方转到银行头上。因此，(通常所谓的)信用证(L/C)是一种由银行代表开证申请人(即买方)向卖方开立的付款承诺。买方是申请人，卖方是受益人。开立信用证的银行就是开证行，开证行一般在买方所在国。向卖方发出信用证通知的银行被称为通知行，它往往在卖方所在国。

如果卖方在指定时间内成功提交了必要的单证，指定银行将进行支付。请注意，银行付款时审核的是单证而不是货物。因此，这个过程对买卖双方都有利。卖方得到了保证，如果卖方交单准时并符合信用证所规定的要求，就可以得到货款；买方也得到了保证，银行将对卖方所提交的单证进行全面审核，并确保单证满足信用证规定的各项条款。

Text B   (Omitted)

Unit 11

Text A

I. Discuss the following questions.
   (Omitted)

II. Analyze the case below and discuss the question.
    (Omitted)

III. Match the terms in column A with the explanations in column B.
   1.—H   2.—A   3.—I   4.—B   5.—D
   6.—C   7.—F   8.—E   9.—G

IV. Fill in the blanks of the following sentences with the words or phrases given below. Make changes when necessary.
   1. service   2. transaction   3. quote   4. participants
   5. consequence   6. anticipate   7. insurance   8. circumvent
   9. interaction   10. unload

V. Put the following into English.
   1. provide insurance to protect against foreign exchange risk
   2. compare the relative prices of goods and services in different countries
   3. invest spare cash for short terms in the foreign exchange market
   4. convert the domestic currency into a foreign currency without any limitations
   5. limit convertibility to preserve the foreign exchange reserve
   6. the rise in import prices resulting from currency depreciation
   7. get a gross profit of 10% from each transaction
   8. import laptop computers from Japan
   9. participate in the foreign exchange market

VI. Translate the following sentences into English.
   1. In general, however, companies should beware of speculation for it is a very risky business; the company cannot know for sure what will happen to exchange rates.
   2. The spot exchange rate is the rate at which a foreign exchange dealer converts one currency into another currency on a particular day.
   3. The value of a currency is determined by the interaction between the demand and supply of that currency relative to the demand and supply of other currencies.
   4. A lot of companies choose countertrade to avoid the nonconvertibility problem.
   5. A country needs an adequate supply of foreign exchange reserves to service its international debt commitments and to purchase imports.

VII. Translate the following passage into Chinese.
   公司可以通过对销贸易来解决货币的不可兑换性问题。对销贸易类似于易货贸易,即以一种货物或服务来换取其他货物或服务的一种协定。当一国货币不可兑换时,可以采用对销贸易的形式。让我们来看一看1984年,当罗马尼亚的货币不可兑换时,通用电器与罗马尼亚政府之间的一项贸易。当时,通用电器在罗马尼亚获得了一项价值一亿五千万美元的发电机工程的合同,双方商定以在国际市场上售价一亿五千万美元的罗马尼亚商品来支付款项。1986年,委内瑞拉政府与卡特彼勒公司签订一项合同,合同规定委内瑞拉将用35万吨铁矿石换取卡特彼勒的大型施工设备。卡特彼勒随即将这些铁矿石换取了罗马尼亚的农产品,然后又将这些农产品在国际市场上出售,换得美元。

Text B (Omitted)

Unit 12

Text A

I. **Discuss the following questions.**
   (Omitted)

II. **Analyze the case below and discuss the questions.**
   (Omitted)

III. **Match the terms in column A with the explanations in column B.**
   1. —E   2. —J   3. —D   4. —C   5. —G
   6. —A   7. —F   8. —B   9. —H   10. —I

IV. **Fill in the blanks of the following sentences with the words or phrases given below. Make changes when necessary.**
   1. implemented   2. broker   3. financed   4. cover   5. issued
   6. variant   7. infer   8. accumulates 9. maturity 10. pool

V. **Put the following into English.**
   1. the place where securities and bonds are issued, bought and sold
   2. a mortgage loan as part of a public placement
   3. to reduce transaction costs
   4. the rate of return that investors require
   5. to purchase a share of the firm's common stock
   6. services provided by the discount brokerage house
   7. the mutual fund is a kind of tool for the collective investment
   8. to negotiate trading commissions with brokers
   9. to hold 4 percent of equity against the portfolio
   10. to conduct all the investment activities through security management firms

VI. **Translate the following sentences into English.**
   1. No secondary market is perfectly liquid.
   2. Most financial markets provide relatively rapid and low-cost opportunities to trade.
   3. Securities that are held by the buyer are referred to as private placements. Securities that are to be traded in secondary markets are referred to as public placements.

4. The rate of return that investors require on a bond issue of AT&T can be calculated by knowledge of the bond's maturity, promised interest payments, and current market price.

5. The people in search of yield are looking increasingly towards mortgage and asset backed paper with the result that the liquidity in the market is growing.

VII. Translate the following passage into Chinese.

  关于二级市场的存在,被广为引用的原因是它们能够改善流动性。理想状态下的流动着的证券可以被立即售出而且不花费任何成本(佣金、税费、价格波动等)。随着时间的推移,成本的上涨,流动性就随之减少。

  拥有流动性市场的好处是显而易见的:当需要现金或者手上有多余的现金时这种市场就允许交易。以某公司的股票为例。假设你购买了这家公司的一股普通股票,你就有权得到该公司将来会付给你的任何股息,但是你不可以卖掉该股票(可能因为没有二级市场)。这样的话,你会愿意购买这种股票吗?也许会,如果股票价格足够低的话!现在,假设存在这样的一个市场,在其中你可以在任何时候以低价迅速地进行股票交易,那么你愿意以比没有二级市场的情况下略高的价格购买这样的股票吗?当然会。由二级市场所创造的交易选择权本身就是有价值的。

Text B (Omitted)

Unit 13

Text A

I. Discuss the following questions.
 (Omitted)

II. Analyze the case below and discuss the question.
 (Omitted)

III. Match the terms in column A with the explanations in column B.
 1.—J 2.—D 3.—F 4.—C 5.—B
 6.—I 7.—E 8.—G 9.—H 10.—A

IV. Fill in the blanks of the following sentences with the words or phrases given below. Make changes when necessary.
 1. being pumped 2. regulating 3. Conversely 4. circulation
 5. collateral 6. initiatives 7. plummeted 8. enactment
 9. sound 10. loosened

V. Put the following into English.
 1. the second major policy instrument for controlling the money supply
 2. full employment and price stability
 3. expansionary monetary policy
 4. tight fiscal policy
 5. to reduce tax rate or increase public investment

6. to put more money into circulation

7. the buying and selling of government securities

8. to supervise and regulate commercial banks

9. to set and administer monetary and fiscal policy

10. to issue securities to reduce the amount of money in circulation

VI. Translate the following sentences into English.

1. A government's not paying attention to improving its fiscal policy will bring about many troubles, or even, in the end, will result in economic crisis.

2. An increase in government spending will increase aggregate demand and reduce the level of unemployment. Conversely, a decrease in government expenditure will reduce the aggregate demand and hence employment.

3. Unlike government spending, tax rates can be changed or varied quickly and have therefore been the government's main instrument of stabilizing fiscal policy in the short-run.

4. Changes in the discount rate cause more subtle shifts in the money supply than do changes in the reserve requirement. Hence, the Fed uses this tool frequently to change the money supply.

5. Chinese government's implementation of prudent monetary policy and proactive fiscal policy ensures the healthy and stable development of China's economy.

VII. Translate the following passage into Chinese.

联储拥有三种主要工具来对经济中的货币和信贷供应进行控制。最重要的工具是公开市场业务,或者称作买卖政府债券。为增加货币供应,联储会向银行、其他商务机构或个人购买政府债券,用支票(联储发行的一种新的货币来源)来支付;联储的支票被存入银行后,就成为了新的存款——银行可以利用这部分储备放贷或投资,这样就增加了流通中的货币量。另一方面,如果联储希望减少货币供给,它就会把政府债券出售给银行,而从银行回收存款。由于银行的存款降低了,它们就必须减少贷款,相应地货币供给也减少了。

Text B (Omitted)

Unit 14

Text A

I. Discuss the following questions.

(Omitted)

II. Analyze the case below and discuss the question.

(Omitted)

III. Match the terms in column A with the explanations in column B.

1.—C 2.—F 3.—G 4.—A 5.—B
6.—H 7.—J 8.—D 9.—E 10.—I

IV. **Fill in the blanks of the following sentences with the words or phrases given below. Make changes when necessary.**

   1. characterizes   2. committed   3. managed   4. elected
   5. discharging   6. sets   7. enhance   8. assesses
   9. representation 10. outside

V. **Put the following into English.**

   1. shareholders, directors and managers of a company and local stakeholders
   2. to transfer the ownership of the state-owned industry from the government to the general public
   3. values of transparency, responsibility, accountability and fairness in corporate governance
   4. Decision-makers in the government are involved in corporate governance.
   5. The responsibility of the Board of Directors is to manage or supervise the business of a company.
   6. The CEO is to coordinate and preside over the management of the company.
   7. Directors must be independent.
   8. to improve the operation of the Board of Directors
   9. investor protection
   10. dispersion of equity ownership

VI. **Translate the following sentences into English.**

   1. Corporate governance of a company includes formal and informal regulations, practices, law enforcement systems of the private sector and the government, etc.
   2. The major challenge in many countries is not how to work out better laws and regulations for corporate governance, which already exist, but how to implement those laws and regulations more effectively.
   3. It is crucial for strengthened corporate governance, improved corporate performance and long-term economic growth of a nation to have a politically-independent judicial system established that has legal empowerment and sufficient funding.
   4. The framework of corporate governance should enhance the transparency and effectiveness of the market, follow the laws and regulations and clarify the responsibilities of supervision, regulation and enforcement.
   5. The framework of corporate governance should ensure its strategic supervision of a company and the effective monitoring of the management by the Board of Directors and accountability of the Board by the company and its shareholders.

VII. **Translate the following passage into Chinese.**

   在中国的公司治理体系中,监理会是个必不可少的公司组织。根据《公司法》的规定,监理拥有以下职责:(1)审查公司财务;(2)监督董事和主管的行为是否违背公司章程;(3)责令董事和主管纠正其损害公司利益的行为;(4)提议召开股东特别会议;以及(5)公司章程规定的其他职责。监理还有权对董事会的会议进行审核。监理会由股东代表和员工代表组成，代表比例由公司章程规定。员工代表由公司的全体员工民主选举。为确保监理的公正性，"董事、经理或财务人员不能同时担当监理"。

Text B (Omitted)

Unit 15

Text A

I. Discuss the following questions.
   (Omitted)

II. Analyze the case below and discuss the questions.
   (Omitted)

III. Match the terms in column A with the explanations in column B.
   1. —C   2. —J   3. —I   4. —H   5. —B
   6. —A   7. —F   8. —E   9. —G   10. —D

IV. Fill in the blanks of the following sentences with the words or phrases given below. Make changes when necessary.
   1. exchange   2. discharge   3. initiate   4. participate   5. appraised
   6. terminate   7. forecast   8. being sifted   9. personnel   10. deploy

V. Put the following into English.
   1. Career Development Advisory
   2. to harmonize enterprise objective with individual objective
   3. factors affecting staff career
   4. enterprise training program
   5. staff allotment
   6. the forecast of the demand for human resources
   7. performance appraisal
   8. larger job autonomy
   9. opportunity for equal employment
   10. to receive vocational technical training

VI. Translate the following sentences into English.
   1. The purpose of human resources management is to use the human resources in a rational way, enhancing its efficiency to the largest degree.
   2. Staff allotment means changes in human resources, decided by the administrative body, which changes the post, unit or subordinate relations.
   3. Enterprise recruitment is a process of getting talented personnel, and a process of CI promotion as well.
   4. In employment, it is forbidden by law to have discrimination in sex, ethics, color, nation, region and age.
   5. Promotion and transfer are direct representation and chief channel of staff career development.

VII. **Translate the following passage into Chinese.**

　　比尔·威尔森被秘书这一行所吸引，因为他认为办公自动化会给工作带来更大的责任、专业技术和更高的薪水。他认为新技术将会提高办公室的生产力，摒弃一些较为乏味的秘书工作，而这会使像他这样的秘书承担更多的管理和决策事务。他认为在一些分散的机构中尤为如此，那里广泛地使用电脑和文字处理器，行政秘书遍布各个部门或项目组。

　　让威尔森非常失望的是，他发现许多公司主管，包括他的老板，在这一问题上的看法相当不同。例如，他的老板认为秘书没有必要分担管理与决策工作，相反，她认为他们应该做一些集中性的工作，这样以后就可以转到专业性的工作或技术岗位上去。

　　那么，为了维护自己关于分散机构的设想，威尔森应该怎么做？

Text B　(Omitted)

Unit 16

Text A

I. **Discuss the following questions.**
   (Omitted)

II. **Analyze the case below and discuss the question.**
   (Omitted)

III. **Match the terms in column A with the explanations in column B.**

   1. —B　　2. —A　　3. —C　　4. —E　　5. —I
   6. —D　　7. —F　　8. —G　　9. —J　　10. —H

IV. **Fill in the blanks of the following sentences with the words or phrases given below. Make changes when necessary.**

   1. approximately　　2. preferences　　3. offset　　4. downsides
   5. susceptible　　6. assume　　7. integrated　　8. coordinate
   9. distribution　　10. alternative

V. **Put the following into English.**

   1. major transportation means
   2. substantial gold reserves
   3. foreign exchange fluctuations
   4. decrease market shares
   5. strengthen competitive advantages
   6. an integrated global logistics system
   7. improve product quality and consumer satisfaction
   8. trans-border pipeline transportation
   9. adhere to the existing product standards
   10. high-density, low-valued products

VI. Translate the following sentences into English.

1. Logistics is vital to the survival and development of a company, and a global manufacturer in particular.
2. Transportation is a key factor in logistics, for any company, whatever it manufactures or sells, needs to transport its goods from one place to another.
3. As competition among companies is becoming more and more intense, a company has to improve logistics efficiency and reduce costs so as to enhance its competitiveness.
4. The rapid development of technology, steady spread of global market and emphasis on service quality and consumer satisfaction are major reasons behind the fast growth of global logistics.
5. Logistics is by no means a protective industry, and it has to be opened up to grow in a healthy manner.

VII. Translate the following passage into Chinese.

生产商很早就意识到,除了生产所必需的零件和原料,留有多余的存货是对时间、场地以及资源的浪费,额外的存货占用了现金,而这些钱原本还可以产生利息。近年来,不仅汽车生产商有这种想法,服务行业,比如零售商、医院、杂货商也很快意识到了这一点。这就意味着,如今企业越来越依赖于能够保障在确切的时间,将确切数量的原料送到所需地点的体系、公司及人员。在利润不高、竞争激烈的行业,能够充分利用物流是一项巨大的竞争优势。对于沃尔玛和戴尔这样的巨头来说,物流不仅起着后勤支持的作用,更是其业务的核心和竞争力的源泉。

Text B (Omitted)

Unit 17

Text A

I. **Discuss the following questions.**
   (Omitted)

II. **Work in groups and discuss the following question.**
   (Omitted)

III. **Match the terms in column A with the explanations in column B.**
   1. —I   2. —F   3. —G   4. —B   5. —J
   6. —H   7. —A   8. —D   9. —C   10. —E

IV. **Fill in the blanks of the following sentences with the words or phrases given below. Make changes when necessary.**
   1. auction   2. purchase   3. facilitate   4. distribute
   5. flexibility   6. sustainable   7. bid   8. retrieve
   9. dispatch   10. refund

V. **Put the following into English.**
   1. recognize their value and use them to create business opportunities

2. follow the links to place an order directly into the merchant's inventory system

3. the rapid integration of technology and commerce

4. the real manifestation of the knowledge society

5. offer a return fare

6. list items for sale with a commercial auction site

7. perform any transactions in almost any location

8. reach narrow markets that traditional businesses have difficulties accessing

9. a competitive advantage provided by inexpensive products and services

10. decrease costs in processing and storing information

VI. Translate the following sentences into English.

1. The latest development of computer technology enables entrepreneurs to realize that the current commercial pattern would be changed by E-commerce.

2. New technology has led the whole economy into a new era, and has a significant impact on the way in which people lead their lives.

3. Rapid economic growth is built on various factors, such as good infrastructure and sufficient manpower.

4. E-commerce provides manufacturers with a platform to show their products and customers with a wider range of choices.

5. By telecommuting, individuals can nowadays work and do their purchasing at home rather than by traveling around.

VII. Translate the following passage into Chinese.

外资银行迟迟不能进入中国快速发展的网上银行业务的原因部分是因为有关网上银行服务的规章制度才刚刚颁布。中国人民银行于2001年7月颁布了"网上银行业务管理的暂行办法"(简称"网上银行办法"),2002年4月颁布的"中华人民共和国有关执行网上银行业务管理的暂行办法的相关规定的通知"提供了进一步的信息和程序说明。网上银行办法要求所有在中国境内成立的银行机构(包含中资银行、合资银行、全外资银行和外国银行的分支等)在国内提供网上银行服务之前必须取得中国人民银行的批准。此外,境外通过网络向中国客户提供银行服务的机构也必须向中国人民银行进行申请。

Text B (Omitted)

Unit 18

Text A

I. **Discuss the following questions.**

(Omitted)

II. **Make a list of other international organizations besides WTO to see what similarities and differences they have.**

(Omitted)

III. **Match the terms in column A with the explanations in column B.**
   1. —D   2. —F   3. —A   4. —I   5. —J
   6. —B   7. —E   8. —C   9. —G   10. —H

IV. **Fill in the blanks of the following sentences with the words or phrases given below. Make changes when necessary.**
   1. enforcing   2. ratify   3. unprecedented   4. consulted
   5. infringes   6. spells out   7. borne out   8. appeal
   9. resolving   10. mapped out

V. **Put the following into English.**
   1. frame and regulate the international multilateral trade policies
   2. conduct multilateral trade negotiations
   3. settle trade disputes between the members
   4. improve transparency in government procurement
   5. eliminate the discriminatory treatment in international trade
   6. resolve disputes through consultation
   7. start a new round of multilateral trade negotiations
   8. reach agreements on telecommunications services
   9. ministerial conferences
   10. reduce trade barriers and increase investments

VI. **Translate the following sentences into English.**
   1. APEC was established in 1989 to further enhance economic growth and prosperity for the region and to strengthen the economic cooperation in the Asia-Pacific community.
   2. The (Dispute Settlement) Understanding of WTO guarantees that every member's exports will be treated fairly in other countries' markets. If they think their rights under the agreements are being infringed, they may bring disputes to the WTO.
   3. On February 15th, 1997, agreement was reached on telecommunications services by 69 WTO members, which will come into force on the same day next year.
   4. In December 1997, 70 members reached an agreement to open their multilateral financial services deal, covering more than 95% of trade in banking, insurance, securities and financial information.
   5. Compared with GATT, WTO is more authoritative and effective in the settlement of the disputes among its members.

VII. **Translate the following passage into Chinese.**
   在世贸组织内部，成员国如果同意开放其商品领域和服务领域，就得对其关税进行约束。对于商品而言，这些约束税率成为海关关税的上限。有时这些国家对进口商品所征收的税率会低于其规定的约束税率。在发展中国家这种情况比较普遍。在发达国家实际征收的税率和约束税率基本是相同的。

   成员国只有在与其贸易伙伴进行磋商以后才可以调整其约束税率，也就意味着要赔偿对方的贸易损失。乌拉圭多边贸易谈判的成果之一就是在约束税率政策的基础上增加贸易量。在农业领域,百分之百的农产品现在都有约束税率。所有的这些都是为了一个目标:为商人和投资者创造一个具有更高安全系数的市场。

这种关税体系同时也是为了以其他的方式来提高市场的可预测性和持续性。一种方式就是不鼓励成员国使用配额以及其他的用以限制进口数量的控制方式——对于配额的控制会导致产生更多的政府干涉以及更多的不公平行为。另一种方式就是要求各成员国尽可能使其贸易规则清晰、公开(透明)。很多世贸组织的协议都要求政府在本国内公开其商业政策和具体的操作步骤或者告知世贸组织。根据《贸易政策审议机制》的内容,世贸组织会定期对成员国的贸易政策进行检查,这也是一种鼓励成员国在国内和多边范围内增加其贸易透明度的方式。

Text B　　(Omitted)

Glossary

A

accelerate	v.	(使)加快,加速,促进	Unit 6
access	n.	接近,进入;通路	Unit 5
accompany	v.	陪伴,伴奏	Unit 10
accord	v.	给予	Unit 14
accountability	n.	责任	Unit 14
accumulate	v.	积聚	Unit 12
accumulation	n.	积聚,累积	Unit 2
accurate	adj.	准确的;精确的	Unit 3
acquire	v.	收购,获得,购买	Unit 1
acquisition	n.	采购,买进	Unit 4
adaptation	n.	适应;改制(物)	Unit 16
additive	n.	添加剂,附加物	Unit 16
administrative	adj.	管理的,行政的	Unit 5
adverse	adj.	不利的	Unit 11
aesthetic	adj.	审美的	Unit 9
affluent	adj.	富裕的	Unit 8
agency	n.	代理处,经销处	Unit 14
agent	n.	代理人	Unit 1
align	v.	联合,与……一致	Unit 14
alignment	n.	联合	Unit 14
allocate	v.	分配	Unit 12
allocation	n.	分配	Unit 5
alternative	adj. & n.	可供选择的;可供选择的事物	Unit 16
aluminum	n.	铝	Unit 16
ancillary	adj.	补助的;副的	Unit 17
anticipate	v.	预期,预见	Unit 15
appeal	v.	指控,控诉,为……提出上诉	Unit 18
appease	v.	平息,缓和	Unit 5

appliance	n.	工具,器具	Unit 8
appraisal	n.	评价,评估	Unit 15
approximately	adv.	近似地,大约	Unit 16
arch-rival	n.	主要竞争对手	Unit 1
article	n.	一件物品;条款,条目	Unit 6
artificially	adv.	人为地	Unit 5
assess	v.	评估	Unit 9
asset	n.	资产	Unit 12
assimilate	v.	吸收	Unit 1
assume	v.	承担;假设	Unit 16
attributable	adj.	可归因的	Unit 3
auction	n.& v.	拍卖	Unit 6
augur	v.	预卜,预示,预言	Unit 8
authorization	n.	授权,认可	Unit 5
automated	adj.	自动化的	Unit 6
avert	v.	转移	Unit 14

B

ban	v.	禁止	Unit 5
bane	n.	毒药,祸害	Unit 14
banking	n.	银行业	Unit 3
barrier	n.	(贸易)壁垒;限制	Unit 18
bartender	n	酒保	Unit 3
base	v.	设立	Unit 3
bauxite	n.	矾土,铁铝矿石	Unit 16
bid	n.	出价,投标	Unit 17
bidder	n.	出价人,投标人	Unit 5
block	v.	妨碍,阻塞	Unit 10
blockholder	n.	大股东	Unit 14
blur	v.	把(界线、视线等)弄得模糊不清	Unit 4
bottom	n.	臀部,屁股	Unit 1
branding	n.	商标,牌子	Unit 7
broker	n.	经纪人,掮客	Unit 3
bureaucracy	n.	行政系统,行政机构	Unit 18
by-pass	v.	绕开,回避	Unit 17

C

cabby	n.	出租车司机	Unit 3
candidate	n.	候选人	Unit 9
capital	n.	资金	Unit 3
capital-intensive	adj.	资金密集型	Unit 3
carbon-paper	n.	复写纸	Unit 8
carrier	n.	运输船；搬运人	Unit 16
carton	n.	塑料盒	Unit 16
cash	n.	现金	Unit 12
cast	n.	演员阵容	Unit 3
catalyze	v.	催化，刺激，促进	Unit 4
categorization	n.	分类	Unit 3
caterer	n.	包办伙食人	Unit 3
CEO	n.	首席执行官	Unit 14
chairperson	n.	董事长	Unit 14
charge	v.	收费；控诉	Unit 5
circulate	v.	流通，循环	Unit 13
circulation	n.	流通，循环	Unit 13
circumvent	v.	设法避免	Unit 11
citizenry	n.	(旧用法)全体公民	Unit 8
claim	n.	要求而得到的东西	Unit 12
close	n.	收盘，交易结束	Unit 12
collateral	n.	担保物，抵押品	Unit 13
combination	n.	结合	Unit 7
commercial	n.	(电视或无线电中的)广告	Unit 9
commercialize	v.	使商业化，使商品化	Unit 7
commission	n.	佣金	Unit 1
commitment	n.	投入，承担的义务	Unit 1
commodity	n.	商品	Unit 5
comparable	adj.	可比较的	Unit 15
compensate	v.	酬报	Unit 14
competitiveness	n.	竞争力	Unit 5
component	n.	成分，组成部分；零部件	Unit 6
composition	n.	构成，组成，结构；组合方式	Unit 6
compromise	n. & v.	妥协，折衷	Unit 10
conceivably	adv.	令人信服地	Unit 12
concept	n.	观念，概念	Unit 7
confidence	n.	秘密(性)；信任	Unit 18

279

confine	v.	限制	Unit 3
conformity	n.	一致	Unit 5
consecutive	adj.	连续的,连贯的	Unit 6
consequence	n.	结果;影响	Unit 11
consignment	n.	托付货物;托运;交付	Unit 6
consistency	n.	一致性,连贯性	Unit 7
consultation	n.	商量,咨询;协商会	Unit 6
contact	v.	接触,联系	Unit 7
container	n.	容器,集装箱	Unit 7
content	n.	含量,成分	Unit 1
continuation	n.	继续,延长	Unit 7
contraction	n.	收缩	Unit 15
conversely	adv.	相反地	Unit 13
conversion	n.	转换,转变	Unit 14
convert	v.	改变(某物)的形式或用途	Unit 11
convey	v.	搬运;传达;转让	Unit 7
coordinate	v.	协调,调整	Unit 16
copyright	n.	著作权,版权	Unit 1
corporate	adj.	公司的,法人的	Unit 14
council	n.	理事会,委员会	Unit 18
counter	v.	反击,反抗	Unit 5
cover	v.	包含;够支付	Unit 12
crack	v.	挤入,闯入	Unit 1
criteria	n.	标准	Unit 7
cumulative	adj.	累积的	Unit 9
curb	v.	控制,抑制	Unit 8
customization	n.	〈计〉用户化,专用化,定制	Unit 17
customize	v.	按客户具体要求制造	Unit 17

D

database	n.	数据库	Unit 3
dealer	n.	商人;交易商	Unit 11
default	n.	拖欠;食言,不履行责任	Unit 10
defer	v.	使推迟,使延期	Unit 10
deficit	n.	赤字,不足额	Unit 2
deliberately	adv.	故意地	Unit 2
deliver	v.	传递	Unit 9
delivery	n.	递送,交付	Unit 17

demand	n.	需求	Unit 13
demander	n.	需求方	Unit 3
demographic	adj.	人口的	Unit 8
dent	n. & v.	凹痕；削弱，削减	Unit 16
depletion	n.	耗尽，枯竭	Unit 8
depository	adj.	存款的，存储性的	Unit 13
depreciate	v.	折旧；贬值	Unit 4
depression	n.	萧条，衰退	Unit 13
derive	v.	取得，得到	Unit 3
deterioration	n.	恶化	Unit 8
determinant	n.	决定性因素	Unit 14
detrimental	adj.	有害的	Unit 5
devalue	v.	(货币)贬值	Unit 1
devoid	adj.	缺乏的，没有的	Unit 9
diaper	n.	尿布	Unit 1
diffuse	v.	散播，传播	Unit 4
diffusion	n.	扩散，传播	Unit 2
disallow	v.	不允许，不接受	Unit 5
discard	v.	丢弃，抛弃	Unit 15
disparate	adj.	不同的，异类的	Unit 14
dispatch	v.	分派，派遣	Unit 17
disperse	v.	(使)分散	Unit 14
display	n.	展示，陈列	Unit 1
disproportionate	adj.	不成比例的	Unit 7
distortion	n.	扭曲，变形	Unit 5
distribution	n.	销售；分配	Unit 7
distributor	n.	分销商，经销商	Unit 1
diversification	n.	多样化	Unit 6
diversify	v.	使不同，使变得多样化	Unit 6
dividend	n.	股息或红利	Unit 12
documentation	n.	文件	Unit 5
domicile	n.	住所，居住地	Unit 10
dominate	v.	支配，占优势	Unit 17
donor	n.	捐赠人	Unit 4
doorman	n.	看门人	Unit 3
downside	n.	底侧；缺点；下降趋势	Unit 16
dramatize	v.	加剧，使激烈	Unit 15
dropout	n.	退学者，中途辍学者	Unit 8
dumping	n.	倾销	Unit 5

duplicate	v.	复制,复印	Unit 8

E

effect	v.	引起,产生	Unit 13
eligibility	n.	适任,合格	Unit 15
eliminate	v.	排除,除去,消除	Unit 7
embody	v.	包含,包括	Unit 3
emission	n.	排放	Unit 8
empirical	adj.	完全根据经验的,经验主义的	Unit 14
employ	v.	雇佣;使用	Unit 16
enact	v.	制定,颁布	Unit 13
encompass	v.	包围,环绕,包含或包括某事物	Unit 17
endow	vt.	捐赠;赋予	Unit 2
enforce	v.	推行,实施(法律等)	Unit 18
enhance	v.	提高,增强	Unit 4
entail	v.	使……成为必需,需要	Unit 1
entity	n.	实体	Unit 1
entrant	n.	新到者;新工作者;新会员	Unit 17
entrench	v.	确立,是处于牢固地位	Unit 14
entrenchment	n.	确立	Unit 14
entrepreneur	n.	企业家	Unit 12
environment-friendly	adj.	有利于环境保护的	Unit 8
environmentalism	n.	环境保护主义	Unit 8
equitable	adj.	公平的,公正的	Unit 14
equity	n.	资产净值;股票;权益	Unit 4
equivalent	adj. & n.	相当的,相等的;等价物	Unit 2
evaluate	v.	评估,评价	Unit 15
even	adj.	偶数的	Unit 7
exceedingly	adv.	非常地,极度地	Unit 10
exceptional	adj.	杰出的,非凡的	Unit 18
excess	adj.	额外的	Unit 12
exchange	v.	交换	Unit 15
exclusive	adj.	独家的,专用的	Unit 1
execute	v.	完成;执行;履行	Unit 11
execution	n.	实行,实施,执行,完成	Unit 17
executive	n.	主管	Unit 3
exercise	v.	运用,行使	Unit 14
exert	v.	施加(压力等);努力	Unit 4

exhaustion	n.	疲惫,竭尽	Unit 15
expansion	n.	扩充,开展	Unit 15
expend	v.	花费,消费	Unit 14
expenditure	n.	消费,开销,开支	Unit 6
explicit	adj.	清楚的,明确的	Unit 5
exploit	v.	开拓,开发	Unit 15
expropriation	n.	征用	Unit 1
extract	v.	得到,提取	Unit 14

F

facilitate	v.	帮助,促使,使容易	Unit 7
facility	n.	设备,机构	Unit 16
feature	n.	特性	Unit 9
finance	v.	供给……经费,负担经费	Unit 12
financier	n.	财政家,金融家	Unit 17
fist	n.	抓住,抓牢	Unit 14
flexibility	n.	弹性,适应性,机动性	Unit 17
fluctuation	n.	波动,起伏	Unit 10
footloose	adj.	自由自在的	Unit 3
forecast	v.	预测,预见	Unit 15
forefront	n.	最前部,最前线	Unit 4
formula	n.	配方,处方	Unit 1
fourfold	adj. & adv.	四倍,四重(性的)	Unit 3
fraction	n.	(小)部分	Unit 14
framework	n.	框架,结构	Unit 16
free-rider	n.	免费搭乘的人,不劳而获者,无本获利者	Unit 14
freight	n.	运输费用,运费	Unit 1
frequency	n.	频率	Unit 16

G

generate	v.	产生,发生	Unit 7
generic	adj.	属的,类的	Unit 4
governance	n.	管理,统治	Unit 14
grant	v.	授予,给予	Unit 1
graphic	adj.	绘画似的,图解的	Unit 7
grip	n.	掌握,控制	Unit 7

H

hamper	v.	阻碍,妨碍,牵制	Unit 1
haphazard	adj.	偶然的,偶尔的	Unit 15
haul	v.	拖,拉	Unit 16
hike	n.	大幅度增加,提高	Unit 13
homogeneous	adj.	同类的,同质的	Unit 2
horizontal	adj.	水平的	Unit 15
hybrid	n.	杂交种,混合物,合成物	Unit 14
hyperinflation	n.	极度通货膨胀,恶性通货膨胀	Unit 13
hypothesize	v.	假设,假定,猜测	Unit 14

I

identical	adj.	同一的,相同的	Unit 2
identification	n.	辨认,识别	Unit 16
identity	n.	个性	Unit 9
illiterate	n. & adj.	不识字的人,文盲;文盲的	Unit 8
image	n.	形象	Unit 9
immense	adj.	巨大的	Unit 15
impede	v.	阻止	Unit 4
implement	v.	贯彻,实现	Unit 4
implication	n.	行动、决定等可能产生的影响	Unit 6
impose	v.	征收;强加	Unit 5
improvement	n.	进展	Unit 12
incentive	n.	激励,奖励	Unit 1
incorporate	v.	使并入,融入	Unit 1
indicator	n.	指示器,记录器,指示物	Unit 6
individual	n.	个人	Unit 9
induce	v.	劝诱,促使	Unit 4
infamous	adj.	声名狼藉的	Unit 7
infer	v.	推断	Unit 12
inflation	n.	通货膨胀	Unit 13
inflow	n.	流入,流入物(量)	Unit 6
infrastructure	n.	基础设施	Unit 5
infringe	v.	破坏,侵犯,侵害	Unit 18
initial	adj.	开始的,最初的	Unit 9
initiate	v.	发起,启动,开始实施	Unit 8

innocuous	adj.	无害的,不得罪人的	Unit 14
insider	n.	内部人士	Unit 14
inspect	v.	视察,检查	Unit 5
institution	n.	机构;制度	Unit 8
institutional	adj.	机构的	Unit 14
insurance	n.	安全保障	Unit 11
insure	v.	保险,投保	Unit 3
intangible	adj.	无形的	Unit 1
integral	adj.	完整的,整体的,基本的	Unit 7
integrated	adj.	综合的,完整的	Unit 16
integration	n.	融合,融入	Unit 6
interaction	n.	相互作用;相互影响	Unit 11
interchange	v.	相互交换	Unit 17
interest	n.	股份,股权	Unit 1
intermediary	n.	中介人,中间商	Unit 1
interpersonal	adj.	人与人之间的,人际的	Unit 15
interrelate	v.	(使)相互关联	Unit 4
intimately	adv.	亲密地,紧密地	Unit 3
intranet	n.	〈计〉内联网	Unit 17
intransit	adj.	在旅途中的	Unit 16
invalid	adj.	无道理的;站不住脚的	Unit 11
inventory	n.	详细目录;存货	Unit 7
irrevocable	adj.	不可撤销的	Unit 10
issue	v. & n.	发行;证券	Unit 12
issuer	n.	发行人	Unit 12

J

jeopardise	v.	使受危险,危及	Unit 14

K

know-how	n.	技术诀窍	Unit 1
knowledge-intensive	adj.	知识密集型	Unit 3

L

labeling	n.	商标,标志	Unit 7

labor	n.	劳动力	Unit 3
leapfrog	v.	超越,越级	Unit 1
legitimate	adj.	合法的,合理的	Unit 5
levy	v.	征收,征税	Unit 5
liability	n.	责任,义务	Unit 8
liner	n.	班轮	Unit 16
liquidity	n.	流动性,灵活性	Unit 10
loan	n.	贷款	Unit 3
logistics	n.	物流,后勤	Unit 16
loose	adj.	宽松的	Unit 13
lower	v.	降低	Unit 5

M

macroenvironment	n.	宏观环境	Unit 8
mainframe	n.	主机	Unit 7
mall	n.	购物中心,商场	Unit 8
managerial	adj.	管理的	Unit 4
mandatory	adj.	强制性的	Unit 8
manifestation	n.	表现,表明	Unit 14
manipulative	adj.	操纵的	Unit 9
manufacturer	n.	制造商	Unit 9
marketer	n.	营销者	Unit 8
marketing	n.	营销	Unit 9
marking	n.	唛头	Unit 16
maturity	n.	成熟期;到期日	Unit 12
maximization	n.	最大值化,极大值化	Unit 7
maximize	v.	使……最大化	Unit 14
mechanism	n.	机制	Unit 5
mechanized	adj.	机械化的	Unit 16
Mercantilism	n.	重商主义	Unit 2
merchandise	n.	商品	Unit 9
meteoric	adj.	流星般的,疾速的	Unit 17
ministerial	adj.	部长级的;行政(上)的	Unit 18
minority	n.	少数民族	Unit 15
miscellaneous	adj.	不同种类的,多种多样的	Unit 6
mix	n.	混合,混合物	Unit 7
moderation	n.	适度	Unit 14
monitor	v.	监管	Unit 14

monopolize	vt.	垄断,独占	Unit 2
monopoly	n.	垄断,垄断者	Unit 2
motivate	v.	激发	Unit 5
move	v.	流动	Unit 3
multilateral	adj.	多边的,多国的	Unit 4
multiple	adj.	多样的,多重的	Unit 5
mutually	adv.	互相地,互助地	Unit 2

N

napkin	n.	餐巾	Unit 8
nationalization	n.	国有化	Unit 16
network	n.	网络	Unit 12
noncontrollable	n.	不可控制的变量	Unit 8
nonpersonal	adj.	非个人化的	Unit 9
norm	n.	标准,规范	Unit 10
nurture	v.	养育,教育	Unit 15

O

obligation	n.	债务	Unit 12
odd	adj.	基数的,单数的	Unit 7
offset	v.	抵消,弥补	Unit 16
optical	adj.	视觉的,视力的;光学的	Unit 6
outlet	n.	出口,出路	Unit 7
outright	adj.	彻底的,完全的	Unit 15
overlap	n.	(两个或两个以上东西的)重叠,互搭	Unit 14
overriding	adj.	压倒一切的,首要的	Unit 18

P

packaging	n.	包装	Unit 3
paradigm	n.	典范,范例,示例	Unit 17
past-due	adj.	过期的	Unit 7
patent	n.	专利	Unit 1
payment	n.	付款,支付,报酬	Unit 12
penetrate	v.	穿透,渗透	Unit 16
penetration	n.	穿透,透过,突入,打入	Unit 6

pension	n.	养老金,退休金	Unit 17
perceive	v.	感知,认识到	Unit 4
performance	n.	表现,业绩	Unit 14
permutation	n.	置换;蜕变;彻底改变	Unit 10
personnel	n.	人员,职员,人事	Unit 15
perspective	n.	观点,看法;前途	Unit 7
pervasive	adj.	渗透的,遍布的,蔓延的	Unit 6
pilot	v.	引导	Unit 14
pipeline	n.	管道	Unit 16
plague	v.	折磨,使苦恼	Unit 15
platform	n.	平台;(车站)月台;讲台,讲坛	Unit 17
plausible	adj.	似是而非的	Unit 2
plummet	v.	突然下降,大跌	Unit 13
polystyrene	n.	聚苯乙烯	Unit 8
pool	v.	共享;集中(钱、力量等)	Unit 12
portfolio	n.	有价证券	Unit 4
posh	adj.	豪华的	Unit 3
potential	adj.	潜在的,可能的	Unit 7
practice	v.& n.	实施,实践;惯例,做法	Unit 5
precautions	n.	预防,警惕,防范	Unit 7
precondition	n.	前提	Unit 5
predominantly	adv.	卓越地,支配地,主要地	Unit 17
preference	n.	偏好	Unit 16
premium	n.	优惠	Unit 8
presence	n.	存在	Unit 3
preserve	v.	保护,保持,保藏	Unit 7
presuppose	v.	推测	Unit 3
primary	adj.	初级的,初级品的	Unit 1
principal	n.	当事人,委托人	Unit 10
priority	n.	优先,优先权	Unit 18
privacy	n.	隐私,秘密	Unit 15
privatization	n.	私有化	Unit 14
problematic	adj.	难处理的	Unit 11
procedure	n.	程序,手续	Unit 5
procurement	n.	(政府的)收买,采购	Unit 17
producer	n.	生产商	Unit 3
productivity	n.	生产力	Unit 12
professional	n.	专业人士	Unit 9
prohibit	v.	禁止,阻止	Unit 5

prominent	adj.	显著的,卓越的,突出的	Unit 6
promise	n.	承诺	Unit 12
promotion	n.	促销	Unit 1
promulgate	v.	公布,颁布(法令、教规等)	Unit 8
proprietary	adj.& n.	所有的;所有权,所有者	Unit 16
proprietorship	n.	所有权	Unit 7
prospect	n.	前程;前景	Unit 11
prospective	adj.	预期的	Unit 15
prototype	n.	原型	Unit 7
proximity	n.	接近,近似性	Unit 3
publication	n.	出版物	Unit 9
pump	v.	抽出(注入)液体、气体等	Unit 13
purchaser	n.	购买者	Unit 9

Q

quality	n.	优质	Unit 8
quantitative	adj.	数量的,定量的	Unit 5
quota	n.	定额,限额,配额	Unit 5

R

radically	adv.	激进的	Unit 13
ratify	v.	批准,认可	Unit 18
rational	adj.	合理的;理性的	Unit 9
rationale	n.	基本原理;理论基础	Unit 11
real asset		不动产	Unit 12
receiver	n.	收货人	Unit 16
recipient	n.	接受者,容纳者	Unit 4
refinement	n.	精致,文雅,精巧	Unit 7
refund	n.	退还;偿还额;退款	Unit 17
regulate	v.	管制	Unit 13
regulation	n.	规章,规则	Unit 15
regulatory	adj.	规范的	Unit 14
reinforce	v.	加强,强化	Unit 8
relaxation	n.	放松,放宽;消遣,娱乐	Unit 6
reliance	n.	依靠,依赖;信任,信赖	Unit 6
remedial	adj.	治疗的,补救的	Unit 15

remit	v.	汇款,汇寄	Unit 3
reprisal	n.	报复	Unit 14
reserve	n.	储备	Unit 13
resident	n.	居民	Unit 11
resolve	v.	解决	Unit 18
responsiveness	n.	响应	Unit 16
restriction	n.	限制,约束	Unit 5
retail	adj.	零售的	Unit 3
retailer	n.	零售商	Unit 8
retain	v.	保留	Unit 15
retaliate	v.	报复	Unit 5
retrieve	v.	重新得到	Unit 17
return	n.	利润	Unit 12
revenue	n.	收入,(国家的)税收,岁入	Unit 1
royalty	n.	专利权税,版税	Unit 3

S

sanitation	n.	卫生;卫生设施	Unit 18
saving	n.	存款	Unit 12
screen	v.	筛选	Unit 15
secretariat	n.	秘书处,尤指国际组织的	Unit 18
secure	v.	获得	Unit 1
securities	n.	有价证券	Unit 3
security	n.	安全	Unit 10
self-contained	adj.	设备齐全的,有独立设施的	Unit 1
set	n.	(一)套	Unit 14
setting	n.	环境,背景	Unit 14
settle	v.	解决;支付	Unit 10
share	n.	份额	Unit 3
share-weight		股份比重	Unit 14
shift	v.	转换	Unit 12
shipment	n.	装载的货物;运输的货物	Unit 11
shipper	n.	托运人,发货人	Unit 16
shipping	n.	航运业,运输业	Unit 3
shortfall	n.	缺点,不足之处	Unit 13
sift	v.	详审;挑选	Unit 15
simultaneously	adv.	同时地	Unit 2
skyrocket	v.	(物价、数量等)猛涨,剧增	Unit 8

slack	v.	松懈,减弱	Unit 15
slant	v.	歪曲	Unit 9
societal	adj.	社会的	Unit 9
soil	v.	损坏,玷污	Unit 14
sole	adj.	单独的,唯一的	Unit 7
sophisticated	adj.	复杂的;精密的;高级的	Unit 6
sound	adj.	合理的	Unit 13
spare	adj.	剩余的;多余的;备用的	Unit 11
specified	adj.	规定的,明确的	Unit 1
specify	v.	规定	Unit 5
spell	v.	带来,意味着	Unit 8
splintered	adj.	分裂的	Unit 3
spoilage	n.	损坏	Unit 7
spot	v.	找出,认出,看出	Unit 8
stability	n.	稳定性	Unit 10
staff	n.	全体职员	Unit 18
stake	n.	股权,股份	Unit 1
stakeholder	n.	股东,享有股份或利润的人	Unit 4
standpoint	n.	立场,观点	Unit 7
state-owned	n.	国有的	Unit 1
static	adj.	静态的	Unit 7
statistics	n.	统计数字,统计资料	Unit 6
stimulate	v.	刺激	Unit 9
stock	n.	股权	Unit 1
stockout	n.	无存货	Unit 16
straightforward	adj.	简单的,易理解的	Unit 9
strategy	n.	战略	Unit 16
submission	n.	提交	Unit 5
subscription	n.	订金,订阅	Unit 17
subsidiary	n.	子公司	Unit 1
subsidize	v.	资助,补贴	Unit 2
subsidy	n.	(国家间的)财政援助	Unit 18
substantial	adj.	大量的,重大的	Unit 6
substitute	n.	替代,替代品	Unit 2
successor	n.	继承者,接任者	Unit 18
succinctly	adv.	简洁地,简便地	Unit 14
superfluous	adj.	多余的,过剩的,过量的	Unit 17
supplier	n.	供应商	Unit 3
supply	n.	供给	Unit 13

surplus	n.	剩余,过剩,[会计]盈余	Unit 2
susceptible	adj.	易受影响的	Unit 16
sustainability	n.	可持续性	Unit 17
systematic	adj.	系统的,体系的	Unit 15

T

takeover	n.	接管	Unit 14
tariff	n.	关税	Unit 18
taxonomy	n.	分类	Unit 3
teller	n.	(银行)出纳员	Unit 13
term	v.	把……称为	Unit 14
termination	n.	终止	Unit 15
tier	n.	层次,等级	Unit 8
tight	adj.	紧缩的;严格的	Unit 13
tradable	adj.	可进行贸易的,可做交易的	Unit 3
trade-off	n.	平衡,协调	Unit 14
trademark	n.	商标,商号	Unit 1
tramp	n.	不定期货船	Unit 16
transaction	n.	交易	Unit 11
transistor	n.	晶体管	Unit 8
transit	n.	运输;中转	Unit 16
transition	n.	转换,过渡	Unit 4
transparency	n.	透明度	Unit 14
trillion	num.	万亿	Unit 16
turnover	n.	成交量;营业额	Unit 6

U

ubiquity	n.	到处存在,(同时的)普遍存在	Unit 17
unanticipated	adj.	意料之外的	Unit 11
under-consuming	n.	压低消费,抑制消费	Unit 2
underlying	adj.	根本的,潜在的	Unit 14
undertaking	n.	承诺,保证	Unit 10
unequivocally	adv.	意思明确地	Unit 14
uniformity	n.	同样,一式,一致	Unit 7
unload	v.	转手	Unit 11
unprecedented	adj.	空前的,前所未有的	Unit 6

unravel	v.	弄清楚	Unit 3
upscale	adj.	上层的，有声望的，有地位的	Unit 8
utility	n.	效用，有用	Unit 7
utilize	v.	利用	Unit 4

V

vacancy	n.	空缺，空白	Unit 15
variant	n.	变量	Unit 12
variation	n.	变化，变异，变种	Unit 10
venture	n.	企业	Unit 12
via	prep.	经，通过，经由	Unit 17
viable	adj.	可行的	Unit 4
violation	n.	违反，违背	Unit 18
volatility	n.	不稳定性，多变性	Unit 14
volume	n.	量，分量	Unit 6
vulnerable	adj.	易受攻击的	Unit 8

W

warehousing	n.	仓储，仓储业务	Unit 1
warrant	v.	使……有正当理由	Unit 14
warranty	n.	担保	Unit 9
wheelbarrow	n.	独轮手推车	Unit 13
whereby	adv.	以……的方式，凭借……	Unit 1
white-goods	n.	白色织物，白色货物	Unit 1
wholesaler	n.	批发商	Unit 9
wholesaling	n.	批发	Unit 3
withdraw	v.	提取，收回	Unit 1
wrapping	n.	包装	Unit 8

X

xerography	n.	静电印刷	Unit 8

《Grammar in Context》(4th Edition)

英语语境语法

系列（第四版）

本套书由美国语言教学研究专家特为非英语母语的英语学习者编写的"英语语境语法系列"（分为"1、2、3级，共6册"和"教师参考用书1、2、3册"）。

本系列丛书特点：

将语法点融入有趣的阅读材料，通过对语境主题的不断练习讲授语法，以促进学生的英语学习和认知发展。

包含大量全新的阅读材料，有关美国日常生活的实例，如简历写作、处理远程交易等，有利于学生获得及扩展对美国文化和历史的了解；涵盖所有语法点的清晰的语法图，便于学生快速查阅和掌握语法知识；大量更新的活动设计，讨论、阅读、作文以及创造性思维技巧训练，帮助全面提高学生的语言和交流技能。

- 英语语境语法 1A / N.艾尔鲍姆·桑德拉 / 32.00
- 英语语境语法 1B / N.艾尔鲍姆·桑德拉 / 32.00
- 英语语境语法 1 教师用书
  　　　　　　　/ N.艾尔鲍姆·桑德拉 / 60.00
- 英语语境语法 2A / N.艾尔鲍姆·桑德拉 / 32.00
- 英语语境语法 2B / N.艾尔鲍姆·桑德拉 / 32.00
- 英语语境语法 2 教师用书
  　　　　　　　/ N.艾尔鲍姆·桑德拉 / 66.00
- 英语语境语法 3A / N.艾尔鲍姆·桑德拉 / 32.00
- 英语语境语法 3B / N.艾尔鲍姆·桑德拉 / 32.00
- 英语语境语法 3 教师用书
  　　　　　　　/ N.艾尔鲍姆·桑德拉 / 68.00

我们还提供注解版的教师用书，包含详细的教学要点和建议；教师同时可获赠含大量题库的CD-ROM和教学指导录像，更加方便教师组织测验和教学。

北京大学出版社

外语编辑部电话：010-62767347　　010-62765014
市场营销部电话：010-62750672
邮购部电话：010-62534449

北大英语辞书

《热门话题汉英口译词典》　　杨大亮　王运祥　主编　　　25.00 元

《常见英语错误例解词典》　　Harry Blamires 著　　　　　26.00 元

《最新通俗美语词典》　　　　高克毅　高克永　主编　　　42.00 元

《英语写作技巧》　　　　　　James Aitchison 著　　　　　26.00 元

《英语常用词组用法词典》　　Rosalind Fergusson 著　　　 45.00 元

《电力科技英汉词典》　　　　涂和平　主编　　　　　　　19.80 元

《当代英汉美英报刊词典》　　周学艺　主编　　　　　　　52.00 元

北京大学出版社

外语编辑部电话：010-62767347　　市场营销部电话：010-62750672

　　　　　　　010-62755217　　　邮购部电话：010-62752015

Email：zbing@pup.pku.edu.cn